Bianca Boteva-Richter, Griet Galle,
Riccardo Pozzo, Bernd Rolf, Markus Wirtz
(Hg./Eds.)
im Auftrag der AIPPh

# The Challenges of Populism
# Die Herausforderungen des Populismus
# Les défis du populisme



*Forum Philosophie International*

is the yearbook
of the International Association for Teachers
of Philosophy at Schools and Universities /

ist das Jahrbuch
der Association International des Professeurs de Philosophie,
Verein zur Förderung philosophischer Bildung e. V./

est la publication annuelle
de l'Association Internationale des Professeurs de Philosophie

(www.aipph.org).

# Forum Philosophie International

*(bis Band 68 Europa Forum Philosophie)*

herausgegeben von der

Association Internationale
des Professeurs de Philosophie

Senior Editor:
Dr. Gabriele Osthoff-Münnix



Band 73

LIT

Bianca Boteva-Richter, Griet Galle,
Riccardo Pozzo, Bernd Rolf, Markus Wirtz
(Hg./Eds.)

im Auftrag der AIPPh

# The Challenges of Populism
# Die Herausforderungen des Populismus
# Les défis du populisme

Senior Editor: Gabriele Münnix

LIT

Titelkarikatur mit freundlicher Genehmigung von Dr. Jan Tomaschoff, Düsseldorf.

Layout: Dr. Bernd Rolf

Redaktion: Bianca Boteva-Richter, Griet Galle,
Gabriele Münnix, Riccardo Pozzo, Bernd Rolf, Markus Wirtz

**Bibliografische Information der Deutschen Nationalbibliothek**
Die Deutsche Nationalbibliothek verzeichnet diese Publikation in der Deutschen Nationalbibliografie; detaillierte bibliografische Daten sind im Internet über https://dnb.dnb.de abrufbar.

ISBN 978-3-643-91710-2 (br.)
ISBN 978-3-643-96710-7 (PDF)
ISSN 1019-9993


Flössergasse 10
CH-8001 Zürich
Tel. +41 (0) 78-307 91 24
E-Mail: zuerich@lit-verlag.ch https://www.lit-verlag.ch

**Auslieferung:**
Deutschland: LIT Verlag, Fresnostr. 2, D-48159 Münster
Tel. +49 (0) 2 51-620 32 22, E-Mail: vertrieb@lit-verlag.de

# Contents / Inhalt / Contenu

# Editorial

Due to increasingly complex global circumstances, seductively simplistic narratives on social media, and the failures of political institutions, populist movements have been rising dramatically across many countries. Consequently, democratic values – rooted in philosophy, from ancient Greece through Montesquieu to the articulation of human rights – are facing multiple threats. Philosophy is therefore tasked not only with examining the manifestations of these populist movements but also with exploring how philosophical education and training in critical thinking can prevent or counteract susceptibility to reductive interpretations of the world. The contributions in this volume aim to provide insights and suggestions in this regard.

Aufgrund immer komplexerer Weltlagen und verführerisch simplifizierenden Angeboten in den sozialen Medien, aber auch durch das Versagen politischer Institutionen, nehmen in vielen Ländern populistische Strömungen dramatisch zu und die Werte der Demokratie – einst in der Philosophie entwickelt, von der griechischen Antike über Montesquieu bis hin zur Entwicklung und Formulierung von Menschenrechten – sind vielfach bedroht. Seitens der Philosophie ist also nicht nur nach Erscheinungsformen dieser populistischen Strömungen zu fragen, sondern auch, wie man mit philosophischer Bildung und Erziehung zum kritischen Denken der Anfälligkeit für vereinfachende Weltdeutungen vorbeugen bzw ihr entgegenwirken kann. Die Beiträge dieses Bandes sollen dazu Anregungen geben.

En raison de situations mondiales de plus en plus complexes et d'offres séduisantes et simplistes sur les réseaux sociaux, mais aussi en raison de l'échec des institutions politiques, les mouvements populistes augmentent considérablement dans de nombreux pays et les valeurs de la démocratie – autrefois développées en philosophie, de la Grèce antique à Montesquieu en passant par le et la formulation des droits de l'homme – sont souvent menacés. La philosophie ne devrait donc pas seulement s'interroger sur les manifestations de ces courants populistes, mais aussi sur la manière dont l'éducation philosophique et la pensée critique peuvent être utilisées pour prévenir ou contrecarrer la susceptibilité aux interprétations simplistes du monde. Les contributions de ce volume ont pour but de fournir des suggestions à cet égard.

The editors / Die Herausgeber / Les éditeurs:

*Bianca Boteva-Richter* *Griet Galle* *Gabriele Münnix*
*Riccardo Pozzo* *Bernd Rolf* *Markus Wirtz*

# 1. Currents / Aktuelles / Actualité

## Interview with Stefan Rummens on Populism and Teaching about Populism

*Stefan Rummens is a full professor of Political Philosophy at the Institute of Philosophy of KU Leuven. His academic work is mainly concerned with a philosophical analysis of the nature of our democratic regime and the problems it is currently facing, such as populism. For the Oxford Handbook of Populism, he wrote an article on "Populism as a Threat to Liberal Democracy" (2017) and (together with Koen Abts) he published "Populism versus Democracy" in Political Studies (2007).*
*Stefan Rummens (SR) was interviewed by Griet Galle (GG) in Leuven on 24 October 2024.*

*GG: How would you describe populism?*
SR: In my work, I usually try to make the distinction between populism as style and populism as ideology and I think that is important for a proper understanding of the phenomenon. On the one hand, many politicians use a kind of populist *style*. With 'populist style' we mean they are against the establishment and pretend to be on the side of the common people, and they often use simplistic slogans or solutions for complex problems. That is the way we use the word 'populist,' but that still is a rather superficial phenomenon. In a mediatized context, a lot of politicians are often tempted to use very simplistic solutions or give a kind of sneer to the establishment.

But at the same time, we have populism as an ideology, and that is a much more worrisome phenomenon. Populists, in the ideological sense, use the same kind of populist style, but for them, something more is at stake. They have a different view of what constitutes political legitimacy. Their key ideological belief is that the people somehow should be seen as a collective with a singular will. They believe that the will of the people exists in the singular and that they know what the will of the people is. From this populism in a much stronger sense, many other things follow. If you believe that, then it follows that politicians from other parties don't really represent the people and are traitors to the people. It also implies that if judges go against the decision that you have made – if you were a populist in power and the courts say no, this is unconstitutional – then you will also say the courts are mistaken and are traitors to the people. Of every kind of critique you get from the media, you will say "Oh, this is fake news" or "This is also a betrayal of the people." So, the logic that automatically follows is that everybody who goes against you is not a legitimate representative of the people. Or all critique, all contestation becomes illegitimate.

This is what you're seeing in Donald Trump very clearly. When the courts go against him, it's the fault of the courts and he's going to go against the courts. Or Hilary [Clinton] is not a legitimate opponent. Hilary should be imprisoned. If the elections turn out the wrong way, then clearly the elections were stolen by the other side. He is the will of the people. Obviously, if the elections don't confirm that, there is something wrong with the elections. All these populist features we see follow from that one single idea: that they consider themselves to be the only legitimate voice of the people. That is what makes populism in that ideological sense so undemocratic.

For me, it's important to make that distinction. When politicians use a populist kind of rhetoric or style, I'm not saying that that's unproblematic, it's usually not a very good idea. It's not very conducive for rational public debate if you use too simplistic slogans etc. But if underlying that rhetoric, they remain committed to the core principles of democracy, then the populist style is not a problem. Remaining committed to the core principles of democracy means that you recognize the legitimacy of a problem, you recognize the legitimacy of critique, you recognize the legitimacy of the courts, you recognize the importance of minority rights, and so you recognize that the people is a diverse community. It becomes a real problem if it becomes this ideological conviction that "I am the only voice of the people."

Sometimes it is said that populists are merely *illiberal*, so they don't respect the rule of law and the separation of powers and minority rights (rights of immigrants, for instance) and all of that is true. It's true that populists like Donald Trump – over here in Europe, you could think of Viktor Orbán – are illiberal, but importantly they're also *undemocratic*, because a real democracy recognizes that the people always speak with many voices at the same time; there's not just one voice. That has to do with how you approach the public debate and how you give respect to your political opponents; all of that is also missing with these populists. So, it's a problem both on the liberal and on the democratic side of liberal democracy. That's the real populism in the ideological sense.

*GG: Which political leaders or parties worldwide do you think are exemplary of populism?*

SR: Donald Trump is really a very good and clear example, also in a pedagogical context, because he fits all the features and people know him very well. You can easily see why he is populist in the ideological sense, so that's by far the easiest example. In Europe, you have Viktor Orban, who is also a good example. Then in Turkey, Erdogan is also considered to be a populist in the literature and I think rightly so. All of these are more rightwing or conservative forms of populism. In Latin America, there's a tradition of left-wing populism as well, going back to Juan Perón in Argentina in the post-war period, and more recently in Venezuela: Hugo Chavez (who is deceased now) was very populist in the way he presented himself, and that also backslided into an awful authoritarian regime. So, you have both left- and right-wing populist leaders who can fit the bill and can be very problematic in that sense.

*GG: Is populism usually related to right-wing or left-wing ideologies?*

SR: Mostly yes. What is typical of populism? Populism is the belief that the people is a homogeneous collective with a singular will. But the populists also have to tell a story about what the will of the people is. So, they need a complementary ideology to make sense of what the people then is. Typically, people on the left will come up with a socio-economic story about who the true people are: it's the poor, the workers, the labourers, the peasants. They have a more socio-economic understanding of the true people and the people's iden-tity. On the righthand side, populism associates itself with more nationalistic ideas and presents itself in cultural terms, referring to the original culture of the people. In more vicious forms of populism, this can also slide into a more ethnic understanding of the true people. Those are the two most prominent ways of coming up with additional ideological inputs of populism.

*GG: Is nationalism usually connected with the extreme right?*

SR: Many of the nationalists in Western Europe, such as Vlaams Belang in Flanders, Rassemblement National (the former Front National) in France, Alternative für Deutschland in Germany, also qualify as populists, precisely because they have this notion of 'the real people.' They consider the original, autochthonous people to be the real people. From this, everything else follows: their antagonism towards minority rights and the way they do politics.

*GG: Do you see a connection between the rise of social media and the growth of populism in Western democracies?*

SR: That's a difficult question. When it comes to merely the populist *style*, I think that the use of social media and the more general mediatisation of politics provide incentives for politicians to use a populist style as a way of attracting attention. So, they come up with more simplistic solutions. Or it's a kind of cult of personalities that comes with it, in a polarized debate in which you must choose sides. When it comes to populism as an *ideology*, I think that social media can make it worse, but I don't think they are the real cause. There is an ongoing academic debate, without clear consensus, about where populism as an ideology comes from. In my view, the mediatisation of politics and social media are not the main cause.

You need to think more deeply about why it is that voters no longer turn to the more traditional parties and somehow don't feel recognized anymore or have the feeling that their concerns are not really being taken up. Many hypotheses point to the fact that there is increasing socio-economic inequality in many societies. So, people are much more economically insecure than they were a couple of decades ago, and they no longer have the feeling that traditional politicians are really concerned about that and taking care of them. The erosion of the welfare state and increasing socio-economic inequalities play a role according to many people and I think it is part of the explanation.

But also on the cultural side, in many Western or European societies, we have seen a rapid, increasingly multicultural society, which puts a lot of cultural pressure on communities. In that sense, there is a kind of backlash of people being worried, feeling threatened, or feeling insecure. I'm not saying that the populist solutions are the good ones, but there is a concern that you need to take seriously, and maybe the traditional parties are not very successful in convincing these voters that they understand the worries and that they will somehow help them deal with those changing social circumstances.

So cultural anxieties and economic worries, I think, are more important in terms of the underlying explanations. It's a very difficult and controversial topic in the academic debate.

*GG: If these traditional parties do not take the people's worries very seriously, is there still a way to curve this populism?*

SR: That's very hard. You would need to think about what could convince voters again that their worries are being taken seriously. What you see traditional parties doing now is simply copying the proposals and the rhetoric of these extremist and populist parties. That's probably not the best way forward, because that will put pressure on our basic democratic principles in society. But then how to do it is unclear. It is a fact that in almost all Western societies inequalities have been increasing for 40 years now. It should be possible to come up with socio-economic policies that curve that evolution again and to go for a more equal and more inclusive society in which people feel more at home and more secure. I don't think traditional parties have done everything they can to come up with proposals in that regard.

*GG: And on the cultural side?*

SR: That's hard to say. Very often, cultural anxieties also have socio-economic causes. I'm not willing to reduce all cultural anxieties to socio-economic ones, but it plays a role. If you're economically secure, you can deal with more cultural diversity in your society than when you are not. Somehow, we need to reach a new understanding of what our social contract implies also in terms of cultural diversity. What are the norms that we share, should share, and should impose on everyone and what kind of diversity do we think is acceptable or desirable? That debate is still ongoing and, of course, has to remain within the constraints of constitutional democracy. But even within those constraints, there is some room for thinking about what the terms of agreements should be.

*GG: Do you think education can play a role in combatting populism?*

SR: I definitely think so, because what is at stake, is our understanding of what democracy is and what citizenship is. Populism really is based on a misunderstanding of what the will of the people is or what it means to decide in a pluralistic context. The underlying idea is that there is a true people that can often be detected through a majority vote and then can decide. But that is, of course, not what democracy is. Liberal democracy is accepting that the people is this pluralistic community. So basically, one way of formulating the difference between a populist and a true democrat, is that they have different ontological understandings of what the people is. A populist believes that the people is this kind of homogeneous collectivity with a singular will, whereas the real democrat should recognize that there is no such thing: A people is a community of free and equal citizens, who will and are allowed to disagree about many things, also about political issues. Political disagreement should not translate into a kind of oppression of the minority or an imposition of a kind of majoritarian view. No, we should deal with that diversity and respect it. That translates into respect for minority rights, for a real public debate, in which every position can and should be criticized. It translates into respect for your opponents and recognizing and accepting that other people might disagree with you and that this does not make them traitors, or that a dissenting view is not the same as fake news.

Concerning how you deal with pluralism, many views and values are at stake that can be discussed and thematised in an educational context, and many skills can be stimulated or trained. What constitutes real debates amongst people who are different and disagree? How do you deal with disagreements in a respectful manner? How do you make decisions in the context of diversity?

*GG: Do you have concrete ideas of how we could deal with populism in class?*

SR: You could do case studies. You could let students analyse actual (e.g., social media) contributions to the public debate: Is this respectful of opponents? What are the underlying assumptions? What is an appropriate way of dealing with conflicting views in society? In addition, you could look at case studies of actual populists and try to find where it goes wrong and what the problem is.

You could organize debates about how we deal with diversity and different views and whether that means we should be able to say everything. Can you defend any view that you want? Under which conditions? Is it allowed to defend an extremist position in a debate, if you have arguments, or are there constraints? You could let students think about that and make them aware of the paradoxes that are sometimes involved.

*GG: Do you think education must deal with populism?*

SR: Education has to prepare young people for their role as citizens more generally and so populism is, I think, an interesting topic in that context, precisely because all of these issues come together. Populism has to do with respect for minority rights, for the rule of law, and for the separation of powers, with the quality of the public debate, and with the quality and the role of the media. In that sense, it is an interesting lens through which you can look at the whole series of dimensions that have to do with citizenship, with the democratic process, and with the public debate.

I'm not saying that good citizenship education should deal with populism, but at the same time, it is becoming one of the most visible and in a way worrisome political phenomena of recent decades. So it's a bit hard not to talk about it. There are many reasons to pay attention to it, I think.

*GG: Philosophy as a subject is a part of the curriculum in many countries. Do you think more specifically that the subject philosophy can discuss populism, and in which way?*

SR: Yes, I think so, because in political philosophy, these are core topics and even tensions. In a democracy, what is the relationship between a majority vote on the one hand and constitutional protections on the other? This is one of the core paradoxes of our democratic system, so it's a core topic in political philosophy, and populism can be used to thematise that kind of tension. Even to young pupils, you can quite easily explain that there is a tension between the will of the majority and basic rights.

There's this other topic, the paradox of tolerance. How tolerant should we be? One of the defining values of our democracy is that we should be respectful. But what does that imply for our relationship with those who oppose tolerance or democracy? Should we be respectful of people like Trump, even if they do not recognize the outcome of the elections and even try to stage a coup? Should we be tolerant towards those who do not share our commitment to tolerance? One point of view is: you should be consistent and be tolerant also towards the intolerants. The argument against that is, of course, that if we are too tolerant of the intolerant and they come into power, then our society will no longer be tolerant. So, tolerance is something that you must actively protect. This is also an important topic in political philosophy that can be raised through the lens of populism.

You could also discuss how populism fits in the philosophical tradition and go back to John Locke on the importance of rights and Rousseau on the will of the people. One specific, contemporary suggestion is the famous book *What is Populism?* by Jan-Werner Müller. He is a professor at Princeton and one of the leading figures in the debate. It's a very accessible book, written for a wider audience, that deals with many interesting aspects of the topic. That could be one way into the debate for students with some more background knowledge already.

Populism is a highly rewarding subject in classes, as it connects to political reality and offers abundant philosophical possibilities. There are many interesting issues at stake, with which you can easily clarify core philosophical problems and are led in philosophical reflection.

*GG: When during philosophical conversations in class, students are defending extreme positions, such as sexist or racist positions, how should teachers deal with this in your opinion?*

SR: Philosophy is a very radical discipline. I think it's an important part of philosophy that we should be able to discuss everything, also extreme positions, but it always has to be based on arguments; you cannot simply claim certain positions. Of course, you have to protect a kind of safe environment in the classroom, in the sense that we always treat each other with respect and debate in a respectful way. But if you're doing philosophy, then ultimately, it cannot be a safe space in terms of the arguments or the topics that are up for discussion. Engaging in philosophy means that you can be confronted with views and arguments you dislike and might find discomforting.

Of course, it depends on the level of students and how far you are willing to take that. If you're in a high school setting, I think it's important that you make sure that there is a safe space in the first sense and that might require that you put some constraints on the discussion. But the philosophical ideal is that the constraints on what can be said should be as minimal as possible and as students grow into more mature philosophers, they should be able to discuss everything. It is part of the training of philosophers. In the master classes at the university level – with students who are much more advanced and have the ambition of becoming professional philosophers – I think all limits are off. I also discuss fascist thinkers in my classes, as it's important to see what their arguments are.

*GG: How do you think society should deal with the paradox of tolerance?*

SR: My colleague Koen Abts and I have advocated a dual strategy: you may never exclude the voters, but you may be more critical towards politicians and parties. This means being more inclusive towards voters, whom you would like to win back, but maintaining an exclusive attitude towards extremist parties, to prevent their proposals from being translated into policy.

If you adopt a concentric model of our political system – with the parliament and government at the centre, encircled by the public sphere and individual citizens – we argue that, at the periphery of this political system, you have to be very tolerant, even towards extremist positions. Here, everything must be open to discussion, you want to know what the people are concerned about, and freedom of expression should be almost unrestricted. But as actors move closer to power, in the centre, where decisions are made, you may not be as tolerant anymore and you should avoid that extremist views are implemented into policy. These views are relevant to the debate but may not shape policy. This is the "guideline of decreasing tolerance": the closer extremists get to power, the less tolerant we should be towards them. This middle position is original within the debate. Usually, you have two positions: either the one that tolerates extremists and does not ignore them; or the militant position that says "no, we ban this party". But in fact, there is a position in between.

*GG: Thank you very much for the interview.*

SR: Thank you for having me.

*Riccardo Pozzo (Rome, Italy)*

# Global Ethics at the 25th World Congress of Philosophy Rome 2024

In a fascinating newspaper article, Roberto Esposito previewed for the general public the nature and objectives of the 25th World Congress of Philosophy, held in Rome at Sapienza University from August 1 to 8, 2024.[1] Esposito did not hesitate to paraphrase the conclusion of Marx's Manifesto: "Philosophers of the world, unite!" in order to emphasize the universalism that philosophy cannot but aspire to, but which must not mean homologation.

With nearly 6,000 registered participants, the Rome Congress did not exceed the nearly 7,000 in Beijing in 2018, but it doubled the 3,000 gathered in Athens in 2013, the last time the Congress was held in Europe. It was good to see that the auditoriums were always full, in a program that started at 9:00 a.m. each day and ended at 7:00 p.m. (with a queue, on three evenings, from 9:00 p.m. to 10:30 p.m. at the Palatine), an extremely packed schedule, searchable on a dedicated app and published in a 552-page online document. What were the most innovative lines seen at the congress? Certainly, as Marina Calloni noted in her evaluation article, the discourse on interculturality, the interdisciplinary approach, and gender issues.[2]

The official languages were those of the United Nations, with the addition of German and Italian, but no Arabic. Note how, for the first time in the history of the World Congress, artificial intelligence applications, along with on-screen transcription of the original language, produced excellent simultaneous translations from one source language into six target languages, i.e., Chinese, French, English, Italian, Russian, Spanish, and German.

## 1. Global Ethics

As Esposito mentioned, philosophers from 109 countries from five continents were present. Globalization demands from philosophy an innovative narrative of inclusion and reflection. Hence the need for a global ethics: what should we choose and what guides our choices? Are ethical outcomes possible? Global

---

[1] Roberto Esposito, "Filosofi di tutto il mondo unitevi! Da domani a Roma il congresso dedicato alla disciplina che per sua natura coltiva il dialogo e il confronto. Parola d'ordine: Attraversare i confini. Evitando le trappole della *cancel* culture," in: *La Repubblica*, 31 July 2024, 26-27.

[2] Marina Calloni, "A Roma la filosofia abbatte i confini: Ritrovando i Quaderni di Gramsci. Al Congresso quasi 6000 partecipanti, provenienti da 109 paesi: con la cultura italiana tornata al centro del dibattito," in: *Il Caffè* 10 August 2024, 24.

ethics considers globalization in the various forms of social activity, including economic, political, and cultural life. In turn, globalization issues call for new approaches to dealing with the conflicts that arise when different cultural norms and practices collide, as Kwasi Wiredu points out.[3]

In the much-awaited plenary session on August 3, 2024, "Living in a Sustainable World," chaired by Carolina Scotto, the renowned economist Jeffrey Sachs asked philosophers to help solve the four global crises in which we find ourselves today, namely: (1) the ecological crisis due to human activity; (2) the ever-changing technological transformations; (3) the geopolitical transformation of a multipolar world due to the end of 500 years of Eurocentrism (since Columbus and Vasco de Gama) that dominated all of Africa and the Americas and most of Asia; and (4) demographics, with half of the world's population living in urban areas.

Consider the 17 goals of the *United Nations 2030 Agenda for Sustainable Development*, most notably SDG1 *No Poverty*, SDG10 *Reduce Inequalities*, SDG5 *Gender*, SDG16 *Peace*, and SDG17 *Cooperation*. Goals for which a mid-term review has been completed, showing that not all of them will be achievable in the originally planned 15-year period, thus calling for their updating in what will become the 2050 Agenda. The new 2050 horizon does not mean a relaxation of efforts. Rather, it means better long-term planning to achieve highly ambitious goals and targets. After all, it's only been nine years since then United Nations Secretary-General Ban Ki Moon declared that we have no Plan B because there is no Planet B, and every new disaster reminds us of that every day.

"So you are well satisfied with the world?" asked the Communist agitator Sarge artfully in Elizabeth Taylor's, *At Mrs. Lippincote's*.[4] In the *Eleventh Thesis on Feuerbach*, Marx accuses philosophers of merely interpreting the world in different ways – when what is needed is to transform it.

While economists can propose technical solutions for sustainable development, it is up to philosophers to convince governments and peoples to implement them. Hence the need for a global ethic: What should we choose, and what guides our choices? Are ethical outcomes possible? Today, philosophers can concretely address the conditions of possibility for ethical governance that respects harmony in diversity, and thus devise strategies to remedy the inefficiencies that persist in multilateral systems.

---

[3] Kwasi Wiredu, "On the Idea of a Global Ethics," in: *Journal of Global Ethics* 1 (2006), 45-51.

[4] ElizabethTaylor, *At Mrs. Lippincote's*, Davies: London 1945, 123.

The most fundamental principle for our new world system must be mutual respect among nations. The world faces profound and unprecedented challenges – environmental degradation, widespread political instability, the weaponization of cutting-edge technologies, and dramatic increases in in-equalities of wealth and power – that can only be met through peaceful co-operation among nations. Yet despite the urgency of cooperation, we are drifting toward larger and more frequent wars.

"World leaders," Sachs suggested in the plenary session of the World Congress, "need a course in moral philosophy – because many are neither responsible nor ethical. We need a global ethic for sustainable development. We need citizen participation and mutual respect in the global community of citizens. We need to find a consensus that will help to define our way forward." The first step was the United Nations' *Universal Declaration of Human Rights* of 1948.

Sachs listed six requirements for establishing global ethical approaches to sustainable development:

(1) study the great traditions, think of Confucius, Buddha, Aristotle, Mohammed, who shared a consensus that human beings can be better;
(2) develop citizenship not only locally but regionally and globally;
(3) promote benevolence and reciprocity, twin concepts;
(4) to increase dialogue, encounter, peaceful problem solving;
(5) to demand accountability of wealth and power, against many who do not tell the truth; let them stop lying; the world is for all, not for the few;
(6) to happiness and well-being. εὐδαιμονία (eudaimonia) and εὖ ζῆν (eu zen), 天命 (tianming); the SDGs should be seen holistically, not selectively.

In a recent paper, Sachs noted that the rapid advancement of technologies in areas such as artificial intelligence, computer science, biotechnology, and geoengineering are profoundly disrupting the world's economy and politics.[5] Hence the need to present a philosophical contribution to the *Summit of the Future* to be held in New York on September 21-22, 2024, a project whose development began with a meeting on *Confucius and Aristotle: The Commons in Intellectual Traditions and Future Practices* held in Beijing and Qufu, the hometown of Confucius, on July 7-12, 2024 and continued on August 3, 2024 with the invited session on *Aristotle-Buddha-Confucius-Islam: Ancient Wisdom for Modern Challenges* at the 25th World Congress of Philosophy.

[5] Jeffrey D. Sachs, "Beyond Hegemony: A New International Order Under the UN Charter," in: *Horizons* 27 (2024), 12-22.

World Congress participants were confronted with the question of the philosophical underpinnings of migration and food security, which is not only a matter of concern for high-income countries, but a phenomenon that directly involves the formula of humanity: "Act in such a way as to use humanity, whether in your own person or in the person of another, always at the same time as an end, never only as a means," as Kant expressed it;[6] not only "never only as a means," but also "never only as a thing or as a threat," as Corinna Mieth and Martin Sticker argued.[7] As Alix Cohen has made clear, if the perfect duty of global ethics remains to "treat others as ends in themselves and not as mere things," we must be careful not to commit the grave moral error of holding beliefs about others that objectify, dehumanize, or even bestialize them.[8] For example, when we adhere to stereotypes and think of others as mere things, reducing them to their natural constitution and thus denying their humanity as a capacity for self-regulation. But we must also guard against the very common epistemic error of accepting beliefs based on stereotypes even though they are illegitimate because they are based on inadequate grounds, i.e., hasty generalizations.

Today, philosophers must speak out on how to achieve Goal 8, decent work and economic growth, which has a very simple corollary: the need to end the exploitation of migrant labor. Work goes beyond mere tasks and serves as a fundamental aspect of human fulfillment and social contribution, intimately linked to the care of the planet. However, the relentless march of technological and economic progress often marginalizes the well-being of workers, a stark reality exemplified by the harsh conditions often faced by migrant workers in the EU agri-food system. According to Eurostat, these workers, numbering between 400,000 and 500,000 in Italy alone, are a vital structural element within the agricultural sector, making up almost half of the EU's workforce. Despite their integral role, many of them continue to face exploitative conditions and a lack of social and political recognition. This plight becomes emblematic of a "globalization of indifference," a term vehemently denounced by Pope Francis on several occasions. In addition to addressing persistent challenges such as exploitation, housing shortages, and social isolation, a recent report identifies and analyzes projects that foster virtuous cooperation between farmers and migrant

[6] Immanuel Kant, *Grundlegung zur Metaphysik der Sitten*, in AA IV, 429.

[7] Corinna Mieth/Martin Sticker, "Kant's Formula of Humanity and Migration," in: *14. Internationaler Kant-Kongress*, Universität Bonn: Bonn 2024.

[8] Alix Cohen, "Thinking as a Mere Citizen of the World (KGS 7:130): Kant on Doxastic Wrong, Epistemic Citizenship and the Republic of Knowledge," in: *14. Internationaler Kant-Kongress*. Universität Bonn: Bonn 2024.

workers in the South and North of Italy.[9] These initiatives seamlessly integrate productivity with social sustainability, offering tangible alternatives to the dehumanization embedded in the "dogma of neoliberal faith."[10]

The question is: did we see at the 25th World Congress only interpretations of the world or also projects for its transformation? Legitimate question, which in the case of thematic session 61 *Philosophy of Food*, unfortunately, is answered in the first horn of the dilemma: richness of interpretations, as Marx put it, but still little awareness of the unacceptability of jeopardizing food security (SDG2 *Zero Hunger*) or the political use of food, increasingly made in the two ongoing wars (SDG16 *Peace*).

## 2. The AIPPH at the 25th WCP Rome 2024

The Association Internationale des Professeurs de Philosophie was present at the World Congress with three events.

First, the Society Session "50 Years AIPPh, Past and Future" was intended to celebrate the half-century milestone by presenting highlights of its history, while informing about the development of its yearbook, its publication series, as well as its annual meetings and hybrid conferences. Above all, the AIPPh is interested in answering questions. The fiftieth anniversary refers to the registration of the AIPPh under Belgian law in 1974 (in its present statutes, however, the AIPPh has been re-registered under German law in 2020). The aims of the AIPPh are:

(1) to promote the teaching of philosophy in schools and universities of the member countries; to provide information on the teaching of philosophy in Europe;
(2) to ensure that the teaching of philosophy is based on the fundamental condition of freedom of thought and expression;
(3) to ensure that the working conditions for the teaching of philosophy guarantee its free and effective development; and finally
(4) to promote the cooperation of national associations concerned with the teaching of philosophy with regard to the formation and implementation of the aims of the association.

---

[9] Maurizio Ambrosini et al. (eds.), *Made in Immigritaly. Terre, colture, culture. Primo rapporto sui lavoratori immigrati nell'agroalimentare*, Agrilavoro/Confronti: Rome 2024.

[10] Francis, *Encyclical Letter Laudato Sì of the Holy Father Francis on Care for our Common Home*, Libreria Editrice Vaticana: Rome 2015; Francis, *Encyclical Letter Fratelli Tutti of the Holy Father Francis on Fraternity and Social Friendship*, Libreria Editrice Vaticana: Rome 2020.

It was time to outline the succession of AIPPh presidents: Marcel Fresco (the Netherlands, 1974-1985); Erich Moll (Austria, 1985-1998); Herman Lodewyckx (Belgium, 1998-2006); Werner Busch (Germany, 2006-2012); Gabriele Osthoff-Münnix (Germany, 2012-2023); Riccardo Pozzo (Italy, 2023-present). Introduced by Riccardo Pozzo, the speakers were Gabriele Münnix, Markus Wirtz, Bianca Boteva-Richter, Riccardo Sirello, Ruth Hagengruber, Ivan Kolev, and Griet Galle.

We are proud to mention the presentation by AIPPh Honorary President Gabriele Münnix on *Image Bans and Intercultural Image Philosophy. How to Reconcile Image Semioticians and Image Phenomenologists*, in which she presented arguments on image phenomenology and image semiotics while proposing a solution to the conflict between sign and presence.

Finally, the AIPPh held a roundtable on democracy and populism in the digital age. Populist movements have been known since antiquity, but today they can be observed with a new quality and global significance. Given the increasing mediatization of politics and the trend towards *politainment*, media and communication studies are also analyzing populist phenomena. However, the frame of reference in this descriptive and prescriptive discourse is philosophical. Philosophers from five countries presented different aspects of populism and discussed the consequences of populism for educational institutions. What can critical reason mean in this context? It is undisputed that philosophical education, with its focus on value formation (as opposed to value teaching), has a key role to play in dealing with populist phenomena and can help to empower against the dangers of simplified worldviews. Moderated by Gabriele Münnix, the speakers and their subjects were Tomas Stølen, *Democracy in Danger?*; Ivan Kolev, *On the Importance of Human Rights*; Griet Galle, *Classroom Detection of Fallacies in Political Discourse*; Riccardo Pozzo, *Migration and Xenophobia*; Marina Calloni, *Prejudice and Resentment: Gender, Populism and Social Media*; Gabriele Münnix and Bianca Boteva-Richter, *Populism and Critical Reason: On the Plurality of Critical Reason*; Daniela Zumpf, *Strategies for Teacher Formation: Didactical Transformations.*

*Michelle Wüthrich (Freiburg, Schweiz)*

# Weiterentwicklung der schweizerischen gymnasialen Maturität: Welcher Stellenwert kommt dem Fach Philosophie zu?

Im Jahr 2018 lancierten die schweizerischen Erziehungsdirektor:innen (EDK) das Revisionsprojekt für die Anerkennung der gymnasialen Maturität.[1] Tiefgreifende gesellschaftliche Veränderungen wie Klimawandel, Digitalisierung und der Anspruch auf partizipative Beiträge bedürfen einer *koordinierten Weiterentwicklung der gymnasialen Maturität* (WEGM). Die Umsetzung dauert voraussichtlich bis 2027. Wie hat sich der *Verband der schweizerischen Philosophie-lehrer:innen an Mittelschulen* (VSPM)[2] daran beteiligt? An dieser Stelle soll zuerst ein Überblick zur gymnasialen Maturität und zum Philosophiefach im Allgemeinen gegeben und im Anschluss auf die Verbandsarbeit der Philosophielehrpersonen zur WEGM eingegangen werden.

Die schweizerische gymnasiale Maturität[3] ist ein Bildungsweg nach der obligatorischen Schulzeit (gerechnet ab dem Kindergarteneintritt), der die Zulassung zu Hochschulen ermöglicht.[4] Da in der Schweiz die Kantone die Hauptverantwortung für die Bildungspolitik übernehmen, sieht auch die gymnasiale Maturität von Kanton zu Kanton, teilweise sogar je nach Gymnasium, unterchiedlich aus. Der gemeinsame Nenner stellt das bundesweite Reglement *Maturitätsanerkennungsreglement* (MAR) aus dem Jahr 1995 dar.[5] Dieses Reglement wurde nun aufgehoben und durch das am 01. August 2024 verabschiedete Reglement MAR/MAV ersetzt.[6] Gleichzeitig mit dem MAR/MAV fand die Inkraftsetzung des neuen Rahmenlehrplans[7] statt.

---

[1] EDK, „Gymnasium. Gesamtschweizerische Anerkennung und koordinierte Weiterentwicklung der gymnasialen Maturität", 2024, https://www.edk.ch/de/themen/gymnasium [14.08.2024].

[2] VSPM–SPES–SIFS, https://www.profphil.ch/ [14.08.2024].

[3] EDK, „Bildungssystem Schweiz. Gymnasium", https://www.edk.ch/de/bildungssystem-ch/nachobligatorium/sek-II/gymnasium, 2023 [30.08.2024].

[4] SKBF, „Bildungsbericht Schweiz 2023", https://www.skbf-csre.ch/bildungsbericht/bildungsbericht/ [30.08.2024].

[5] Fedlex, „Verordnung über die Anerkennung von gymnasialen Maturitätsausweisen", 2018, https://www.fedlex.admin.ch/eli/cc/1995/1001_1001_1001/de [22.08.2024].

[6] EDK, „Reglement der EDK über die Anerkennung von gymnasialen Maturitätserzeugnissen (Maturitätsanerkennungsreglement, MAR)", 2023, file:///C:/Users/u0003341/Downloads/A_PLE-2023-2_d_03_gymnasiale-maturitaet.pdf [22.08.2024].

[7] EDK, „Gymnasium".

Der neue Rahmenlehrplan setzt die allgemeine Studierfähigkeit und die vertiefte Gesellschaftsreife als hauptsächliche Bildungsziele, die *kompetenzorientiert* zu erreichen sind. Somit zerfallen die Bildungsziele in einzelne Kompetenzen. Zwar verläuft die Gliederung wie bisher disziplinär, darüber hinaus gewinnen auch inter- und transdisziplinäre Bereiche an Bedeutung. Die transdisziplinären Bereiche *Basale fachliche Kompetenzen für die allgemeine Studierfähigkeit*, *Wissenschaftspropädeutik*, *Digitalität*, *Bildung für nachhaltige Entwicklung und politische Bildung* sollen in jedem Fach und eben auch in interdisziplinären Gefässen gelehrt und gelernt werden.

Angeordnet durch verschiedene, teilweise langwierige Etappen (Vorbereitungs-, Einarbeitungsphase, Vernehmlassung, Anhörung, Inkraftsetzung) arbeiteten zahlreiche Expert:innen, Fachgruppen und Verbände über Jahre hinweg an diesen beiden Referenztexten (MAR/MAV, Rahmenlehrplan). Der Dachverband *Verein der Schweizerischen Gymnasiallehrer und Gymnasiallehrerinnen* (VSG)[8] waltete als eines der Konsultationsorgane für die EDK. Sämtliche Kanntonal- und Fachverbände des VSG beteiligten sich in einem intensiven Prozess an der Vernehmlassungsantwort des VSG. Beim VSG prallten unterschiedliche Partikularinteressen und Gesinnungen aufeinander, so dass sich die gemeinsame Stellungnahme aus dem aufreibenden Tauziehen herauskristallisierte. Dennoch: Eine gebündelte eigene Stellungnahme über einen Verband beim VSG einzugeben, wurde für die Lehrpersonen zur effektivsten Art, um Einfluss zu nehmen. Dies gilt auch für Philosophielehrpersonen, die sich an den VSPM wandten.

Der VSPM ist mit ca. 70 Mitgliedern ein verhältnismässig kleiner Fachverband, doch er deckt mit Mitgliedern aus allen Sprachteilen ein schweizweites Spektrum von Anliegen ab.

Die Heterogenität der schweizerischen Bildungskultur schlägt sich besonders auf das Unterrichtsfach Philosophie nieder: Ob Philosophie als Grundlagen-, obligatorisches, Schwerpunkt- oder Ergänzungsfach angeboten wird, hängt von den Kantonen und von regionalen Charakteristika ab.[9]

Da schweizerische Philosophielehrpersonen ihr Unterrichtsfach in ungleichen Gefässen und kulturellen Prägungen ausgestalten, überrascht es kaum, dass die Meinungen über das Unterrichtsprogramm auseinandergehen: Geht es in der Philosophie vor allem um analytische Arbeit? Wie wichtig ist Philosophiegeschichte? Inwiefern können philosophische Fähigkeiten in Kompetenzen zer-

[8] VSG, https://www.vsg-sspes.ch/ [22.08.2024].

[9] Vgl. Christoph Dejung (1990). „Philosophie-Unterricht in der Schweiz“, in: *L'enseignement philosophique* 40 (1990), https://www.profphil.ch/der-vspm-d/dejung-d [22.08.2024].

gliedert werden? Am durch die VSPM organisierten Kolloquium im Jahr 2021 wurde intensiv über Fragen dieser Art diskutiert.[10]

Die divers geprägten Philosophielehrer:innen eint jedoch eine gemeinsame Überzeugung: Das Fach Philosophie birgt ein immenses Potential, was die gesellschaftlichen Herausforderungen des 21. Jahrhunderts angeht. Sie versammelt sämtliche sogenannte *21. century skills* in einem.[11] Die Philosophie ist *definitionsgemäss* die Disziplin, in der sich Lernende nach Aneignung epistemischer Güter wie Wahrheit und Wissen streben. Welche Disziplin, wenn nicht die Philosophie, gibt den Lernenden also den gewünschten epistemischen Anker, um im Zeitalter zunehmender Komplexität, Krisen und tiefschürfender Veränderungen eine *mentale Resilienz* zu kultivieren?

Erfreut nahmen die VSPM-Mitglieder zur Kenntnis, dass der Zentralvorstand des VSG in seiner Anhörungsantwort den Vorschlag unterbreitete, Philosophie als schweizweites *Grundlagenfach* zu etablieren. Der VSPM hat sich über ein Jahr aktiv für diesen Beschluss eingesetzt. Nachdem die Delegierten in der VSG-Versammlung den Vorschlag übernommen hatten, setzte der VSPM mit einer schweizweiten Kampagne fort, in der die VSPM-Vorstandsmitglieder beharrlich an alle Erziehungsdirektor:innen Argumente für die Einführung des Grundlagenfachs Philosophie herantrugen und sich mit kantonalen Fachschaften vernetzten.

Der Ausgang fiel mit einem im Reglement enthaltenen *Vorschlag*, dass Kantone, Philosophie als Grundlagenfach anbieten dürfen, nicht wie erwünscht aus, da Philosophie damit nicht verbindlich in den Grundfächerkatalog aufgenommen wurde. Doch immerhin haben die Entscheidungsträger:innen den Status der Philosophie auch nicht heruntergesetzt. Die Entscheidungsgewalt liegt somit weiterhin bei den Kantonen.

In der Tradition von Sokrates erlaubte sich der VSPM zudem, sich als ärgerlicher Stachel im Geschehen zu gebaren. Die (philosophisch) anspruchsvolle Leserschaft monierte an der provisorischen Version die begriffliche Vagheit und konzeptuelle Ambiguität. Deswegen formulierte der VSPM neben einer konstruktiven Kritik, insbesondere am Fachrahmenlehrplan Philosophie, auch eine mehrseitige Grundsatzkritik am neuen Rahmenlehrplan.[12] Die Grundsatz-

---

[10] VSPM–SPES–SIFS, „Erstes Schweizer Kolloquium zur Philosophiedidaktik – Freiburg 2021", https://www.profphil.ch/der-vspm-d/kolloquium-2021 [14.08.2024].
[11] Unesco, "TVETIpedia Glossary. 21st century skills", https://unevoc.unesco.org/home/TVETipedia+Glossary/lang=en/show=term/term=21st+century+skills [26.08.24].
[12] VSPM–SPES–SIFS, „Stellungnahme zur Vorlage des Rahmenlehrplans", 17.11.23, https://www.profphil.ch/stellungnahme-des-vsmp-zum-rlp [22.08.24].

kritik enthält die Kritik am Kompetenzbegriff und den Vorschlag, den Text mithilfe von Philosoph:innen zu überarbeiten.

Die 2024 verabschiedete erneuerte Version des Rahmenlehrplans enthält nur einige konstruktive Ergänzungen durch den VSPM. Die Wirkung der Grundsatzkritik auf die Entscheidungsträger:innen bleibt im Dunkeln. Wie dem Austausch unter den VSPM-Mitgliedern zu entnehmen ist, erweist sich die ausformulierte Kritik immerhin als Wohltat für diese.

Die meisten Kantone sind bis 2027 im Begriff, die Referenztexte auf kantonaler Ebene umzusetzen. Nun ist das Engagement der Philosophielehrpersonen auf kantonaler Ebene gefordert: durch partizipative Beteiligung können sie den Stellenwert des Philosophiefachs kantonal mitbestimmen.

Es gibt aber auch über die Revision hinaus Möglichkeiten, die Wichtigkeit des Unterrichtsfachs Philosophie aufzuzeigen. Der VSPM organisierte im Jahr 2023 die Weiterbildung 'OpenAI und wissenschaftsphilosophische Grundlagen'.[13] Für das Jahr 2025 ist in Kooperation mit der Pädagogischen Hochschule Bern die Weiterbildung *Maschinenbewusstsein – Können Roboter ein Bewusstsein haben?* geplant.[14] Die Künstliche Intelligenz ist eine der folgenreichsten Veränderungen des 21. Jahrhunderts. Philosoph:innen ergründen seit Jahrzehnten die Eigenschaften, Möglichkeiten und Gefahren von KI. Eine kritische Distanz wie in der Philosophie ist nicht zuletzt dann wichtig, wenn KI-Phänomene wie Chat-GPT eine grosse mediale Aufmerksamkeit erhalten.[15] Dies ist nur einer von vielen Gründen, die zeigen, warum das Unterrichtsfach Philosophie am Gymnasium wichtiger ist denn je. Dafür steht der VSPM anhaltend ein.

*Für den VSPM: Michelle Wüthrich (Vorsitz)*

[13] Michelle Wüthrich (2023), „OpenAI und wissenschaftsphilosophische Grundlagen. Tagung des VSPM am 7. Juni 2023 im Freien Gymnasium Bern", https://www.vsg-sspes.ch/fileadmin/user_upload/publikationen/Gymnasium_Helveticum/GH-Digital/GH-digital_2023-04_d/GH_2023_04_d_21_OpenAI.pdf [22.08.2024].

[14] PH Bern, „Zur Weiterbildungssuche. Maschinenbewusstsein – Können Roboter ein Bewusstsein haben?, https://www.phbern.ch/weiterbildung/20343281-maschinenbewusstsein-koennen-roboter-ein-bewusstsein-haben [22.08.2024].

[15] Vgl. Daniel Dennett, *I've Been Thinking*, Penguin Random House: New York 2023, 117-118.

*Petra Šebešová*
*(České Budějovice/Budweis, Czech Republic)*

# Philosophical and Critical Thinking in the Context of the Czech Educational System

This article aims to provide an overview of the role of philosophy within the Czech educational system, particularly in the secondary school system, and to discuss current approaches to teaching philosophy in these schools. As we shall see, philosophy holds a relatively minor position among other school subjects, being integrated into a broader subject called Basics of Social Studies and Civics. I would like to argue that philosophical thinking closely aligns with critical thinking, both of which are highly relevant for civic life and education. The second aim of this article is to compare philosophical thinking with critical thinking and explore how they can mutually reinforce each other. The article's final section presents a specific teaching activity that applies a critical thinking method to a philosophical problem, aiming to show how fruitful the combination of both approaches can be.

## 1. Philosophy Education in the Czech Republic

The Czech educational system, like many others, is structured into three levels. Elementary school is compulsory and lasts for nine years, covering ages 6 to 15. Secondary education is differentiated, offering students a choice among various schools, most of which are four years long. These include general schools (grammar schools or gymnasiums) which prepare students for further academic study, and specialized vocational schools which offer a narrower range of subjects. Many gifted students leave elementary school earlier, either after fifth or seventh grade, and finish their compulsory education at six- or eight-year gymnasiums, continuing up to the thirteenth grade. After completing the final secondary school examination, students are eligible to apply for university studies.[1]

Both elementary and secondary education are based on a competence-oriented approach, granting schools considerable autonomy in shaping their curricula and distinguishing themselves from each other. The Framework

[1] For more detailed information on the Czech education system, see for example Embassy of the Czech Republic in Washington, D.C., "Education System in the Czech Republic," https://mzv.gov.cz/washington/en/culture_events/education/education_system_in_the_czech_republic/index.html [30.09.24].

Educational Programme (FEP) serves as the foundational curricular document across these two educational levels, with each school type having its own FEP. The FEP is designed around a competency-based framework, with the overarching goal of fostering the development of seven key competencies: learning competency, problem-solving competency, communication competency, social and personal competency, civic competency, entrepreneurial competency, and digital competency. The FEP outlines mandatory general outcomes, which are then elaborated by each school through the creation of a School Educational Programme (SEP). The SEP specifies the expected outcomes and establishes the school's overall educational framework of the school, including subject selection, course designation, and the allocation of instructional time within predefined limits. The FEP structures for both elementary and secondary education are comparable, with key competencies serving as a cross-disciplinary objective. Educational content is organized into distinct educational areas, each with specified expected outcomes, and is further enriched by cross-curricular subjects designed to shape students' attitudes, values, and behaviours. These cross-curricular subjects include moral, character, and social education; education in European and global contexts; multicultural education; environmental education; and media education.[2]

Philosophy, as such, is only taught at the secondary level in the Czech Republic. However, two initiatives aim to introduce philosophical thinking at the elementary level. First, some institutions promote the Philosophy for Children programme.[3] One such institution, Pink Box, has started publishing translations of French introductory books for children about famous philosophers from the series "Les petits Platons."[4] Second, there is a supplemental school subject called Ethical Education for elementary schools in the FEP. While not mandatory, schools willing to develop ethical and moral understanding as well as prosocial behaviour can use the guidelines from the FEP or textbooks and other resources from the specific website on Ethical education.[5]

---

[2] FEP = Collective of Authors, *Framework Education Programme for Secondary General Education (Grammar Schools)*, Research Institute of Education in Prague – VÚP: Prague 2007, https://www.edu.cz/wp-content/uploads/2020/08/RVP_G-anj.pdf.

[3] For example the University of South Bohemia in České Budějovice (http://www.p4c.cz/), the NGO People in Need (https://www.peopleinneed.net/what-we-do/varianty-educational-programme/philosophy-for-children?_ga=2.55147627.1953715167.1690792098-236285065.1690792097) or private company Pink Box (https://www.pinkbox.org/).

[4] See https://www.lespetitsplatons.com/.

[5] Etická výchova, "Portál pro etickou výchovu ve školách v ČR," http://www.etickavychova.cz/ [30.09.24].

At the secondary level, philosophy is part of a broader educational area called Basics of Civics and Social Sciences, which encompasses introductions to the following disciplines: psychology, sociology, political science, law, international relations, philosophy, and religious studies.[6] As stated above, the FEP provides general expected outcomes that are then specified within the SEP, which divides the subject matter of different educational areas into particular school subjects. At most schools, there is a subject called Basics of Social Studies, taught throughout the four years of secondary education with an average time allocation of one to three lessons per week, usually taught by the same teacher. Philosophy is typically covered in the fourth year over a period of six to eight months.

The content of the philosophical part of the aforementioned educational area is specified in the FEP as follows:

INTRODUCTION TO PHILOSOPHY AND RELIGIOUS STUDIES

*Expected Outcomes*

The pupil shall:

- explain the principles of philosophical questioning, compare the bases of philosophy, myth, religion, science and art for depicting reality and man,
- identify the main philosophical movements, list their key representatives and compare how basic philosophical questions were dealt with in the individual stages of the development of philosophical thinking,
- argue correctly in terms of ethics and facts in dialogue and discussion, approach arguments of others reasonably and critically, identify incorrect arguments and manipulative strategies in interpersonal communication,
- evaluate the importance of scientific knowledge, technology and new technologies for practical life as well as possible risks of their abuse,
- assess the conduct of people in terms of ethical norms and individual conscience, elucidate the variability of basic ethical terms and norms over the course of history,
- distinguish between important religious systems, identify manifestations of religious and other kinds of intolerance and recognise indications of sectarian thinking.

Subject Matter:

- Principles of philosophy – basic philosophical questions, the relations of

[6] In the following, I am focusing on philosophy as outlined in the FEP for general education (grammar schools) because it is the most elaborated there.

philosophy and myth, philosophy and religion, philosophy and science, and philosophy and art

- Philosophy in history – key stages and movements of philosophical thought
- Faith in human life – forms of faith, signs of religious faith; religious systems, Churches; sects.[7]

As we can see, the subject matter of philosophy is rather unspecified and vague. On the one hand, the history of philosophy is explicitly stated as a part of the educational content, on the other hand, the expected outcomes focus more on the development of certain skills. These two aspects of teaching philosophy do not necessarily have to be viewed as a dichotomy, but in reality, it is often difficult to engage students in thinking and developing their thinking skills when the subject matter is foreign to them and perceived as irrelevant to their own lives, which is often the case with the history of philosophy. Though philosophy at secondary schools has traditionally been taught as an overview of its history – and at many schools and according to most textbooks still is – there has been some development in recent years towards a problem-oriented and competence-based approach to teaching that aims to enhance philosophical thinking. This approach primarily focuses on argumentative, interpretative and reflective skills of the pupils and situates historical texts within a contemporary context.[8]

One possible way to shift the focus towards developing thinking skills, not only in teaching philosophy but also in other social sciences, might be through an emphasis on critical thinking, which is viewed as a key component of civic competencies.[9] At the same time, the term is likely overused and easily reduced to the rather technical skill of recognising disinformation or assessing resources. I would like to show in the following that when taken seriously, critical and philosophical thinking have much in common, and philosophy may thus gain a more prominent position among the social sciences.

[7] FEP, 42.

[8] For a more detailed description of the contemporary conception of teaching philosophy, see Petra Šebešová, "Teaching Philosophy and Environmental Education the Czech Republic," in: *Philosophie und Umweltbildung/Philosophy and Environmental Education*, ed. Werner Busch/Gabriele Münnix/Bernd Rolf, Bautz Verlag: Nordhausen 2024, 93-109.

[9] Martyn Barrett et al., *Reference Framework of Competences for Democratic Culture*, vol. 1, *Context, Concepts and Model*, Council of Europe Publishing: Strasbourg Cedex 2018, http://rm.coe.int/prems-008318-gbr-2508-reference-framework-of-competences-vol-1-8573-co/16807bc66c.

## 2. Critical and philosophical thinking[10]

To begin with, we need a definition of critical thinking, which is not an easy matter. I find the following conceptions of critical thinking the most useful to work with, for they provide an operationalised account of both skills and affective dispositions that are needed to think critically in a complex way. These conceptions are those of Robert Ennis,[11] a consensual conception provided by the American Philosophical Association[12] and a conception focused on the elements of thought by Richard Paul and Linda Elder,[13] proponents of the Foundation for Critical Thinking. Ennis uses a general definition that critical thinking is "reflective and deliberative thinking that focuses on deciding what to believe or do".[14] We can elaborate this definition, in an attempt to provide a synthesis of the other conceptions, and distinguish between three main components of critical thinking: 1) specific knowledge (e.g., the knowledge needed to correctly analyse and evaluate information or arguments), 2) skills (analysis, interpretation, argumentation and evaluation that take into account the various elements of thinking), and 3) affective dispositions (open-mindedness towards different viewpoints, pursuit of true knowledge, trust in the processes of reasoned inquiry, honesty in facing one's own biases, prudence in suspending, making or altering judgments etc.).[15]

Let us now see how critical thinking is related to philosophical thinking. I will briefly summarize the conclusions I reached in my dissertation[16] regarding the specification of philosophical thinking. On the basis of the analysis of selected introductions to philosophy (Karl Jaspers, Ladislav Hejdánek, Simon Blackburn and others) and the concepts of German didacticians of philosophy (Ekkehard Martens, Jonas Pfister, Johannes Rohbeck), two basic features of philosophical

---

[10] This part of the article is based on my recent article written in Czech, focusing on the relationship between philosophical and critical thinking: Petra Šebešová, "Kritické myšlení v kontextu didaktiky filosofie a základů společenských věd", in: *Orbis Scholae* 17 (2023), 85-102.

[11] Robert Ennis, "Critical Thinking. A Streamlined Conception," *Teaching Philosophy* 14 (1991), 5-24.

[12] Peter Facione (ed.), *Critical Thinking. A Statement of Expert Consensus for Purposes of Educational Assessment and Instruction. Research Findings and Recommendations*, Insight Assessment 1990.

[13] Linda Elder/Richard Paul, *A Guide for Educators to Critical Thinking Competency Standards.* The Foundation for Critical Thinking 2005, https://www.criticalthinking.org/resources/pdf/ct-competencies%202005.pdf.

[14] Ennis, "Critical Thinking," 6.

[15] Peter Facione (ed.), *Critical Thinking.*

[16] Petra Šebešová, *Jak učit filosofii na gymnáziích? Příspěvek k didaktice filosofie* [dissertation], Charles University: Prague 2016,
https://dspace.cuni.cz/bitstream/handle/20.500.11956/2929/140055390.pdf.

thinking emerge on which all the examined authors agree: reflection and critical examination of thought content. Reflection can mean both a turning of attention towards the object of thought and an examination of this object in its entirety, i.e. including its assumptions, context and related concepts, as well as a turning to oneself as the subject of thought (then we speak of self-reflection) and an examination of e.g. our assumptions, perspectives and other aspects that influence our thinking. At the same time, this reflection leads us to recognize the limitations of our knowledge and the need to examine the content and correctness of our thinking, our knowledge and our beliefs.

Reflection and critical examination or validation of the correctness of thought is a fundamental feature of philosophical thinking also according to Paul, who defines the philosophical approach as opposed to the non-philosophical approach as follows: "The philosophical mind routinely examines the foundations of its own thinking, realizing that its thinking is determined by its basic concepts, goals, assumptions, and values."[17] Through this reflection, the philosophical mind gains distance from its own thinking, becomes aware of its framework and thus of other possible perspectives. At the same time, according to the author, it is not afraid to not only examine but also to change the basic principles, concepts, methods, etc., with which it works.

If philosophical thinking is not specified in terms of its content, but in terms of its thought process, then in its basic features it has much in common with critical thinking. Both are driven by the pursuit of true knowledge or correct understanding, presuppose reflection, and consist in analysing and evaluating the correctness of thought processes and contents. The close relationship between critical thinking and philosophy is also evident from the literature on critical thinking. For example, Jennifer Mulnix states that critical thinking "is the very practice of philosophy."[18] Similarly, Marie-France Daniel and Emmanuelle Auriac see the similarity between critical and philosophical thinking, suggesting that the basis of philosophy is "the exchange of arguments in a reflective and critical manner" and that critical thinking is "reflective and judgmental thinking focused on what to think, what to believe, and what to do."[19] The goal of both philosophy and critical thinking, then, is to develop autonomously thinking

---

[17] Richard Paul, "Critical and Reflective Thinking. A Philosophical Perspective," in *Dimensions of Thinking and Cognitive Instruction*, ed. Beau Jones/Lorna Idol, Lawrence Erlbaum Associates 1990, 445-494 (p. 448).

[18] Jennifer Mulnix, "Thinking Critically about Critical Thinking," *Educational Philosophy and Theory* 44 (2013), 464-479 (p. 472).

[19] Marie-France Daniel/Emmanuelle Auriac, "Philosophy, Critical Thinking and Philosophy for Children," In: *Educational Philosophy and Theory* 43 (2011), 415-435 (p. 420).

individuals capable of reflection, complex reasoning, logical argumentation, and constructive scepticism.[20]

How then do philosophical and critical thinking differ? I believe that methodologically they are the same[21] and consist of a comprehensive analysis and evaluation of a certain problem, including reflection of different possible points of view, assumptions, consequences, concepts used, etc. What differs is the focus, the type of question to which both ways of thinking seek to answer. The philosophical mode of enquiry (and it does not have to be focused only on the classical philosophical questions falling under ontology, epistemology, etc.) remains at an abstract, theoretical level: philosophical enquiry aims to clarify general concepts or general structures of reality and the relations between them in order to be better able to understand reality.[22] Philosophical inquiry is not empirical. There are different answers to philosophical questions, and it is not empirical evidence but the strength and persuasiveness of the arguments that determines which ones are considered true. This is also why the history of philosophy has a different status than, say, the history of science. Plato's or Aristotle's arguments or conceptual distinctions can still be as relevant to certain topics today as they were in the past.

Critical thinking is more concrete in this respect; we usually use it in a particular situation, in answering a particular question or solving a particular problem, which, moreover, is often related to some field of human knowledge. Its aim is to find an answer, a position or a decision that is based on true information, supported by good arguments and in which we are aware of our possible biases or value preferences. For example, I can decide who I will vote for in the parliamentary elections. Critical thinking leads me to analyse the programs of political parties (in terms of their achievability, coherence and specificity of elaboration), to analyse the statements and actions of the representatives of these parties (based on comparing reports from various reliable sources, etc. ), but also to reflect on my own assumptions (what points of the programme are important to me and why; what I need as a citizen and which party has the greatest potential to fulfil these needs; to what extent my preferences are influenced by personal sympathies for individual politicians or by pressure from the environment, etc.), and on the basis of all this I evaluate the situation and lean towards one party. Philosophical thinking would lead me

---

[20] Daniel/Auriac, "Philosophy, Critical Thinking and Philosophy for Children," 420-421.

[21] See also Paul, "Critical and Reflective Thinking."

[22] Similarly, Daniel/Auriac, "Philosophy, Critical Thinking and Philosophy for Children"; Colin McGinn, "The Science of Philosophy", in: *Metaphilosophy* 46 (2015), 84-103.

to ask questions such as: What are the basic values of the political parties and which values are essential for me? Why go to the polls at all? What is the role of the citizen in a democracy? In what sense are elections free and not free?

However, the line between the two ways of thinking can be very thin, because reflection on our (or the examined) assumptions can very quickly lead to some values that we consider fundamental (in the example above, e.g. education, consideration for the socially disadvantaged, maximum individual freedom, etc.) or other general concepts (here, e.g. the concept of freedom and democracy). These general concepts have a fundamental impact on our understanding of reality. By examining them, we find ourselves already on the ground of philosophy. Thus, a summary of the exploration of the relationship between philosophical and critical thinking could be the claim that philosophical and critical thinking share a common intersection in their analytical methodological approach. Critical thinking, however, is not defined by content in any way, whereas philosophical thinking focuses on the examination of general concepts or structures in order to better understand reality. At the same time, philosophical thinking is not exhausted by this critical aspect and includes other forms of thinking, such as creative or speculative thinking.

### 3. Application

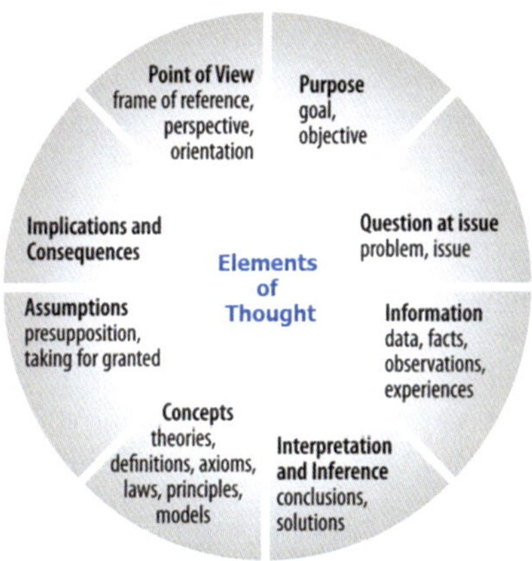


I have tried to show that critical and philosophical thinking consist of similar thought processes but differ in their subject matter. I would now like to show how a method coming from the critical thinking sphere can promote and enrich deeper reflection that is the basis of philosophical thinking.

I like to work with the "wheel of reason",[23] which lists eight elements of thought that should be analysed and evaluated when we want to think critically about an issue. The ele-

[23] The Critical Thinking Community, "Wheel of Reason," https://community.criticalthinking.org/wheelOfReason.php [30.09.24].

ments of thought can be worked with in different ways. I will now present a unit on topic of surrogacy that has been taught both at secondary school and within a university course on critical thinking.

*Lesson objectives:*

*Students:*

- state the possible arguments for/against the surrogacy from the moral point of view
- analyse the given situation from different perspectives
- formulate their own position toward the problem and try to reflect on their underlying values
- learn how to use the elements of thought in the process of critical thinking

*Lesson description:*

Context: The lesson has been developed as a part of a critical thinking course, as an introduction to the elements of thought and reflection. It can be used in philosophy classes concerned with practical ethics, too.

1. We begin the lesson by naming the topic, i. e. the issue of surrogacy. Students then individually read a one-page description of a real case, known as the "Baby M" case.[24] The case involves breaking an agreement between the childless pair and the surrogate mother, who wants to keep the baby after giving birth. The question is whether, from the moral standpoint, the agreement should be enforced. Students write down their answer and their reasons for it. They can share their answers in pairs, when they are finished.

2. As a next step, we do not yet discuss the issue. First, we let the students show a) what their standpoints are and b) how certain they are of their view (by placing their hand on a virtual scale between the desk and their head).

3. Before the expected discussion we complete one further step. We try to analyse the situation and understand it more deeply using the elements of thought. After a brief introduction to the meaning and purpose of the elements of thought, students divide into groups according to the element they want to use for the analysis of the situation. Then they sit together with their group, briefly share their positions and arguments towards the situation, and then try to answer the following questions pertaining to their element of thoughts (they write them down in an online form that will, later on, be projected for the whole class):

- What is your intention in this task? What are the intentions of each character in the story?

[24] I work with the description coming from: Michael Sandel, *Justice: What's the Right Thing to Do?*, Penguin Books: London 2010, 91-92.

- What questions are relevant to solving the problem? What questions will help you better decide in this case?
- What information do we have about the problem? How reliable is this information? What information would we still need?
- What arguments do you base your conclusion on? What assumptions underlie these arguments? What other conclusions/arguments would be possible?
- What are the main concepts relevant to this situation? What concepts need to be explained?
- What assumptions do you base your position on? Are these assumptions justified? How can you verify them?
- What consequences would your position lead to for the individual characters in the story and for society as a whole?
- From what perspective do you view the situation? What would be the viewpoints and positions of the individual characters in the story?

4. After the teamwork, the groups share and comment on their answers which the teacher supplements by other possible answers. Throughout the sharing, we can discuss the issue, ask further questions etc.
5. Each of the students writes down their final position. We then repeat the scale showing how certain they are of their viewpoint and then reflect on the whole process.
6. As a final step in the lesson, we look at the real outcome of the court case (I use the arguments for and against, as discussed in the mentioned M. Sandel's book) and briefly discuss it. Finally, students learn about the laws governing surrogacy in the Czech Republic.

## 4. Conclusion

I have tried to show that critical thinking is a complex process, based on reflection. Methodologically, it is very close to philosophical thinking because it does not only include the evaluation of information but also the examination of the concepts used, of our assumptions and values, possible consequences and the skill to formulate and assess arguments. Because philosophy is taught as a part of a broader subject together with social sciences and civics in the Czech Republic, I find it important to interconnect all these disciplines through a common objective that might be the development of autonomous and correct thinking among the pupils. Both philosophy and the critical thinking movement can provide useful methods and approaches to reach this aim.

*Dorothy Oluwagbemi-Jacob*
*(Calabar, Nigeria)*

# Philosophical Education in Nigeria: History, Current Challenges and Trends

## Introduction

There is no single definition of philosophy that is universally acceptable. Simply put, philosophy is characterized by the curiosity of the human mind to acquire knowledge of both itself and the universe. The philosophical activity begins in wonder. What the human being observes and experiences daily are objects of wonder. Such inspire humans to raise questions regarding the nature of ultimate reality, existence, the phenomenon of death, the essence of morality, politics, justice and the human condition. As a discipline, philosophy investigates the fundamental questions about ultimate reality or existence, knowledge, morality, reason, and human nature.

Generally, philosophical education refers to the formal teaching and learning of philosophy. It goes beyond the mere acquisition of knowledge about historical philosophers and their ideas but involves cultivating a method of thinking critically, reflecting on concepts, and questioning assumptions. This type of education goes beyond the confines of the classroom.[1] It is impactful and transformative as an individual's ability to reason, make judgments, and understand complex ideas are developed in the process. It was in this connection that Jaspers (1959) defines philosophical education as the education of the whole person, focusing not only on intellectual development but also on ethical and moral maturity. For Jaspers, philosophy serves as the foundation of all educational endeavors because it helps individuals reflect on their own learning processes and integrate knowledge from various disciplines into a coherent worldview.[2]

In the Nigerian context, philosophical education combines both the study of Western philosophical traditions and African philosophical thought, which emphasizes communal values, justice, and harmony. Nigerian philosophers like Peter Bodunrin and Sophie Oluwole have worked to assert the importance of African philosophy as a legitimate and necessary part of the philosophical

---

[1] Raphael J. Njoroge/Gerard Bennaars, Godfrey (eds.), *Philosophy of Education in Africa*, Transafrica Press: Nairobi 1986.
[2] Karl Jaspers, *The Idea of the University*, Peter Owen: London 1959.

education landscape.[3] The importance of philosophical education cannot be overemphasized as it develops critical thinking,[4] fosters ethical reasoning, and promotes societal development, as well as interdisciplinary integration. Any nation that ignores this type of education does so at its own peril because such an education plays a vital role in the holistic development of individuals and societies. The integration of both Western and African philosophical traditions into Nigeria's educational system is particularly important, as it allows students to engage with a broad spectrum of intellectual traditions that are relevant to both their local context and the global arena.

The purpose of this paper is to explore the history, current challenges and trends of philosophical education in Nigeria. To accomplish its purpose, this paper is divided into three sections. In section one, I give the historical overview of philosophical education in Nigeria tracing its root to colonial period and the introduction of Western Philosophy in Nigeria, the post-independence and the development of African philosophy. In section two, I make an attempt to highlight the current challenges that philosophical education faces in Nigeria. Section three discusses the current trends of philosophical education in Nigeria. This section also embodies the conclusion.

## 1. Historical Overview of Philosophical Education in Nigeria

It is important to indicate from the onset that what is referred to as philosophical education in Nigeria is not just the product of the imposition of Western education. This is because prior to the advent of colonialism and formal education, Nigeria had rich traditions of philosophical thought embedded in its cultural and communal practices. This indigenous philosophy was largely communicated through oral traditions, proverbs, folktales, and communal values. The pre-colonial era witnessed sophisticated systems of thought, including metaphysical ideas, ethical norms, and political structures that guided everyday life. Such philosophical ideas in pre-colonial Nigeria embodied communal values ranging from shared humanity, integrity and responsibility and collective cooperation. These ideas conveyed metaphysical and moral principles like the interdependence of human beings, the nature of existence, and the role of individuals within society.

They were also embedded in proverbs by means of which complex philosophical ideas about life, death, justice, and human relationships were

[3] Sophia Olúwọlé, *Philosophy and Oral Tradition*, Ark Publications: Lagos 1999.
[4] Mathew Lipman, *Thinking in Education*, Cambridge University Press: Cambridge 2003.

communicated from one generation to another. In his *An Essay on African Philosophical Thought*, Kwame Gyekye explores the way traditional African societies expressed philosophical concepts through non-written forms, emphasizing communalism and moral responsibility[5] while Kwasi Wiredu discusses the importance of oral traditions in maintaining and communicating African philosophical values, highlighting the shared metaphysical beliefs that shaped pre-colonial African societies.[6]

With the establishment of colonial rule in Nigeria in the late 19th and early 20th centuries, formal Western-style education and its associated philosophical traditions were introduced. The British colonial administration set up schools and universities, which were modeled after European institutions. These schools emphasized Christian doctrine and European ways of thinking. As the colonial government extended its influence, the formalization of Western education spread, culminating in the establishment of the University of Ibadan in 1948, which became Nigeria's first tertiary institution. The curriculum of the University of Ibadan was dominated by Western philosophical traditions particularly the analytic tradition. Students were introduced to classical Greek philosophers like Socrates, Plato and Aristotle, as well as modern philosophers such as Descartes, Hume and Kant. The teaching of philosophy was primarily oriented toward logic, epistemology and metaphysics. This curriculum did not reflect indigenous African philosophical ideas. Western philosophy became the standard for teaching and scholarly inquiry.[7]

The postcolonial period saw the rise of universities across Nigeria and the formalization of philosophy as an academic discipline. After Nigeria gained independence in 1960, the University of Ibadan was followed by the creation of other (first generation) universities including the University of Nigeria, Nsukka in 1960, Ahmadu Bello University in 1962, University of Ife between 1961 and 1962, later renamed Obafemi Awolowo University. The other (second generation) universities were established in the 1970s. As at 4th September 2024, Nigeria had 270 Universities: 149 private universities, 63 and 62 state and Federal Universities respectively.[8] These institutions have become centres of

---

[5] Kwame Gyekye, *An Essay on African Philosophical Thought: The Akan Conceptual Scheme*, Temple University Press: Philadelphia 1995.
[6] Kwasi Wiredu, *Philosophy and an African Culture*, Cambridge University Press: Cambridge 1980.
[7] Barry Hallen, *A Short History of African Philosophy*. Indiana University Press: Bloomington 2002; Emmanuel Eze, *Postcolonial African Philosophy: A Critical Reader*, Blackwell Publishing: Hoboken 1997.
[8] https//www.statistica.com.

academic learning and philosophical discourse. Notably, Western philosophy has remained dominant in the curriculum, even in the post-colonial period. However, efforts have been made to integrate African philosophy into academic programmes.

Philosophy became a recognized academic discipline in Nigerian universities during the 1960s and 1970s. Departments of philosophy were established, and scholarly inquiry began to explore not only Western thought but also African philosophical traditions. This marked a turning point in the intellectual history of Nigeria, as African scholars sought to reclaim and validate their indigenous knowledge systems. In his *Philosophy in Nigeria: A General Introduction,* Chukwudum Momoh outlines the evolution of philosophy as an academic discipline in Nigeria, noting the challenges faced in integrating African philosophical ideas into the formal educational structure.[9]

In 1989, the Nigerian National Universities Commission (NUC) made the study of "philosophy and logic" compulsory for all Nigerian undergraduates irrespective of their major areas of study in Nigerian Universities. In the current CCMAS released by the National Universities Commission (NUC) the course is titled, 'Philosophy, Logic and Human existence.'

It was in the post-colonial era that Nigerian philosophers began to advocate for the recognition of African philosophy as a legitimate academic field. This led to the emergence of the African Philosophy Movement, a scholarly effort to demonstrate that African societies had developed their own rich philosophical traditions, independent of Western influences. An intense debate was generated in the 1970s and 1980s, among African philosophers regarding the existence of African philosophy. Key Nigerian philosophers such as Peter Bodunrin argued that much of what was considered African philosophy lacked the formal rigour associated with Western philosophical traditions. He argued that African philosophy should meet the same criteria of logic and rationality applied to Western philosophy and that philosophy must be critical and systematic. He contended whether traditional African thought met these criteria.[10] In contrast, Sophie Oluwole emphasized the validity of African modes of thought, arguing that African philosophy needed to be understood on its own terms, reflecting indigenous epistemologies and metaphysical beliefs.[11]

---

[9] Chukwudum Momoh, *Philosophy in Nigeria: A General Introduction*, University of Lagos Press: Lagos 1989.

[10] Peter Bodunrin, "The Question of African Philosophy", in: *Philosophy* 56 (1981), 161-179.

[11] Sophie B. Olúwọlé, *Socrates and Orunmila: Two Patron Saints of Classical Philosophy*. Ark Publishers: Lagos 2014.

The curriculum in Nigerian philosophy departments is designed to provide students with a broad understanding of philosophical traditions, both African and Western, while equipping them with critical thinking skills. The African Philosophy component of the curriculum covers indigenous concepts such as Ubuntu, communitarianism, and some metaphysical beliefs. The curriculum examines the relevance of these philosophies in contemporary African societies and their interaction with Western philosophical thought. Courses in ethics address both Western and African moral theories. Topics such as utilitarianism, deontology, virtue ethics, and African communitarian ethics are central to understanding moral reasoning in different cultural contexts. Students are encouraged to explore how ethical theories apply to issues like corruption, governance, and human rights in Nigeria. Logic is a foundational component of the philosophy curriculum. Nigerian universities emphasize formal logic, teaching students principles of valid reasoning, symbolic logic, and argumentation. Critical thinking has also been introduced as a course on its own.This is crucial in developing students' analytical abilities and their capacity to evaluate arguments critically.

Courses in metaphysics cover topics like the nature of reality, being, causality, and the existence of God. Epistemology addresses theories of knowledge, the nature of belief, and the distinction between justified belief and opinion. Both fields are taught with reference to both Western and African perspectives. This points to a balanced curriculum.[12]

## 2. Current Challenges Facing Philosophical Education in Nigeria

In Nigeria, philosophical education faces several challenges that hinder its development and the broader acceptance of philosophy as a critical academic discipline. These challenges range from institutional issues, such as a lack of resources, to societal perceptions regarding the value of philosophy. In what follows, I make an effort to highlight some of these challenges. These include:

### *2.1. Limited Access to Philosophical Texts and Journals*

Scarcity of resources reflects in the lack of comprehensive libraries that house the latest philosophical publications and lack of access to databases. This hampers students' and faculty members' ability to effectively access and explore issues in contemporary philosophical debates. In addition, many philosophy departments lack the resources to maintain subscriptions to international jour-

[12] Hallen, *A Short History of African Philosophy*; Eze, *Postcolonial African Philosophy*; Kwasi Wiredu, *Cultural Universals and Particulars: An African Perspective*. Indiana University Press: Bloomington 1996.

nals, limiting access to current research in both Western and African philosophy. Consequently, students are constrained to rely more on limited physical texts some of which may be outdated.

*2.2. Inadequate Research Funding*

The lack of adequate funding for research in Nigerian universities is a systemic problem and poses a serious challenge for philosophical education. In the absence of financial support, philosophers in Nigeria find it challenging to participate in global philosophical communities through conferences and publications. This affects the availability of philosophical materials in Nigerian institutions and impedes progress in philosophical research.[13]

*2.3. Low Enrollment and Interest*

This has to do with the perception of philosophy as a discipline that lacks practical value. Following this, many students and their families prefer fields that are likely to offer immediate employment opportunities on graduation such as law, engineering, pharmacy or medicine. This is the reason why philosophy as a discipline suffers low enrollment rates and declining interest compared to these other fields of study. In a country where there is an emphasis on vocational and technical education following the stark economic realities, philosophy is dismissed as an abstract discipline that does not lead to lucrative employment in the job market.[14]

But is it really true that philosophy lacks practical value? From the perspective of critical thinking, this misconception has been the bane of Nigeria regarding insecurity, corruption and persistent economic woes. Philosophy is, in fact, essential for developing the critical thinking, ethical reasoning, and intellectual rigour needed to address Nigeria's complex socio-economic problems. So many challenges in Nigeria's socio-economic landscape at present can be attributed to wrong decisions, which a little application of critical thinking principles would have solved. Courses in ethics, political philosophy, and logic provide students with tools to critically evaluate government policies, engage in ethical decision-making, and promote good governance. Philosophy may not

---

[13] Theophilus Okere, *African Philosophy: A Historico-Hermeneutical Investigation of the Conditions of Its Possibility,* University of Nigeria Press: Nsukka 1983, Joseph Oguejiofor, *Philosophy and the African Experience: The Contributions of African Thought to Global Philosophy,* University of Nigeria Press: Nsukka 2001.

[14] Godwin Azenabor, *Philosophy and Logic in African Philosophy*, University of Lagos Press: Lagos 2009, Olusegun Oladipo, *The Idea of African Philosophy*, Molecular Publishers: Ibadan 1992.

directly bake bread but it gives the individual ideas and insights that will enable such bake bread.

Philosophers such as Oluwole and Wiredu have argued in this connection that philosophy has practical value when applied to African contexts, where it can challenge corrupt practices, promote ethical leadership, and foster dialogue about justice and human rights.[15] But unfortunately, many refuse to see it in this light.

## 3. Trends of Philosophical Education in Nigeria

Contrary to some misperceptions, philosophical education in Nigeria has a lot of promise in terms of being the elixir for treating Nigeria's social and political malaise. It has the capacity to meet Nigeria's contemporary challenges and enriching its intellectual discourse. With the new National Universities Commission's CCMAS strategic reforms in curriculum design, public engagement and interdisciplinary collaboration, philosophy can play a transformative role in Nigeria's academic and socio-political landscape.

One noticeable trend in philosophical education in Nigeria at present is its integration of more African philosophical traditions into the curriculum. Given its colonial history, Western philosophy dominated Nigerian academic programmes, but there is a growing recognition of the need to decolonize philosophical education and give African philosophy the prominence it deserves. At present, philosophical education tends to be more contextualized and more impactful by exposing students to courses on traditional African concepts like Ubuntu, communalism, and African metaphysics that reflect their cultural heritage. There is a greater recognition that African students need to study philosophies rooted in their own cultural experiences to fully understand and engage with their identities.[16]

Another trend in philosophical education in Nigeria pertains to its inclusion of contemporary global issues such as climate change, ethics of artificial intelligence, and global justice. In exploring these topics, philosophy students get exposed to global debates while addressing issues that directly impact Nigeria, such as environmental degradation, technological advancements, and international human rights. This integration has gone a long way to show that philosophy is relevant to the public domain, not just an affair of the classroom.[17]

---

[15] Olúwọlé, *Socrates and Orunmila*; Wiredu, *Cultural Universals and Particulars*.
[16] Wiredu, *Philosophy and an African Culture*; Olúwọlé, *Socrates and Orunmila*.
[17] Eze, *Postcolonial African Philosophy*.

Further, beyond the classroom, there is an integration of the town and the gown as shown in the organization of conferences, public lectures, and symposia by universities and philosophical associations that engage philosophers, public intellectuals, and policymakers in philosophical discussions on current societal issues. This encourages the dissemination of philosophical ideas beyond academic circles and fosters a culture of critical thinking in broader society.[18]

Worth mentioning also is the trend of interdisciplinary collaboration. Such courses as philosophy of law, which combines philosophy and law provides law students with the critical thinking skills necessary for sound legal reasoning, philosophy and politics which offers insights into governance, democracy, and the role of justice in society, create well-rounded policymakers who are equipped to critically assess government policies, political structures, and human rights issues. In the area of business and technology, several philosophy departments have incorporated business ethics exposing students to the ethical implications of emerging technologies and addressing issues such as corporate responsibility, ethics of artificial intelligence, and the moral dimensions of economic inequality. This fosters critical thinking across disciplines.[19]

## Conclusion

This paper set out to discuss philosophical education as this pertains to Nigeria. It tried to trace the various stages of evolution of philosophical education from the precolonial, colonial to the postcolonial period. It made the point that philosophical education in Nigeria is not the child of Western colonial imposition alone but rather had its origin in the indigenous philosophical ideas as captured in the oral traditions and proverbs transmitted from one generation to another. Having noted that the curriculum of the philosophy departments (University of Ibadan) established prior to and after independence was dominated by Western philosophy, the paper made the point that such at present incorporates both the Western and the indigenous or African philosophy. The paper also highlighted the challenges philosophical education is facing in Nigeria to include lack of adequate resources for research, misconception regarding the practical value of philosophy and the marginalization such has suffered as a result. On the positive side, however, the paper pointed out the current trends in philosophical education that position it for societal impact.

---

[18] Kwame Anthony Appiah, *Cosmopolitanism: Ethics in a World of Strangers,* Penguin: London/ New York 2006.

[19] Martha Nussbaum, *Cultivating Humanity: A Classical Defense of Reform in Liberal Education,* Harvard University Press: Cambridge 1997.

From the foregoing, it can be said that philosophical education in Nigeria has the potential for growth and impact. As Nigerian philosophers continue to engage with global and African thought, the discipline of philosophy is positioned to contribute significantly to both local and international philosophical debates. Making 'philosophy and logic' and now 'philosophy, logic and human existence' a compulsory course for all the undergraduate students in Nigeria irrespective of their field of study has brought philosophical discussions into the mainstream and can foster a culture of critical thinking. Interdisciplinary collaborations between philosophy and fields like law, politics, and technology do enhance the application of philosophical reasoning in various sectors. If these current trends are anything to go by, one can say that philosophical education in Nigeria can become a powerful force for societal transformation.

# 2. The Topic / Zum Thema / Le sujet

*Ewa Nowak (Poznań, Poland)*

## Populist Philosophy of Law and its Colonial Legacy

### 1. Populism

In his book *A Lacanian Conception of Populism*, Timothy Appleton identifies an analogy between the Freudian question: "What does woman want/desire" and the question "What does the people want/desire"[1]. The latter roughly frames the semantic field of the term *populism* (from *populus, population, people*). Well, the object of populist ideology (politics, discourse) is that which serves to satisfy the desires of 'people'. But this is an incomplete meaning of populism: populist politics, discourse, narrative can produce and promote 'imaginaries', utopias, or promises of a better, desirable, and sometimes utopian order offered by governors who are themselves, by definition, vocated to be servants of the people.[2] More generally, a doctrine promising to improve the life standard of people who are unsatisfied with can be populist. The populist imaginary may portray society as a homogenous and harmonious totality, but according to Appleton, Laclau and Mouffe[3], there is an unbridgeable division in this totality between elite and people, 'us vs. them'[4], classes, castes, or camps. Between the two there occurs an antagonism as "the fundamental ontological aspect of populism (i.e., of politics as such)"[5], with various socio-economic, normative, and political consequences, including the hegemony of one class (or camp). Thus, populist doctrine or imaginarium generates and legitimises various forms of inequality, injustice, exclusion, stigmatisation ("The corresponding normative eliminativism

---

[1] Timothy Appleton, *A Lacanian Conception of Populism*, Routledge: London/New York 2023, 269.

[2] A colonial utopia "under their own [colonizers', – E.N.] laws" was designed by Thomas Moore, see Susan Bruce, "Utopian Justifications: More's 'Utopia', Settler Colonialism, and Contemporary Ecocritical Concerns", in: *College Literature* 42(1) (2015), 23-43; Lyman Tower Sargent, "Colonial Utopias/Dystopias", in: *The World Novel in English to 1950*, ed. Ralph Crane/Jane Stafford/Mark Williams, Oxford University Press: Oxford 2016, 300-312; Randall Holcombe, "Populism. Promises and Problems", in: *The Independent Review* 26(1) (2021), 27-37.

[3] Ernesto Laclau, *On Populist Reason*, Verso: London 2005.

[4] Axel Mueller, "The Meaning of Populism", in: *Philosophy and Social Criticism* 45(9-10) (2019), 1026; also, Jan-Werner Müller, *What Is Populism?* De Gruyter: Berlin 2016.

[5] Appleton, *A Lacanian Conception of Populism*, 272.

(or nihilism) also underwrites populism's preference for non-cooperative, adversarial zero-sum politics"[6]), rather than merely the differences inherent in an agonistic model of democracy.[7] This would be a schematic account of populism, which is not an easy-to-define phenomenon. It is even more challenging to grasp it in the context of a colonial philosophy of law – which is precisely the focus of this article.

## 2. Populist philosophy of law in the early modern era

Populist doctrines and imaginaries were also produced by modern political philosophy and philosophy of law. Some of them significantly influenced the politics and legislation of colonial empires, while shaping "social imaginaries [...] shared by large groups of people, if not the whole society"[8]. The contents of these colonial imaginaries revolved around the discovered and conquered lands of the New World, its inhabitants and the colonisers' attitude towards them – initially cognitive, but soon also practical and regulative. "The social imaginary is that common understanding that makes possible common practices and a widely shared sense of legitimacy"[9], Taylor explains. But here, in the context of colonisation, such a sample imaginary included an understanding – or, more often, a misunderstanding – of the extra-European others and forms of practice and cooperation emerging from it. Their authors were aiming to establish some kind of relationship between 'us' and 'them': this relationship was based on the hegemony of 'us'. Therefore, the genealogies of colonial imaginaries were different from the bottom-up and immanently communal imaginaries as described by Taylor. Early modern, colonial proto-imaginaries fed first on accounts of explorers and conquerors, translated to Latin and circulating among literate and influential elites. On 3 August 1492, Columbus created the first imaginarium in which the Taíno (indigenous inhabitants of the islands included in the West Indies) are all "destitute of arms [...] because they are timid and full of terror [...] when they see that they are safe, and all fear is banished, they are very guileless and honest, and very liberal of all they have [...]. They manifest the greatest affection towards all of us, exchanging valuable things for trifles, content with the very least thing or nothing at all. [...] They might become Christians and inclined to love our King and Queen and Princes and all the people of Spain; and that they might be eager to search for and gather and give to us

[6] Mueller, "The Meaning of Populism", 1034.
[7] E.g., Chantal Mouffe, "Deliberative Democracy or Agonistic Pluralism?", in: *Prospects for Democracy* 66(3) (1999), 745-758.
[8] Charles Taylor, *Modern Social Imaginaries.* Duke University Press: Durham/London, 2004.
[9] Ibid., 23.

what they abound in and we greatly need"[10]. Epistemic false and cruel imperial (respectively, colonial) claims inscribed in reports of figures such as Columbus, Diego Velázquez, Francisco López de Gomara, and (after 1540) Hernán Cortés, law graduate of the University of Salamanca[11], will be questioned by Bartolomé de las Casas in his *New Laws*[12] and Spanish courts.

Reports such as the one referenced above reached Renaissance legal scholars, and these were elaborating on foundations of the colonial rule of law, including *jus gentium* (the common law of nations). Inspired by ancient Roman and biblico-theological sources, they created visions of order and even democracy brought to the overseas lands by enlightened – and armed – European elites, who were to first civilise and christianise the 'Sauvages'. Many philosophers until the 20th century believed that the inhabitants of non-European territories were ignorant not only of metallurgy (so argued Columbus and Locke, among others), but also of autonomy, moral virtues, the idea of rights and humanity, and even eagerness, which inherently predisposed them to a condition of slavery and servitude. In such thinking, the ethno-racial and normative – typical for populism – antagonism between the colonial elite and the colonised populations was pronounced from the beginning.

Against this backdrop of antagonism, the colonial rule of law was officially addressed to all members of this supposedly inclusive, yet forced community or 'commonwealth' (usually located in a state's colonial province). Such a community was further antagonised by the commercialised, racialised, inherited slavery[13] and forced labour, all connected to the permanent settlement.[14] The theory and practice of colonial rule of law at the time thus owed[15] a great deal to the

[10] Christopher Colombus, "Epistola Christofori Colom ... de insulis Indie supra Gangem" (Pamphlet). Rome, April 1493", in: *The Gilder Lehrman Collection* GLC01427, www.gilderlehrman.org; see also Bernard Cohen, "What Columbus 'Saw' in 1492", in: *Scientific American* 267(6) (1992), 100-107.

[11] A slightly later law graduate from the same university, Francisco Suárez, objected to colonisation.

[12] Matthew Restall, "'There Was a Time When We Were Friends': Las Casas and Cortés as Monstrous Doubles of the Conquest Era", in: *Bartolomé de las Casas, O.P. History, Philosophy, and Theology in the Age of European Expansion*, ed. David Thomas Orique O.P./Rady Roldán-Figueora, Brill: Leiden/Boston 2019, 58–70; Henry Wagner, "Francisco López de Gomara and His Works", in: *American Antiquarian Society* 58(2) (1948), 263-282.

[13] Mary Elliot, Jazmine Hughes, "Four hundred years after enslaved Africans were first brought to Virginia...", in: *The New York Times Magazine*, 19 Aug 2019, https://www.nytimes.com/interactive/2019/08/19/magazine/history-slavery-smithsonian.html.

[14] Patrick Wolfe, "Settler Colonialism and the Elimination of the Native", *Journal of Genocide Research* 8(4) (2006), 387-409.

[15] Nicola Lacey, "Populism and the Rule of Law", *Annual Review of Law and Social Science* 2019, vol. 15, pp. 79–96, Megan Morell, "Between Populism and Settler Colonialism: A US Case

philosophy of law; not just legitimacy – given that the scholars representing it were often jurists and influenced their states' legal policies. For example, the dispute between Juan Gines de Sepúlveda and Bartolomé des las Casas waged in 1550 before the court of Valladolid over whether Indians had a soul and whether they could be enslaved officially limited the colonial power of the Spaniards. Meanwhile, the "new ethno-nationalist populisms which justify exclusivist nationalisms or white supremacy"[16] are rooted in the historical dominance of legal thought inspired by de Sepúlveda.

In decolonial studies to date, we find few references to *populist theory and philosophy of law* and its impact on the colonial rule of law.[17] Hence, the present paper is exploratory in nature. Among philosophers with significant influence on the social imaginaries of modern political space, Taylor mentions Hugo Grotius and John Locke[18]: "It often happens that what start off as theories held by a few people come to infiltrate the social imaginary, first of elites, perhaps, and then of the whole society. This is what has happened, *grosso modo*, to the theories of Grotius and Locke"[19]. Incidentally, Grotius and Locke – in the large company of other modern philosophers (e.g., Montesquieu, Voltaire, Mill) – also promoted colonial "commanding power(s)"[20] and colonial rule of law with a variety of factual, epistemic, normative, and identity aspects[21], including populist aspects. This article contributes to identification of this trend in the early modern philo-

Study", *Culture, Society and Praxis* 16(1) (2024), art. 1; Kevin Bruyneel, *Settler Memory: The Disavowal of Indigeneity and the Politics of Race in the United States*. University of North Carolina Press 2021; Charles Forsdick, James Mark, Eva Spišiaková, "Introduction. From Populism to Decolonisation: How We Remember in the Twenty-First Century", *Modern Languages Open* 1(17) (2020), 1-34; Aline Sierp, "EU Memory Politics and Europe's Forgotten Colonial Past", *Interventions* 22(6) (2020), 686-702; Roxanne Dunbar-Ortiz, *An Indigenous Peoples' History of the United States*. Beacon Press 2014.

[16] Ch. Forsdick *et al.*, "Introduction...", 16.

[17] See Dani Filc, "Colonialism and Populism", in: Y. Stavrakakis, G. Katsambekis (eds.), *Research Handbook on Populism*. Edward Elgar, Cheltenham, UK – Northampton, MA 2024, 494-505.

[18] E.g., James Farr, "Locke, Natural Law, and New World Slavery", *Political Theory* 36 (2008), 495-522; James Tully, "Rediscovering America: The *Two Treatises* and Aboriginal Rights", in: J. Tully, *An Approach to Political Philosophy: Locke in Contexts*. Cambridge 1993, 137-176; Barbara Arneil, *John Locke and America: The Defence of English Colonialism*. Oxford 1996; Johan Olsthoorn, Laurens van Appeldoorn, "'This Man Is My Property': Slavery and Political Absolutism in Locke and the Classical Social Contract Tradition", *European Journal of Political Theory* 21(2) (2022), 253-275.

[19] Ch. Taylor, *Modern Social Imaginaries*, 24.

[20] Amartya Sen, *Identity and Violence. The Illusion of Destiny*. Cambridge 2005, 47.

[21] Ch. Taylor, *Modern Social Imaginaries*, 24.

sophy of law.[22] To put it in Axel Honneth's words, its "long shadow"[23] extends also to the imaginaries underlying white supremacy and apartheid.[24] Related philosophical accounts have some common denominator, namely epistemic and juris-hermeneutical violence as a strategy for (1) questioning moral subjectivity, self-governance and jurisgenerative skills[25] of Indigenous 'Savages' as well as their natural law ('if they had any', it was more a law of Mother Nature than of human reason)[26], and (2) placing into the vacant space a new, hegemonic, often deceptive (e.g., covering up colonial crimes) model of the rule of law[27] and its 'equal' addressees. Philosophers of law are indebted to themselves and their students for a little reflection on this topic.[28]

## 3. Juris-Hermeneutical Violence, Early Modern Populist Philosophy of Law and Coloniality

A. Honneth exemplifies the colonial, both epistemic and juris-hermeneutical violence, with Hobbes (among others). Hobbes "repeatedly emphasizes his concept of the state of nature to be meant as purely fictitious and therefore serving only methodological purposes, but then does not hesitate to describe the Indigenous peoples of North America as being in a state similar to nature, in order

---

[22] Jan Nederveen Pieterse, Bhikhu Parekh (eds.), *The Decolonization of Imagination: Culture, Knowledge and Power*. London 1995.

[23] Axel Honneth, "Der lange Schatten des Kolonialismus. Ein Literaturessay über *Colonialism and Modern Social Theory*", *WestEnd. Neue Zeitschrift für Sozialforschung* 20(1) (2023), 165-179.

[24] Ch. Forsdick *et al.*, "Introduction..."; also, "The Doctrine of *Apartheid*. Native Policy of the South African Nationalists", *The Round Table. The Commonwealth Journal of International Affairs* 39(153/156) (1948), 33-35.

[25] Kristen Carpenter, Angela Riley, "Indigenous Peoples and the Jurisgenerative Moment in Human Rights", *California Law Review* 102 (2014), 173-234.

[26] Murray Simpson, "From Savage to Citizen: Education, Colonialism and Idiocy", *British Journal of Sociology of Education* 28(5) (2007), 561-574; Annick Samibaden *et al.*, "Afterimages of Savages: Implicit Associations between Primitives, Animals and Children", *British Journal of Social Psychology* 49(1) (2010), 91-105.

[27] Such a deceptive model, exemplified by a painting promoting British rule of law during the uprising of the aboriginal Tasmanians against the invaders, was described by Desmond Manderson, "The Law of the Image and the Image of the Law: Colonial Representations of the Rule of Law", *New York Law School Law Review* 57(1) (2012/2013), 153-168. The painting was intended to suggest to the wider publicity that colonisation promoted the rule of law, and to the colonised, in their pictographic convention, to suggest that colonial rule of law established equal rights for all. For colonial epistemic hegemony see Grant Silva, "Comparative Philosophy and Decolonial Struggle: The Epistemic Injustice of Colonization and Liberation of Human Reason", *Philosophy Faculty Research and Publications* 2019, 781. https://epublications.marquette.edu/phil_fac/781

[28] Bernard Matolino, "Philosophers' Debt to Their Students: The South African Case", *Transformation in Higher Education* 5 (2020), article 87.

to justify their colonial settlement and exploitation by properly constituted states"[29]. Aforementioned epistemic and juris-hermeneutical violence involves the denial of politico-legal status to Indigenous peoples, classified in terms of primitivism and savagery[30]. As I have already indicated, such violence produces a gap to be managed by politico-legal doctrines legitimising the hegemony of the colonial rule of law over the customs and practices of a people who supposedly have not yet left the state of nature and it is uncertain whether they will ever do so. To such people – as we shall see with Hugo Grotius – a lifelong and even hereditary condition of slavery will be institutionalised in law.

In general, "the notion of epistemic violence refers to the different ways in which violence is exercised in relation to the production, circulation and recognition of knowledge: the denial of epistemic agency for certain subjects, the unacknowledged exploitation of their epistemic resources, their objectification, among many others"[31]. Medina refers to the maximum-degree of hermeneutical violence – namely hermeneutical death – "when subjects are not simply mistreated as intelligible communicators, but prevented from developing and exercising a voice, that is, prevented from participating in meaning-making and meaning-sharing practices"[32] – here practices of traditional indigenous law transmission and administration. For example, if, as a result of long-term of forced education of Indigenous children in colonial residential schools, one generation fell out of the oral, intergenerational transmission of knowledge that also covered laws, this knowledge would perish also in subsequent generations[33]; thus, the indigenous voice in legal matters will be silenced for centuries.[34]

---

[29] A. Honneth, "Der lange Schatten des Kolonialismus", 168.

[30] Olive Patricia Dickason, *The Myth of the Savage: and the Beginnings of French Colonialism in the Americas*. University of Alberta Press 1997. This myth, though, seems older and not limited to the French circle, where it is represented by the „bon Sauvage" in Rousseau, Montaigne, and Diderot, see Bernard Mouralis, *Montaigne et le mythe du bon Sauvage*. Pierre Bordas et Fils 1989; Denis Diderot, "Le supplément au voyage de Bougainville", in: *Correspondance Littéraire*, ed. F.-M. Grimm, issues of September and October 1773, March and April 1774; first published openly in Denis Diderot, *Œuvres*, vol. III, ed. Naigeon. Paris, Desray et Déterville 1798, 382-384.

[31] Moira Pérez, "Epistemic Violence: Reflections between the Invisible and the Ignorable", *El lugar sin límites* 1(1) (2019), 83.

[32] José Medina, "Varieties of Hermeneutical Injustice", in: I. J. Kidd, J. Medina, G. Pohlhaus Jr. (eds.), *Decolonial Praxis and Epistemic Injustice. The Routledge Handbook of Epistemic Injustice*. London, Routledge 2017, 41; Andrea Pitts, "Decolonial Praxis and Epistemic Injustice", in: I. J. Kidd *et al.* (eds.), *Decolonial Praxis…*, 149-157); Gaile Pohlhaus Jr., "Relational Knowing and Epistemic Injustice: Toward a Theory of Willful Hermeneutical Ignorance", *Hypatia* 27(4) (2012), 715-735.

[33] Joanna Gierak-Onoszko, *27 śmierci Toby'ego Obeda* [27 deaths of Toby Obed]. Warszawa, Dowody na Istnienie Publishers 2019; Konstantin Petoukhov, "'They Just Let Us Rot to Death:' Anti-Colonialism, Contestation, and Resistance to Reparations for Indian Residential School

Questioning the existence and quality of laws in New World peoples, conquered and then governed by colonial institutions but never properly explored for their normativities, as well as denying cognitive and moral faculties in these peoples (widespread by Aristotle[35]) exemplify blatant juris-hermeneutical ignorance. Further, the forceful invalidation of indigenous legal systems by colonial rule of law for whatever reason – be it humanitarian, paternalistic, educative, civilisational – is an act of juris-hermeneutical violence.[36] Such violence has found support in legal theories and philosophies, legitimising the implementation of colonial law and translating this kind of juris-hermeneutical violence into *the language of justice*. In contrast, the task of decolonial philosophy of law is to translate it into the *language of injustice*. In turn, questioning the existence and quality of laws in New World peoples, conquered and then governed by colonial institutions but never properly explored for their normativities, as well as denying cognitive and moral faculties in these peoples (popularised by Aristotle) exemplify blatant juris-hermeneutical ignorance. Further, the forceful invalidation of indigenous legal systems by colonial rule of law for whatever reason – be it humanitarian, paternalistic, educative, civilisational – is an act of juris-hermeneutical violence. Such violence has found support in legal theories and philosophies, legitimising the implementation of colonial law and translating this kind of juris-hermeneutical violence into *the language of justice*. In contrast, the task of decolonial philosophy of law is to translate it into the *language of injustice*.

The strategy of colonial juris-hermeneutical violence has, in fact, a broader background than Hobbes's. Two Spanish legal scholars: de Sepúlveda (1490-1573)[37] and – to a lesser extent – de Vitoria (1483-1547) were its precursors. Half a century later, it was applied with tremendous success by Hugo Grotius (1583-1645). This strategy fits into the projects of colonial rule, including *the jus gentium*, introduced by a variety of means: from open or preventive war, conquest and enslavement through treaties with the natives ("It would be easy to

---

Abuse", *Social & Legal Studies* 32(5) (2023), 737-755; The Royal Canadian Geographical Society 2018.

[34] Carsten Stahn, "Law's Complicity In Cultural Takings and Colonial Violence: Double Standards, Discursive Silencing, and Social Transformation", in: idem, *Confronting Colonial Objects*. Oxford University Press 2023, 286-344.

[35] Against Socrates' argument in Plato's *Meno*: "But if [the slave] were repeatedly asked the same questions in various ways, you know that in the end his knowledge about these things would be as accurate as anyone's".

[36] David Applebaum, "Violence and the Rule of Law", *Journal of Offender Counseling, Services and Rehabilitation* 5(2) (1981), 5-18; D. Manderson, "The Law of the Image and the Image of the Law…".

[37] José Fernández-Santamaria, "Juan Ginés de Sepúlveda on the Nature of the American Indians", in: *The Americas* 31(4) (1975), 434-451.

enumerate here the many wars waged by the Greeks and Romans for this reason, with much approval from the people, whose consensus must be considered to be a law of nature"[38]) to educational surveillance (colonial *Bildung*), hegemonic rule, settlement, and finally plantations and factories based on slave labour. Measures based on voluntarism and contractualism may seem benevolent and 'democratic' at first glance, until one realises what asymmetrical contractualism means in Grotius and that centuries later ca. 400 federal treaties concluded by Thomas Jefferson with Amerindian Tribal Nations were rarely respected.

In his ficticious dialogue with Leopold titled *Democrates Alter, or on the Just Causes for War against the Indians*[39], de Sepúlveda presented in a nutshell the doctrine of the colonial commonwealth patterned on juris-hermeneutic violence:

> I believe that the jurist speaks with seriousness and great prudence, but this word slavery means quite a different thing for the jurist than for the philosopher. For the former slavery is an accidental thing, born of superior strength and from the laws of peoples, sometimes from civil laws, while philosophers see slavery as inferior intelligence along with inhuman and barbarous customs. [...] If, by the laws of nature, the reign is to be reserved for the more prudent and virtuous men, suppose that the kingdom of Tunis (I wish to seek examples of misfortune among the infidels and not among our own peoples) were to fall, by virtue of patrimony and by rights of age, into the hands of a prince less prudent and virtuous than his younger brothers. Do you not think, according to your doctrine, that the kingdom should be given to the best of all of them and not to the least worthy? [...] You can well understand, Leopold, if you know the customs and manners of different peoples, that *the Spanish have a perfect right to rule these barbarians of the New World and the adjacent islands, who in prudence, skill, virtues, and humanity are as inferior to the Spanish* as children to adults, or women to men, for there exists between the two as great a difference as between savage and cruel races and the most merciful, between the most intemperate and the moderate and temperate and, I might even say, between apes and men.[40]

Thus,

> What is more appropriate and <u>beneficial</u> for these barbarians than to become subject to the rule of those whose wisdom, virtue, and religion have converted them from barbarians into civilized men (insofar as they are capable of becoming

[38] Juan Ginés de Sepúlveda, *Democrates Alter*. Orig. *Demócrates segundo o de las justas causas de la guerra contra los Indios* (1547). Trans. M. Menéndez y Pelayo, *Boletin de la Real Academia de la Historia* 21 (1892), 257-369. English: "The Second Democrates", http://www.columbia.edu/acis/ets/CCREAD/sepulved.htm
[39] Ibid.
[40] Ibid. (emphasis mine).

> so), from being torpid and licentious to becoming upright and moral, from being impious servants of the Devil to becoming believers in the true God? (...) The man rules over the woman, the adult over the child, the father over his children. That is to say, the most powerful and most perfect rule over the weakest and most imperfect [...]: legem naturalem philosophi eam esse definiunt.[41]

At the same time, de Sepúlveda "appreciates the difference between the juridical position of the Indians who submit peacefully" due to their "natural servitude" and of "those who resist"[42] the colonial *derecho indiano*[43] including the *katechon*-based colonial law.

Another classic of the Renaissance, a theologian and jurist Francisco de Vitoria, referred to Christian charity, good faith and virtue, aby uzasadnić moderate – epistemic and juris-hermeneutical – colonial discipline w odniesieniu do praktyk of American aborigens. Here the presumption was that indigenous laws were largely malevolent and barbaric. The implementation of colonial law invalidated "tyrannical laws which work wrong to innocent"[44], but did not discredit all Amerindians as bestial natures, irrational or potentially rational beings. On the contrary, de Vitoria believed in actual rationality[45] and protection of native populations against demoralisation. In his eyes, this humanitarian and emancipatory aims justified colonial intervention described by him as "colonisation as a trust" and "protectorate". These institutions – also legitimised by theological reasons – should be accepted by "voluntary choice" of their addressees. It is possible that Vitoria was also guided here by the testimonies of those conquistadors who were supposed to have observed among Amerindians practices

---

[41] Ibid., 49 and 68. The phrasing "what is beneficial for these barbarians..." originates from de Vitoria (see below) and was adopted modern philosophers of law as European colonizers' civilizing mission beneficent for the colonized. According to Mill, Kant and Hegel, Indigenous peoples are much less skilled when it comes to the 'rule of law' creation than Europeans, who in turn have a moral obligation to educate and civilize the former. In J. S. Mill's *A Few Remarks on Non-Intervention* (orig. 1859) we read: "for their benefit that they should be conquered and held in subjection by foreigners" Mill and Hegel's views on this subject are related and were summed up by Tunick: "Mill emphasizes two ways in which civilized societies overcome nature: through the establishment of the rule of law and the development of cooperative ventures", Mark Tunick, "Tolerant Imperialism: John Stuart Mill's Defense of British Rule in India", *The Review of Politics* 68 (2006), 7.

[42] J. A. Fernández-Santamaria, "Juan Ginés de Sepúlveda on the Nature...", 449.

[43] Luigi Nuzzo, "Between America and Europe. The Strange Case of the *derecho indiano*", in: T. Duve, H. Pihlajamäki (eds.), *New Horizons in Spanish Colonial Law*. Frankfurt am Main, Max Planck Institute for European Legal History 2015, 161-192.

[44] Francisco de Vitoria, *De Indis*, de tit. leg., para. 15.

[45] Camilla Boisen, "The Changing Moral Justification of Empire: From the Right to Colonise to the Obligation to Civilise", *History of European Ideas* 39(3) (2013), 335-353.

such as cannibalism, human sacrifice, and native ritual violence.[46] Putting an end to these practices was the official justification for later colonial interventions in the role of a civilising or preventive mission, undertaken *for the benefit of* the colonised. According to de Vitoria, colonial law should in so doing inflict "as little harm to the barbarians as possible"[47] and be „done for the benefit and good of the barbarians, and not merely for the profit of the Spaniards"[48]. In turn, indigenous law showing convergences with European law was to be respected by the colonial authorities.

For instance, "the people in question (the Indian aborigines) were in peaceable possession of their goods, both, publicly and privately. Therefore, unless the contrary is shown, they must be treated as owners and not be disturbed in their possession unless cause be shown [...] Unbelief does not prevent anyone from being a true owner [...] The Indian aborigines are not barred on this ground [...] from the exercise of true dominion"[49]. By means of the juris-paternalistic discipline and education outlined here, colonial (or colonial-federal) rules could even instil "a democracy" in the colonized, "that is – popular rule"[50]. However, educational missions in the manner of de Vitoria and egalitarian declarations were usually accompanied by abuses on the part of colonial governments[51], additionally demoralising for native inhabitants.[52]

As can be seen, de Vitoria's colonial *Jus gentium* diverged considerably from de Sepúlveda's account, but with regard to the natural law justifying slavery these differences were minor.[53] According to the latter, some people are by na-

---

[46] Between 1492 and 1493, Columbus and his crew were confronted eight times with mentions by natives of 'Caribs' with one eye, dog's nose, and eating men; "it seems clear that Columbus's'understanding' was based on the answers he wanted to hear, on the expectations that he brought with him, rather than on any genuine communication with the natives", Peter Hulme, "Columbus and the Cannibals: A Study of the Reports of Anthropophagy in the Journal of Christopher Columbus", *Ibero-Amerikanisches Archiv* 4(2) (1978), 119.

[47] F. de Vitoria, *De Indis*, para. 3.1.5.

[48] Ibid., para. 3.8.

[49] Ibid., sect. I, para. 4 and 23-24.

[50] Francisco de Vitoria, *De pot. civ.*, para. 11.

[51] In 1792, Jefferson signed "The Non-Intercourse Act" with the government's official policy to civilise the native populations; see also Miguel Bandeira Jerónimo, *The 'Civilising Mission' of Portuguese Colonialism*, 1870-1930. Palgrave Macmillan 2015; Larry McGrath, "Bergson, Servant of Colonialism: Education and Empire in North Africa under the French Third Republic", *Bergsoniana* 2 (2022), 41-54.

[52] Wolfgang Gabbert, "Human Sacrifice, Ritualised Violence and the Colonial Encounter in the Americas", in: R. Antony *et al.* (eds.), *The Cambridge World History of Violence*. Cambridge University Press 2020, 96-116.

[53] Joseph Capizzi, "The Children of God: Natural Slavery in the Thought of Aquinas and Vitoria", *Theological Studies* 63(1) (2002), 31-52.

ture slaves (*physei doulos* according to the Aristotle's *Politics*; *natura servi*); according to the former, some people require the governance – including moral – of more rational subjects than them. For instance, "the Indians are either (1) sinners, (2) unbelievers, (3) irrational, (4) childlike, or (5) madmen"[54]. The presumption of natural slavery, founded on Thomistic-Aristotelic premises, challenged even Roman law, where slavery was an institution of the common law of nations (*jus gentium*) and the private law as well, primarily established for humanitarian reasons: namely to save the lives of captured innocent people. As "by nature all men are born free, the Romans said [...] In Institutes 1,3,3 and 4 we find an outline of the origins of slavery as rooted in the *jus gentium*: gradually supplementing the older custom of killing the vanquished in war, people all over the world had got accustomed to saving the lives of the conquered in order to use or sell them as slaves instead. *Servus* ('slave') was said to be derived from the word *servare* ('to save')"[55]. Nevertheless, there have been many more ways[56] of enslavement known to the law since Roman times. Let us finally consider which of the modern legal scholars contributed to the most controversial ones.

### 4. Hugo Grotius

In this nexus of modern populist legal scholars, another influential one – already in terms of the legalization of colonial slavery – was Hugo Grotius. Third Book of his *The Rights of War and Peace* categorises Romanera slavery in multiple ways, including 1) the institution of penalisation: particular persons with a criminal status can be enslaved and their enslavement "extends no farther than their own selves, because crimes are personal" and remains "private". People "should be as much punished in war as in peace; and this last is the law of nations"[57]. "[...] it is just that they should suffer by arms, who have taken up arms, but the innocent should not be touched"[58]. Moreover, "the ravishing of women is sometimes permitted in war, and sometimes not. They that permit it, respect only the injury done to the body of an enemy, which by the law of arms

---

[54] Ibid., p. 48.

[55] Gustaaf van Nifterik, "Arguments Related to Slavery in Seventeenth Century Dutch Legal Theory", *The Legal History Review* 89 (2021), 163-164.

[56] Peter Van den Berg, "Slaves: Persons or Property? The Roman Law on Slavery and Its Reception in Western Europe and Its Overseas Territories", *Osaka University Law Review* 63 (2005), 171-188; Alice Rio, "Self-sale and Voluntary Entry into Unfreedom, 300-1100", *Journal of Social History* 45(3) (2012), 661-685; Alice Rio, "Self-sale, Debt Slavery, and Penal Enslavement", in: ibidem, *Slavery after Rome, 500-1100*. Oxford University Press 2017, 42-74.

[57] Hugo Grotius, *The Rights of War and Peace,* Book II. Indianapolis: Liberty Found 2005, 1300.

[58] Ibid., 1443.

they think should be subject to all acts of hostility"[59]. And 2) national slavery which is "public", "perpetual", and "founded on the voluntary law of nations"[60].

What interested Grotius most, however, was the institutionalisation of slavery in his time, when colonial expansion (in particular, but not only, carried out by the Netherlands) was gaining momentum. This interest was sparked by his studies on Roman law and by the presumption that a portion of humanity was by nature cognitively limited, lacking certain virtues and the ability to manage own conduct, but at the same time capable of voluntarily rendering itself into slavery under the terms of an unequal contract, of which Grotius would be the architect.[61] Needless to stress, interest in such institutions was growing in the world, and Grotius – as the 'face' of early modern rationalism, universalism, liberalism (self-determination, voluntarism), contractualism founded on consent, reciprocity, equality – as well as the Calvinist entrepreneurial mindset – gave them a legitimacy drawn from natural law, which not even God can change. He also legitimised the right of conquest and preventive seizure of foreign territory (which was to protect it from occupation by the enemy), the right to expropriate indigenous peoples from their lands due to inappropriate cultivation (becoming *terra nullius* because of this)[62], etc.

This institutionalisation was, according to Grotius, indispensable because slavery does not exist in a state of nature, but results from divisions generated by people meeting standards of rationality, in particular "a will governed and directed by reason"[63] (as well as being Christian) towards people who do not meet such standards. The former make up a class of masters (*lord*, *pater familias*[64]) and therefore dominate. The latter form a class of servants, servitus ("the words servitus and slavery, however, cover a wide scope of historical varieties of bondage and serfdom, including kinds of unfreedom in a philosophical way"[65]), which is in possession and under governance of the first. However, Grotius does not underpin this relationship with the coercion exerted by the

[59] Ibid., 1300.
[60] Ibid., 565.
[61] Inge Van Hulle, "Grotius, Informal Empire and the Conclusion of Unequal Treaties", in: *Grotiana* 37 (2016), 43-60.
[62] See Mikki Stelder, "The Colonial Difference in Hugo Grotius: Rational Man, Slavery and Indigenous Dispossession", in: *Postcolonial Studies* 25(4) (2022), 564-583; José Eisenberg, "Cultural Encounters, Theoretical Adventures: The Jesuit Missions to the Jesuit World and the Justification of Voluntary Slavery", in: *History of Political Thought* XXIV(3) (2003), 375-396.
[63] H. Grotius, *The Rights of War and Peace*, Book I, 567.
[64] M. Stelder, "The Colonial Difference...".
[65] Gustaaf van Nifterik, "Hugo Grotius on 'Slavery'", *Grotiana (New Series)* 22/23 (2001/2002), 233-244.

masters over the enslaved subjects. Its foundation is to be a voluntary act of surrender to slavery, sealed by an asymmetrical contract with the master. Asymmetry and inequality are not a matter of mere contract here, since the contract reflects cognitive and moral asymmetries and inequalities between parties.

Each party embodies specific but different virtues. Some are predisposed by their virtues to reflection, prudence, self-control, etc.; others are predisposed by their virtues (and vices, for example, irrationality) to servitude, Grotius elucidates. In the Roman manner, he also emphasises the beneficence of such an unequal contract, which endows the enslaved with a privilege – for otherwise they would be murdered. However, the contract in question is also supposed to institutionalise, not least in the light of international law, new inequalities between the status, rights and duties of the parties. Grotius' idea of an unequal contract has been repeatedly enacted in various variants, most often in the context of the colonial slavery and dispossession.[66] In *De Indis*, Grotius explained that "some are naturally inclined to enter into contracts that do not benefit them in the same way as the other signee. This is especially pronounced within the colonial context in which such contracts were based on the ontological predisposition to rule and be ruled. European colonizers readily employed Grotian ideas on absolute and perpetual contract to coerce Indigenous peoples into signing away all or parts of their lands and livelihoods, and to procure captive Africans on the African continent"[67]. Unequal contracts – and there were countless of them on several continents – were broken when Indigenous signees realised that they had been dispossessed of land or other resources by means of a pseudo-contract. In such cases, colonial sanctions and penalties for breaking the 'contract' by enslaved, colonised, or dispossessed signees were applied. "Grotius transformed aggressive acts of (dis)possession and conquest into acts of volition, due to the so-called natural disposition of enslaved and Indigenous people to be ruled"[68]. In fact, Grotius introduced his colonial contract into the international legal circuit which was not publicly debated for, as van Welie puts it, "what happened in the colonies stayed in the colonies"[69]. It is noteworthy that the contract under discussion which is primarily concerned with

[66] E.g., William Waller Henlng, "Virginia Slave Laws", in: ibid., *Statues at Large; Being a Collection of All of the Laws of Virginia*, vol. II. Richmond: Samuel Pleasnats 1809-1823, 170, 260, 266, 270.
[67] M. Stelder, "The Colonial Difference...", 11.
[68] Ibid., 13.
[69] Rik van Welie, "What Happened in the Colonies Stayed in the Colonies: The Dutch and the Slave-Free Paradox", in: P. Misevich, K. Mann (eds.), *The Rise and Demise of Slavery and the Slave Trade in the Atlantic World*. University of Rochester Press 2016, 181-227.

the exploitation and management of slave labour (referred to in Grotius as paternalistic care), goes hand in hand with one of the central premises of populism. This premise is concerned with the satisfaction of people's wishes by their benefactors, that is, the elite in power. This elite is both political and, even predominantly economic, and will effectively capitalise slavery and slave labour. "Now perfect and utter slavery, is that which obliges a man to serve his master all his life long, for diet and other common necessaries; which indeed, if it be thus understood, and confined within the bounds of nature, has nothing too hard and severe in it; for that perpetual obligation to service, is recompensed by the certainty of being always provided for; which those who let themselves out to daily labour [as a freeman, – E.N.], are often far from being assured of [...] who is the owner of the thing, is naturally the owner of all its produce"[70].

As if the controversies surrounding the perversion of the ideal of contractualism were not enough[71], Grotius also adapted the Roman institution of inherited slavery for women. This included reproductive capacity, the so-called *servitio subiectum uterum*. Thus, one may speak of a modern legitimisation of reproductive slavery by this Dutch jurist and natural law thinker. "Neither do only they themselves become slaves, but their posterity for ever; for whosoever is born of a woman after she is a slave, is born a slave: and this is what *Martian* said, that by the law of nations those that were born of bond-women are accounted slaves. And *Tacitus* speaking of the wife of a *German* prince (taken prisoner) said, she had *servitio subjectum uterum, a womb subjected to bondage,* that is, her child would be a bondslave"[72]. During five centuries of slavery and slave labour's capitalisation, as well as of demographic growth of societies with colonial and slavery background, the scale of reproductive slavery (in the meantime legitimised by Grotius), of "predation of millions of bodies on the African continent" and "dispossession of women's wombs"[73] must have been considerable. In the context of colonial slavery, women were valued less due to

---

[70] H. Grotius, *The Rights of War and Peace*, Book II, 557 and 693; labour will also be racially determined, see Nicholas de Genova, "A Racial Theory of Labour: Racial Capitalism from Colonial Slavery to Postcolonial Migration", *Historical Materialism* 21(3) (2023), 219-251.

[71] Mark Strasser, "Mill on Voluntary Self-enslavement", in: *Philosophical Papers* 17(3) (1988), 171-183; John Kleinig, "John Stuart Mill and Voluntary Slavery Contracts", in: *Politics* 18(2) (1983), 76-83.

[72] H. Grotius, *The Rights of War and Peace*, Book III, 1362. Also, see Emma D. Velez, The Colonial Contract and the Coloniality of Gender: Decolonial Feminist Reflections on Charles Mill's Racial-Sexual Contract", *Critical Philosophy of Race* 12(2) (2024), 366-381; Teneile Warren, "Black Womb: Genderless", *Briarpatch* 2024, Feb 7, 30–33.
https://briarpatchmagazine.com/articles/view/black-womb-genderless.

[73] Françoise Vergès, "The Wombs of Black Women, Capitalism, and the International Division of Labor", in: idem, *The Wombs of Women*. Duke University Press 2020, 50.

their lower physical strength compared to men. However, their value was recalculated in terms of sexual availability[74] and reproductive capacity. "Women knew that enslavers valued and depended upon their ability to bear children and increase the slave population"[75]. On the other hand, "before abolitionism, slaveholders showed little interest in women as mothers. Their willingness to pay more for men than for women, despite the fact that any children born to enslaved women would also be the slaveowners' property and would thus increase their wealth, suggests that they preferred to buy new enslaved people from Africa rather than bear the costs of raising children. Women who did have children, therefore, always struggled with the impossible conflict between, on the own hand, their own physical needs and their children's need for care and, on the other, the requirements forced on them by plantation work regimes"[76].

## 5. Concluding Remarks

Due to the fundamental nature of his ideas on legislation and policies designed to support modern colonial expansion and slavery, separations, hierarchical citizenship (or "legal anti-citizenship"[77]) and relations in social formations with colonial background, Hugo Grotius has no equal when it comes to "what we call justifying reasons"[78]. His influence on the related regulatory practices was also

---

[74] Sally McKee, "Slavery", in: J. Bennett, R. Carras (eds.), *The Oxford Handbook of Women and Gender in Medieval Europe* 2013, 282-294; Kathleen Sheldon, "Women and Colonialism", *Oxford Bibliographies / African Studies* 2018, DOI: 10.1093/obo/9780199846733-0067; for sexual colonization and slavery, forced marriage, coercive traffic, see Andrea Smith, "Not an Indian Tradition: The Sexual Colonization of Native Peoples", *Hypatia* 18(2) (2003), 70-85; Juliana Barr, "From Captives to Slaves: Commodifying Indian Women in the Borderlands", *The Journal of American History* 92(1) (2005), 19-46. "With women, there was something more practically important in their biology than skin color – their position as childbearers – but this was not enough to account for the general push backward for all of them in society, even those who did not bear children, or those too young or too old for that. It seems that their physical characteristics became a convenience for men, who could use, exploit, and cherish someone who was at the same time servant, sex mate, companion, and bearer-teacher-ward en of his children", Howard Zinn adds, *A People's History of the United States, 1492*-Present. Harper Perennial Modern Classics 2005.

[75] LDHI, "Hidden Voices…", 2024. https://ldhi.library.cofc.edu/exhibits/show/hidden-voices/resisting-enslavement/reproduction-and resistance.

[76] Diana Paton, "Enslaved Women and Slavery Before and After 1807", *History in Focus*, 2024. https://archives.history.ac.uk/history-in-focus/Slavery/articles/paton.html; Alan M. Klein, "The Plains Truth: The Impact of Colonialism on Indian Women", in: *Dialectical Anthropology* 7(4) (1983), 299-313.

[77] Guno Jones, "What Is New about Dutch Populism? Dutch Colonialism, Hierarchical Citizenship and Contemporary Populist Debates and Policies in the Netherlands", *Journal of Intercultural Studies* 37(6) (2016), 605-620.

[78] H. Grotius, *The Rights of War and Peace*, Book I, 390.

far greater than that of the two pioneers of such regulations, also on the scale of *the ius gentium*. If contemporary international law is still based on the foundations laid by these scholars, its decolonisation[79] as well as decolonisation of legal philosophy insofar as it refers uncritically to its Renaissance founders is recommendable. But what would the depopulisation of their philosophy, which introduces, normatively perpetuates and legitimises forms of separation based on discrimination due to indigenousness, ethnicity, non-European descent, culture, and later, skin colour, and race (left out here, as the racial anthropology is a later creation of European philosophy), consist in?

In the colonial context, separation and hierarchisation initially applied to populations from outside European political formations. Over time, they were internalised in formations dominated by colonial settlers, based on apartheid or finally in European and American formations whose elites treated Indigenous groups, slavery's descendants[80], migrants, etc., as inferior. Today, we already realise that republicanism and democracy can also have populist rights[81] at their core. Also, we know that – contrary to Grotius – the neo-Roman legal thought should advocate for freedom "as non-domination or non-dependency"[82], and that Europe remains the progenitor of both universalist human rights acts (starting with the 1789 French Declaration of the Rights of Man) and the denial of such rights to many people of non-European origin, from the Third World, Global South, etc. Global as well as local forms of separation have a populist basis, legitimised also by philosophy and theory of law despite declarations of universalism, rationalism, natural law.

---

[79] Anthony Anghie, "Toward a Postcolonial International Law", in: P. Singh, B. Mayer (eds.), *Critical International Law*. Oxford University Press 2014.

[80] Dionne Ford, Jill Strauss, *Slavery's Descendants: Shared Legacies of Race and Reconciliation*. Rutgers University Press 2019.

[81] Guy Aitchison, „Three Models of Republican Rights: Juridical, Parliamentary and Populist", *Political Studies* 65(2) (2017), 339–355.

[82] Ibid., 341.

*Gabriele Münnix*
*(Düsseldorf, Deutschland)*

# Kritische Rationalität und populistische Vernunft

Populistische Bewegungen sind seit der Antike bekannt, auch wenn man sie noch nicht so benannt hat. Jeder Kanaldeckel in Rom etwa (SPQR: Senatus Populusque Romanorum) bezeugt, dass es schon zur damaligen Zeit eine Trennung zwischen den herrschenden Senatoren und den freien männlichen Bürgern der Stadt Rom gab. Und es galt als durchaus nicht unehrenhaft, die Rechte des normalen Volkes gegenüber den Herrschenden (meist adliger Herkunft) zu vertreten. (Man unterschied übrigens auch noch zwischen *plebs* und *populus,* zum letzteren zählten nur die männlichen Bürger, Frauen und Sklaven waren von den Bügerrechten wie im antiken Griechenland ausgenommen.) Weshalb aber ist „das Volk" überhaupt elevant? Mit welchem Recht berufen sich die heutigen populistischen Strömungen, die durch ihre vielfältigen Mediatisierungen auch im Bereich der sozialen Medien eine völlig neue Dimension und Brisanz gewonnen haben, in vielen Ländern auf „das Volk"?

## I. Einige Fragen

1. „Wir sind das Volk": mit diesem Slogan gelang in der ehemaligen DDR eine unblutige Wende hin zur Demokratie, jedenfalls konnte man aus einem totalitären System mit Bespitzelung in ein (vermeintlich) besseres freiheitliches System ausbrechen. Da der Slogan so erfolgreich war, wurde er von Pegida-Bewegung in Ostdeutschland missbraucht, um „gegen die Islamisierung Deutschlands" zu protestieren, in Ausblendung der Tatsache, dass im offeneren, nicht von der Welt abgeschnittenen Westen der Republik gut integrierte MigrantInnen , oft in 3. Generation, und oft mit deutscher Staatsangehörigkeit, lebten und leben. Pars pro toto, diese Technik wird auch von Ernesto Laclau als interne Universalisierungstendenz des Populismus beschrieben[1], der einfach nur eine Art ist, das Politische passend zu konstruieren. Wer genau aber ist „das Volk"?

2. „Demo"-„kratie": Volks-herrschaft durch eine an den Menschenrechten orientierte Partizipation von Bürgern in einer parlamentarischen oder repräsentativen Demokratie, in die man sich über verschiedene Institutionen einbringen und verschiedensten Meinungen Gehör verschaffen kann, bleibt in vielen Ländern ein

[1] Ernesto Laclau, *Die populistische Vernunft*, Passagen Wien/Graz 2022, 23.

anzustrebendes Ideal. Doch zunehmend fühlen sich weite Teile der Bevölkerung, und nicht nur in Deutschland, von demokratischer Partizipation abgeschnitten und außen vor, besonders wenn, wie in Frankreich oder England, ein althergebrachtes System der Eliten (durch ENS und ENA qualifiziert, oder durch die Eton/Oxbridge-Tradition) die Regierungskaste stellt. Wie kann man die für Demokratien gefährliche Ausschließungsfunktion von Eliten vermeiden oder ihr entgegenwirken?)

3. „Vox populi, vox dei“: Dieser latinisierte Spruch des griechischen Dichters Hesiod[2] wird in der Demokratietheorie gelegentlich als Beleg dafür zitiert, dass sich in der vielfachen Stimme des Volkes eine quasi göttliche Vernunft artikulieren könnte, mit der z. B. auch antike Helden als solche identifizierbar wurden (oder Verdikte legitimisiert wurden). Spricht da aber wirklich eine quasigöttliche Stimme, die demokratischen Wahlen Ihren Sinn geben kann? Der Spruch wurde zudem auch karikiert zu „vox populi, vox bovi“ (dem preußischen General Wrangel wurde „vox populi, vox Rindvieh“ zugeschrieben). Es ist also zu fragen: ist „Volkes Stimme“ immer vernünftig? Oder artikuliert sich in ihr, wie Karl Hepfer in Bezug auf im Netz kursierende Verschwörungstheorien meint, eine Unvernunft, der man kaum beikommen kann[3]? Kann man gar, wie Ernesto Laclau, doch von „populistischer Vernunft“ sprechen und ihr eine gewisse innere Logik zusprechen? Was also ist „Volkes Stimme“? Wo und wie artikuliert sie sich zu recht, wo zu unrecht? Spricht aus ihr eine wie auch immer geartete Vernunft, die einer inneren Logik folgt? Was hieß in diesem Zusammenhang „vernünftig“? Und wer ist überhaupt „das Volk“?

Und wie können wir auf Kulturen der Rationalität in unserem Denken zurückgreifen und sie für gegenwärtige Situationen in erhitzten Debatten fruchtbar machen? Und was ist überhaupt Wahrheit, in „postfaktischen Zeiten“ Was darf man glauben, wem darf man vertrauen? Wie kann man Fakten von Fiktion trennen?

## II. Drei Antworten und darüber hinaus: Gibt es eine populistische Vernunft?

1. Der ursprünglich aus Argentinien stammende Ernesto Laclau, mit einem Hintergrund aus der gegen Oligarchen gerichteten südamerikanischen Befreiungsphilosophie, argumentiert zwar im Sinne eines linksgerichteten Populismus[4] und

[2] Hesiod, Werke und Tage, Reclam: Stuttgart 2004, 763f.

[3] Karl Hepfer, *Verschwörungstheorien. Eine philosophische Kritik der Unvernunft*, transcript: Bielefeld, [3]2021, 18.

[4] Laclau, ibid., siehe das Vorwort von Chantal Mouffe, 11.

rechnet sich selbst dem Postmarxismus zu. Da er aber strukturanalytisch vorgeht (und übrigens sich im ersten Drittel des Buches mit der Psychologie der Massen beschäftigt, was sich wie eine Betriebsanleitung für PopulistInnen liest), lassen sich seine Analysen sehr gut auch für populistische Bewegungen überhaupt verstehen. Laclau legt dar, dass es für diese wesentlich ist, eine Grenze zu ziehen zwischen „denen da oben" und „uns, hier unten", wobei es absolut erforderlich sei, dass diese Grenze extrem unscharf bleibt. (Migrationsfeinde, Querdenker und Impfgegner in der Pandemie, sowie Gegner einer maßlosen Unterstützung und Alimentierung von Arbeitslosen und Migranten, aber auch diese in prekären Verhältnissen Lebenden selber – die Liste ließe sich fortsetzen – sollen sich gleichermaßen entrüsten und angesprochen fühlen.) Unter Verwendung einer Unterscheidung aus de Saussures Linguistik zwischen *signifiant* und *signifié*, einem bloßen Namen, einer Bezeichnung, und dem was sie inhaltlich bedeutet, auf was genau sie sich bezieht, macht Laclau deutlich, dass „das Volk" ganz wesentlich ein *leerer* Signifikant bleiben muss, besser noch, wie er später spezifiziert, ein *flottierender* Signifikant , der seinen Bezug von Mal zu Mal wechseln kann[5], ohne dass es groß auffällt. (daher die bewusst unscharfe Grenze!)

Der „Staat" wird so zur Projektionsfläche für enttäuschte Erwartungen aller Art, ohne dass eventuelle Mitwirkungsmöglichkeiten an politischen Prozessen in Rechnung gestellt werden. Das „Volk" wird immer als politischer und kollektiver Akteur allererst konstruiert. Für diese Konstruktion des jeweiligen „Volkes" braucht es interne Äquivalenzen, und ebenso wesentlich Differenzen nach außen[6], um Entrüstung produzierende Affekte zu nutzen etwa gegen „Staat", „Eliten", „Establishment", „Kapitalismus", „Kommunismus" , „Ausländer" etc., um die Menschen zu einer politischen Bewegung zusammenschweißen können. Dabei entstehe dann eine besondere Art von Ganzheit, die sich nicht etwa aus Teilen zusammensetzt, sondern in der „ein Teil als das Ganze fungiert („..mit einer *plebs*, die beansprucht, mit dem *populus* identisch zu sein"[7]). Dabei gehen Laclaus Analysen bis zurück in die Antike („Demagogie"), und können als Beitrag zur linken Strategiedebatte gelesen werden.

2. Während Laclau strukturanalytisch vorgeht, sind Bernd Stegemanns Untersuchungen genetistisch. Er macht – nicht nur in Deutschland, auch andernorts – die Entwicklung des (Neo-)Liberalismus für das Erstarken des Populismus verantwortlich, was de facto einer immer mächtigeren Wirtschaft in die Hände spie-

[5] Ibid.,167ff.
[6] Ibid.,144.
[7] Ibid.,145.

le, die sich politischer Institutionen nach Belieben bedienen könne (was natürlich der Rede von „denen da oben“ Vorschub leistet). Die kürzeste Definition sei, dass der Populist einfache Antworten auf komplizierte Fragen gebe[8]. Neben linkem und rechtem Populismus (der erste gerichtet gegen soziale Ungleichheit und Ausbeutung[9], der zweite gerichtet gegen Migration und kulturelle Veränderungen, die die nationale Identität und die damit verknüpften Werte bedrohen[10]) unterscheidet er noch den liberalen Populismus (vielleicht besser: Populär-Liberalismus?)[11]: der möglicherweise ein Missverständnis dessen, was Freiheit meint, beinhalte. Nämlich eben als Absage an Kantsches Willkürhandeln; doch Kants Freiheitsbegriff ist in der angelsächsischen Philosophie wenig rezipiert worden. Hier geht es mit der Freiheit um den „pursuit of happiness“, oft mit einer utilitaristischen Ethik verknüpft, und oft auf Kosten der Schwachen. (Wie einst Otfried Höffe bemerkte, hat der hedonistische Kalkül ein Gerechtigkeitsproblem.[12]) Doch, so Stegemann, dergestalt erledige sich der Liberalismus selbst und leiste der Entwicklung an den Rändern Vorschub. Aber die Populismen sind in vielen Ländern kaum noch als Randerscheinungen abzutun, eher kann man das vom allerorts schwächelnden Liberalismus annehmen: Eine globale Änderung der Lebensgewohnheiten angesichts von Finanzkrise, Klimakrise, Pandemie und nun auch noch Kriegen, mit Kriegs- und Klimaflüchtlingen, sei schwer zuzumuten und erzeuge Entfremdungserfahrungen und – typisch für den Populismus nach Stegemann – ein System von Narrativen, die Sicherheit und Gemeinschaft schaffen sollen.

3. Die österreichische Politologin Natascha Strobl hingegen diagnostiziert auf der rechten Seite einen „radikalisierten Konservatismus“. Im Gegensatz zum normalen Konservativismus, der die bestehenden ungleichen Verhältnisse zwecks eigener Privilegierung bewahren wolle[13] (hier wird ihre SPÖ-Mitgliedschaft deutlich), strebe der radikalisierte Konservatismus danach, die Demokratie zu verändern und auszuhöhlen, bzw. zu unterwandern. Es dürfte sich also um Rechtspopulismus handeln. Im Vergleich von Sebastian Kurz und Donald Trump stellt sie fest, dass beide eine Bewegung der politischen Gefolgschaft geschaffen hätten, die fast Züge einer bedingungslos folgenden Fangemeinde

---

[8] Bernd Stegemann, *Das Gespenst des Populismus*, Theater der zeit: Berlin 2017, 13.
[9] Ibid., 41-36.
[10] Ibid., 94-137.
[11] Idid., 64-93.
[12] Otfried Höffe (Hg.), *Einführung in die utilitaristische Ethik,* Francke: Tübingen ²1992, 13, 45.
[13] Natascha Strobl, Natascha Strobl, *Radikalisierter Konservatismus*, Suhrkamp: Berlin 2021, 11.

annehme. Dazu brauche es einen kulturkampfähnlichen permanenten Wahlkampfmodus, der strahlende Held werde im Falle von Kritik als Opfer ungerechtfertigter, sogar bösartiger Verleumdungen stilisiert. Bewusst werde eine Gegenrealität geschaffen, der man sich zugehörig fühlen könne, nicht ohne Leidenschaften zu bedienen. Gezielte Tabu- und Regelbrüche machten jeden Auftritt der Führer zu einem Event und befeuerten Fremden- und Frauenfeindlichkeit, wobei gleichzeitig Ängste geschürt werden (wie z. B. bei Kurz' von den Identitären übernommene Rede vom „großen Bevölkerungsaustausch") und demgegenüber Sicherheit auf der „richtigen" Seite suggeriert werden solle.[14] Die Fixierung einer Partei auf den „Führer" kehre die Machtverhältnisse um, die demokratische Kontrolle schwinde[15], und so könnten ungehindert wichtige Posten in Exekutive und Judikative und auch in der vormals freien Presse neu und passender besetzt werden. Doch heute, und das analysiert Strobl eindrücklich, verfüge man mit einer individualisierten Medienwelt noch über andere geschicktere Instrumente der Beeinflussung. Der bereits erwähnte Ex-Berater Trumps, Steve Bannon, wird zitiert mit einer Maßgabe „Flood the zone with shit", um bei den Mediennutzern eine kaum noch zu durchdringende Vermischung von fact und fiction zu erzeugen.[16] Erstmals gehe, so Strobl, in einem fundamentalen Sinn die Basis einer geteilten Wirklichkeit (oder war das auch Fiktion?) verloren; die Instrumente fehlen, um Einzelfälle – wie es die New York Times mit den Lügen Trumps tut – zu verifizieren. Strobl zitiert Quellen, nach denen nur 12% der Trump-Aussagen wahr oder größtenteils wahr seien und kommentiert, dass dies zur Überflutung des medialen Diskurses und somit zu seiner Zerstörung beitrage.[17] Es würden damit eben keine Probleme gelöst, wie man es von gewählten Politikern erwartet bzw. erhofft, sondern gezielt Leidenschaften bedient.

Die Harvard-Politologen Steven Levitsky und Daniel Ziblatt beschreiben in ihrem Buch „Wie Demokratien sterben" gleich an zwei Stellen 4 Schlüsselindikatoren für autoritäres Verhalten:

1. Ablehnung demokratischer Spielregeln (oder schwache Zustimmung zu ihnen);
2. Leugnung der Legitimität politischer Gegner;
3. Tolerierung von oder Ermutigung zu Gewalt, und

[14] Ibid., 71.
[15] Ibid., 81.
[16] Ibid., 121
[17] Ibid., 122.

4. Bereitschaft, die bürgerlichen Freiheiten von Opponenten, einschließlich der Medien, zu beschneiden.[18]

Natürlich haben die Autoren sehr detailreich die amerikanische Politik im Visier, vergleichen aber auch mit einstigen oder jetzigen Machthabern in anderen Ländern. (Immer im Vergleich mit Trump: Chavez, Fujimori, Peron, Viktor Orban, Marcos, Erdogan, Berlusconi, Kaczynski und natürlich Putin, und sie präsentieren eine vergleichende Tabelle – jeweils nach dem 1. Amtsjahr – auf dem Weg zur Aushöhlung der Demokratie)[19]. Das Kapitel am Ende zum Untertitel des Buchs „Was wir dagegen tun können" bleibt ab er leider seltsam ideenarm.

### III. Kann kritische Rationalität helfen?

Ich möchte hier daher auf drei Strömungen des letzten Jahrhunderts eingehen, die immer noch nachwirken und vielleicht angesichts dieser Sachlage hilfreich sein könnten. Es geht dabei um Modelle bzw. Schulen kritischen Denkens, die in der Nachfolge von Kants „Selberdenken" um neue aktuellere Formen von Rationalität bemüht sind. Aufklärung muss als ein andauernder Prozess gesehen werden, so auch die Kuratorin der aktuellen Ausstellung zur Aufklärung in Berlin[20], gerade angesichts der Bedrohung von Errungenschaften, die man lange als gesichert ansehen konnte. Auch in der diesjährigen Kant-Ausstellung in der Bundeskunsthalle wurden die Schattenseiten der historischen Aufklärung thematisiert, u. a. Kants Rassismus, der dazu geführt habe, dass in Europa weißen gebildeten Männern Rechte zugestanden wurden, die man anderswo, z.B. in den „Kolonien", brutal missachtete.

Ich schildere hier also in der gebotenen Kürze drei Strömungen kritischen Denkens aus der zweiten Hälfte des letzten Jahrhunderts, die um aktuelle Formen kritischer Vernunft bemüht waren, und die bis heute nachwirken:

1. Die „Kritische Theorie" der sog. „Frankfurter Schule",
2. Die gegen jeden Dogmatismus gerichtete evolutionäre Wissenschafts- und Gesellschaftstheorie Poppers, die auch auf totalitäre Tendenzen im eigenen, philosophischen Denken aufmerksam machte, und schließlich
3. die postmoderne Rationalismuskritik, die sich keineswegs gegen die Vernunft selber richtete, sondern mit dem Paradigma der Pluralität in die

---

[18] Steven Levitsky & Daniel Ziblatt, *Wie Demokratien sterben. Und was wir dagegen tun können*, Zeitverlag Gerd Bucerius: Hamburg 2024, 25f und 66f.

[19] Ibid.,184.

[20] Liliane Weissberg, „Ordnen kann auch gefährlich sein. Was bleibt von der Aufklärung? Wie rassistisch war sie? Und wer sind ihre Erben?", in: DIE ZEIT, Nr. 44 vom 17.10.24 , 49.

interkulturelle Philosophie führte21 und so als neue Welle der Aufklärung verstanden werden kann. Wie kann man sich von ihnen anregen lassen?

*ad 1: Kritische Theorie*

Schon in der „Dialektik der Aufklärung", einem der Gründungsdokumente der sogenannten „Kritischen Theorie" der sog. „Frankfurter Schule", hatten Horkheimer und Adorno von einer der Vernunft innewohnenden Dialektik von Aufklärung und Gegenaufklärung („Mythos") gesprochen.[22] Diese Dialektik wurde im Sinne des Linkshegelianismus mit einer „Aufwärtsbewegung" hin zu mehr Fortschrittlichkeit gedacht, so dass am Ende die aufklärerische Vernunft sich auch selber hinterfragen müsse, so Adorno in seiner späteren „negativen Dialektik"[23]. In seiner „Kritik der Instrumentellen Vernunft" , die auch heute wieder angesichts der zunehmenden Technokratisierung von Gesellschaft und Politik und angesichts der massiven Umweltzerstörungen aktuell bleibt, hatte Horkheimer – wie übrigens auch Heidegger auf der anderen Seite des politischen Spektrums – von einer unstatthaften Verengung der Vernunft gesprochen, was sie ihres kritischen Potenzials berauben könne.

Es geht der Kritischen Theorie nicht darum, technologischen Fortschritt abzulehnen oder zu verhindern, aber darum, „Widerstand zu leisten, indem sie dafür sorgt, dass das, was einmal Kultur war, von der Technik nicht einfach ausgewischt wird."[24] (Der angeblich so rationale Verlust von Spielräumen für Kinder, die digital kompensiert werden, die Digitalisierung der Arbeitswelt, die mit Verarmung von Sozialkontakten einhergeht, die touristische „Aufwertung" von Landschaften zum Zweck ihrer marktwirtschaftlichen Ausbeutung, ja die Unterordnung alles Handelns unter Prinzipien der Zweckrationalität sind ja tatsächlich zu betrauern.) Marcuse hatte im „Eindimensionalen Menschen" einst mit großem Einfluss auf die Studentenbewegung der 70er Jahre eine Dialektik des Positiven, Gegebenen, in einer von Konsum dominierten Gesellschaft, und einer negativen, kritischen Dimension der sich dagegen stellenden Vernunft gesprochen, die affirmativ Freiheit nur noch als Wahlfreiheit unter Konsumgütern er-

[21] Z. B. Heinz Kimmerle, *Interkulturelle Philosophie*, Junius: Hamburg 2002, 66.

[22] Theodor W. Adorno & Max Horkheimer, *Dialektik der Aufklärung*, Querida: Amsterdam 1947, 22–57. Auf S.1 44 ff. wird angesichts vielfältiger Manipulation Aufklärung als „Massenbetrug" und als „totalitär" (S. 37) bezeichnet.

[23] Theodor W. Adorno, *Negative Dialektik*, in: Theodor W. Adorno, *Gesammelte Schriften,* Bd. 6, Suhrkamp: Frankfurt 1970, 160. Aber: „Die Selbstreflexion der Aufklärung ist nicht deren Widerruf." (ebd.)

[24] Max Horkheimer, *Zur Kritik der instrumentellen Vernunft*, Fischer: Frankfurt/Main 1967, damals schon mit einem Kapitel über „Die Revolte der Natur" (93-125).

kennt und sich doch kritisch gegen den eindimensionalen „Konsumterror“ und andere Systemzwänge wehren müsse.[25]

Doch auch durch bürokratische Geschäftigkeit politischer Institutionen werden Zielsetzungen und Werte oft kaum noch be- oder hinterfragt, kritisch denkende Individuen werden als unliebsam abgewehrt, da sie die alltägliche Praxis stören. Je instrumentalisierter die Ideen werden, desto weniger kann ein mit „common sense“ begabter Mensch in ihnen Sinn erblicken. Jedenfalls nicht in einer zweckrationalen instrumentellen Vernunft, die sich ihrer kritischen Kompetenz beraubt hat.

Die an Grundrechten orientierte Demokratie ist und bleibt also gefährdet. Problematisch am Konzept der kritischen Theorie ist nur, dass sie auf der Basis einer neomarxistischen Weltsicht kritisch gegen die „bürgerliche Moral“, z. B. bei Kant, argumentiert, was einen dogmatischen Kern enthüllt. Nicht Pflichtbewusstsein und „rechte Gesinnung“ (im Dienst wofür?), sondern die „richtige“ Theorie sei entscheidend, und das ist natürlich die eigene, materialistische.[26] Ein utopischer Entwurf einer besseren gerechteren Gesellschaft ohne Kapitalismus gehört zentral zur Kritischen Theorie, die als einziges Mittel für eine Änderung der durch und durch pervertierten Verhältnisse eine Revolution der bestehenden Ordnung sah, und mit ihrer Philosophie, so eine spätere Bewertung, in der Nachkriegszeit zur „intellektuellen Gründung der Bundesrepublik“ nach der Katastrophe des Nationalsozialismus beigetragen haben soll.[27] Und heute Argumentationshilfen auch für linke Strategen aller Art bietet.

*ad 2.: Kritischer Rationalismus*

Einer solchen Dogmatisierung der Vernunft versucht der Kritische Rationalismus Poppers entgegenzuwirken. Popper hatte den Marxismus in jungen Jahren attraktiv gefunden, aber dann doch als dogmatisch verworfen. Einst hatte er, vom sogenannten „Wiener Kreis“ um Carnap und Schlick angeregt, das empiristische Sinnkriterium verworfen: Aussagen könnten nur sinnvoll sein, wenn sie sich verifizieren ließen. Das geht z. B. mit einzelnen Existenzaussagen, gilt aber nach Popper nicht für allgemeine wissenschaftliche Theorien, die sich so nicht begründen bzw. verifizieren lassen. Daher entwickelte er in seiner „Logik der Forschung“ , die heute als Standardwerk moderner Forschung gilt, mit dem zentralen Prinzip der *Falsifikation* eine alternative evolutionäre Wissenschaftstheo-

---

[25] Herbert Marcuse, *Der eindimensionale Mensch*, Luchterhand: Berlin [8]1976, 139-214.

[26] Max Horkheimer, *Materialismus und Moral*, in: Zeitschrift für Sozialforschung 2 (1933), 161-197; https://search.app/n4k3uUJRo7HsXUA59 [23.10.24].

[27] Clemens Albrecht, Günter C. Behrmann et al., *Die intellektuelle Gründung der Bundesrepublik. Eine Wirkungsgeschichte der Frankfurter Schule*, Campus: Frankfurt a.M. 2007.

rie.[28] Apriorische Grundlagen verwirft auch er, anders als noch Kant, als dogmatisch und nicht überprüfbar, sie werden im Sinne eines „common sense", aber oft nur von Angehörigen der eigenen kulturellen Tradition, eingesehen und scheinen evident, entziehen sich aber kritischer Prüfung. Auch Theorien sind nicht sakrosankt, sie können Irrtümer enthalten und müssen immer „wahrheitsähnlicher" gemacht werden. Dabei gilt Wahrheit als regulative Idee und Ziel eines Denkprozesses, auch in den Wissenschaften, die sich in Erklärungen nicht nur von Naturphänomenen versuchen. Und das gilt daher auch für Theorien über unsere Gesellschaften.

Sein zweites Hauptwerk „Die offene Gesellschaft und ihre Feinde" ist nicht nur ein Grundlagenwerk der Demokratietheorie und des Rechtsstaats geworden, indem es u. a. jedem mit Denkvermögen begabten Wesen als Quelle möglicher guter Argumente zu respektieren empfiehlt, womit auch normative Standards für politische Diskurse gesetzt werden. Darüber hinaus aber werden in beiden Bänden auch Totalitarismustendenzen innerhalb des philosophischen Denkens aufgezeigt, in Band 1 wird „Der Zauber Platons" für das politische Denken in seinem total reglementierten Musterstaat untersucht[29] (der Herrscher darf „Lügen verbreiten und die Feinde sowie die eigenen Bürger zum Besten des Staates täuschen." [30]) . Im 2. Band denkt er über „Hegel, Marx und die Folgen" ideologiekritisch nach. Es geht Popper um die Vermeidung von Despotie und Totalitarismus, die nur durch die andauernde Wachsamkeit derer verhindert werden können, die für Freiheit und Verantwortlichkeit zu kämpfen bereit sind.

Die aus der Wissenschaftstheorie gewonnene evolutionäre Erkenntnistheorie wird bei Popper in ein evolutionäres Gesellschaftsmodell überführt, in dem es statt um holistische Sozialutopien stückweise um nötige Reformen („Sozialtechnik der kleinen Schritte") gehen muss (Vorwurf der Frankfurter: „Stückwerktechnologie" sei systemstabilisierend [31]), was es verbietet, jede sich absolut setzende Theorie auch für die Zukunft festzuschreiben. Eine Theorie, die sich gegen Kritik zu immunisieren sucht, z. B. durch Perfektionierung ihrer Begründungszusammenhänge, und sich verschließt gegen andere Sichtweisen, ist für

[28] Karl Raimund Popper, *Logik der Forschung*, Mohr/Siebeck: Tübingen ³1969, 47–59.
[29] Karl Raimund Popper, *Die offene Gesellschaft und ihre Feinde*, Bd. I, Mohr Siebeck: Tübingen ⁸2003, z. B. Kap.6: „Die totalitäre Gerechtigkeit" (104–163). Siehe dazu Platon, *Politeia*, 389b.
[30] Platon, Politeia, 389b.
[31] Popper, *Die offene Gesellschaft*, 4; s. auch ders., *Das Elend des Historismus*, Mohr /Siebeck: Tübingen 1979, 51–73, sowie Theodor W. Adorno et al. (ed.), *Der Positivismusstreit in der deutschen Soziologie*, Luchterhand: Berlin 1976.

ihn unwissenschaftlich. Das Erkennen solcher Immunisierungsstrategien kann also beim Identifizieren von Ideologien und Weltanschauungen helfen und aufklärerisch wirken.

Es darf daher in der Demokratie also nicht um Autoritäten und Axiome, sondern es muss um Sachargumente gehen, nur so macht die Wissenschaft und auch die Gesellschaft Fortschritte, und auch unser tägliches politisches Leben zwischen fake news und sog „Lügenpresse“ kann vom Prinzip der Falsifikation und schrittweisen Verbesserungen profitieren.

*ad 3: Postmoderne Rationalismuskritik*

„Anything goes“: mit diesem unzutreffende Schlagwort wurde das postmoderne Denken gerade in Deutschland gerne abgetan, mit einem Vorwurf der Beliebigkeit verknüpft und so gar nicht erst in Betracht gezogen. Es hat aber in der philosophischen Theorie, ganz anders als bei dem eklektischen Nebeneinander von Stilen in der Kunst, eine ganz und gar nicht beliebige an Gewaltlosigkeit und Gerechtigkeit orientierte Wert-, um nicht zu sagen Pflichtethik (Lyotard: „Dem Einzelnen gerecht werden“), und nimmt das Paradigma der Pluralität auch für die Gesellschaft ernst.[32] „Anything goes“, das war einst bei Feyerabend eine Maxime gegen Dogmatismus und Schuldenken im Wissenschaftsbetrieb, es sollten auch alternative als die gängigen Methoden ausprobiert werden, um Forschungsfortschritte zu erreichen, während doch plurale Ansätze in allen Wissenschaften, auch wenn sie derzeitigen Schulmeinungen oder Dogmen nicht entsprechen, im Hinblick auf ihre Wirksamkeit bzw. Aussagekraft ohne Denkverbote erforscht werden sollten. (Wie bei Nietzsches „Fröhlicher Wissenschaft“ weist mir diese Wissenschaftstheorie jenseits ihres kritischen Potentials am Methodendogmatismus zu wenig Sozialbindung auf, weswegen ich mein Konzept einer multiperspektivischen Erkenntis als „joint venture“ dagegengesetzt habe.[33]) Auch „*die* Rationalität“ habe sich, so die postmoderne Kritik, z.B. bei Lyotard[34], monopolisiert und schreib ihre je eigenen eurozentrischen Methoden als allgemeingültig und universal fest.

Hingegen soll, so auch bei Lévinas, das und der/die Andere in seinem/ihrem Wert erkannt und anerkannt werden, andere Denkweisen sind zu erforschen.

---

[32] Vgl. Gabriele Münnix, “Anything goes? Zum Schlagwort von der ‚postmodernen Beliebigkeit‘“, in *Freiheit, Moral, Beliebigkeit. Was sollen wir tun?*, ed. Karin Farokhifar, Brigitta Fuchs, André Schütte, CMZ: Rheinberg 2014, 43–60, sowie ausführlicher Gabriele Münnix, *Zum Ethos der Pluralität. Postmoderne und Multiperspektivität als Programm*, LIT: Münster ³2020, mit zwei Kritikpunkten schon in der Einleitung.

[33] S. Münnix, *Zum Ethos der Pluralität*, 183. Postmoderne und Multiperspektivität als Programm, LIT: Münster (3 Aufl.) 2020, 183.

[34] Jean-Francois Lyotard, *Der Widerstreit*, Fink: München 1987.

Dazu gehört eine vor allem von Derrida propagierte Methode und Bereitschaft zur Dekonstruktion der eigenen Denkgebäude im abendländischen Denken. Das Wort hat er von Heidegger übernommen, und es meint keineswegs Destruktion (Husserls „eidetische Reduktion“ meinte dasselbe) . Heidegger hatte ja schon vor langer Zeit behauptet, das abendländische Denken habe seinen Begriff von Vernunft schrittweise verengt (Logos war noch weitergefasst als die römische Ratio, z. B. und spätere Verengungen hin zur Zweckrationalität folgten.) Nötig ist also nach Heidegger „ein Schritt zurück“, um das früher Mitgemeinte wieder einzuholen und einem reicheren Denken verfügbar zu machen.

Dieser „Schritt zurück“ veranlasste damals Habermas zu einer Polemik gegen Lyotard, mit einem Vorwurf der (reaktionären) Rückwärtsgewandtheit, was für lange Zeit die Beschäftigung intellektueller (linker) Kreise mit dem postmodernen Denken jenseits von vereinfachenden Klischees verhinderte. Es ist für viele aber, so auch z. B. für Heinz Kimmerle[35], eine Vorstufe der interkulturellen Philosophie geworden und hat postkoloniale und feministische Diskurse ermöglicht. Denn die Dekonstruktion und kritische Befragung eigener Denktraditionen erzeugt mehr Offenheit für andere Denkmuster und –traditionen. Dabei entwickelt Derrida eine textkritische Methode durch Gegeneinanderstellen von unterschiedlichen Texten, um Inkonsistenzen und implizite Voreinstellungen aufzudecken. So z. B. untersucht er einen weniger bekannten Aufsatz von Kant, in dem dieser die kraft eines höheren Gefühls philosophierenden „Mystagogen“ ironisiert. Die Vernunft wird so nach Kant „kastriert und entmannt“, was „die Polizei im Reiche der Vernunft nicht zulassen kann.“[36] (Die so verstandene Vernunft ist also männlich, Derrida spricht hier kritisch von „Phallogozentrismus“). Die vergleichende Analyse seiner textkritischen Methode der Dekonstruktion macht einen Vernunftbegriff deutlich, der heute – so das Anliegen – gegen alle Ausschlüsse ausgeweitet werden muss.

Das postmoderne Denken, das sich ernsthaft um Pluralität bemüht, auch mit einem nichthegemonialen Denken, dass über europäische Traditionen hinauswächst, speist sich aus Quellen bei Heidegger, Nietzsche und dem amerikanischen Pragmatismus, der sich auch gegen jedes sich selbst immunisierende Systemdenken wendet und sich im Namen des Pragmatismus einem „Multiver-

---

[35] Kimmerle, *Interkulturelle Philosophie*, 66

[36] Jacques Derrida, „Von einem neuerdings erhobenen vornehmen Ton in der Philosophie. No Apocalypse, not now“, in: Jacques Derrida, *Apokalypse*, ed. Peter Engelmann, Passagen: Wien 1972, zitiert hier Kants Aufsatz „Von einem neuerdings erhobenen vornehmen Ton in der Philosophie“, in: z. B. Weischedel-Gesamtausgabe Bd. 3, WBG: Darmstadt 1971, 377-397 (A 387-A 425).

[30] Ibid., A 417 und A 421.

sum“[37] und einer an Tatsachen orientierten Philosophie des „und“ [38] jenseits von Systemen zuwendet. Den postmodernen Strömungen geht es daher zentral um eine Offenheit gegenüber anderen Denkschemata als den eigenen liebgewordenen, und sie können daher als neue Welle aufklärerischen Denkens gegen jeden Dogmatismus auch in der Philosophie gesehen werden, das sich nebenbei auch über die eigene Gewordenheit aufklärt, wozu auch Foucault mit seiner „Archäologie des Wissens“ beigetragen hat. Und das muss nicht in Relativismus und Beliebigkeit enden: Das Ernstnehmen auch anderer als der eigenen historisch gewachsenen Perspektiven kann man als Bereicherung im Bemühen um eine umfassendere Wahrheit sehen[39], auch wenn ich selbst auf zwei Kritikpunkte hingewiesen habe[40]. Man kann daher durchaus von einer Dialektik von Moderne und Postmoderne[41] sprechen. Beide brauchen einander als Reflexionspotential. Und Habermas, der sich später mit Derrida getroffen hat, hat sich heute auch anders positioniert.

Alle drei beschriebenen philosophischen Denktraditionen wirken bis heute nach. Gemeinsam ist ihnen, dass sie sich gegen jeden Dogmatismus richten und dabei das kritische Denken in je anderer Weise für die Gegenwartsgesellschaft aktualisieren und fruchtbar machen wollen.

## IV. Fazit

Kann kritische Vernunft helfen? Unbedingt! Und man kann sich von dem geschilderten Strömungen anregen lassen.

Natürlich bleibt die „Kritik der instrumentellen Vernunft“ (das galt ja schon als Vorwurf an die Adresse der Vorsokratiker) gültig und wichtig, gerade in Zeiten, da eine arbeitsschaffende Industrie sich zur Bedrohung unserer natürlichen Lebensgrundlagen entwickelt hat[42], Menschen vom „Kapital“ instrumentalisiert werden bzw. in Billiglohnjobs ausgebeutet werden, und wildwuchernde Bürokratie sich manchmal fast selbstzweckhaft in eine Sprache verirrt, die normalgebildete Bürger kaum noch verstehen. Horkheimers Buch hilft, die Aggression der Abgehängten, oder derer, die sich so fühlen, besser zu verstehen, der durch die Technik der Massenproduktion ausgepressten „Opfer der instrumentellen Ver-

[37] So William James kritisch in seinem Buch *Das pluralistische Universum. Vorlesungen über die gegenwärtige Lage der Philosophie*, WBG: Darmstadt 1994.
[38] William James, *Der Pragmatismus*, Meiner: Hamburg 1994, 79ff.
[39] Münnix, *Zum Ethos der Pluralität*, 129–190.
[40] Ibid., z. B. Einleitung, ii.
[41] Albrecht Wellmer, *Zur Dialektik von Moderne und Postmoderne*, Suhrkamp: Frankfurt 72015.
[42] Werner Busch, Gabriele Münnix, Bernd Rolf (ed.), *Philosophie und Umweltbildung*, Bautz: Nordhausen 2024, darin als Einleitung, Gabriele Münnix, „Natur als Ressource? Zur Bedeutung philosophischer Reflexion in der Klimakrise“, 12ff.

nunft"[43], und es macht auf bedenkliche Auswüchse im politischen Diskurs aufmerksam. Poppers „offene Gesellschaft und ihre Feinde" als eine der Bibeln der Demokratie hat angesichts der internationalen Migrationsbewegungen und zunehmenden populistischen Strömungen wieder neue Aktualität gewonnen. Und sein Prinzip der Falsifikation ist nicht nur wissenschaftstheoretisch bedeutsam geworden, sondern kann auch helfen, fake news und Vorurteile zu widerlegen. Schließlich hat die postmoderne Rationalismuskritik darauf aufmerksam gemacht, dass eine sich monopolisierende westliche Vernunft Gewaltpotential haben kann[44] und potentielle Diskursteilnehmer vom Diskurs ausschließt, die sich in ihm artikulieren wollen, aber es nicht können.

Poppers Überzeugung, dass man jeden Menschen als Quelle vernünftiger Argumente achten müsse, hat zu postkolonialen und feministischen Diskursen geführt, die sich nun über epistemische Gewalt austauschen.[45] Und dabei wird deutlich, dass wir mehr über unterschiedliche Rationalitätstypen wissen müssen, die man nicht einfach als unvernünftig abtun kann, nur weil sie der eigenen Denktradition nicht entsprechen.[46] Doch wichtig bleibt angesichts aller Diversität, dass wir eine Basis an Gemeinsamkeiten suchen müssen, auf der man für Diskurse aufbauen kann. Kritische Rationalität in diesem erweiterten Sinn ist also auch für eine Populismuskritik unabdingbar und steht in der Tradition der Aufklärung, muss also mit bestimmten Techniken der Kritik einhergehen, die gelehrt werden können.[47] Es geht mir hier um eine Didaktik logischer Methoden der Sprachkritik, wie ich sie schon früher vorgeschlagen habe.

Doch wir müssen m. E. noch über rationale Diskurse und kritische Rationalität hinausgehen: Populistische Bewegungen zielen, wie deutlich wurde, weniger auf Argumente, sondern bewusst auf Gefühle wie Angst, Ärger, Wut, Enttäuschung und suchen sie für sich zu befeuern und auszunutzen. Doch was Kant einst als „pathologisch affiziert" abqualifizierte, weil so vernünftige Entscheidungen beeinträchtigt werden könnten, ist nicht einfach irrational, sondern

---

[43] Horkheimer, *Kritik der instrumentellen Vernunft*, 119.

[44] Vgl. Gabriele Münnix, „Kontradiktion und Komplementarität. Ist *die* Logik universal?", in: *Tradition und Traditionsbruch zwischen Skepsis und Dogmatik*, Studien zur interkulturellen Philosophie (SIP) Bd. 16, ed. Claudia Bickmann, Hermann-Josef Scheidgen, Tobias Voßhenrich u. Markus Wirtz, Rodopi: Amsterdam/New York 2006, 265-280.

[45] Claudia Brunner, „Ungerechtigkeit, Unterdrückung oder doch Gewalt? Feministische Konzeptionen der epistemischen Grundlagen globaler sozialer Verhältnisse", in_ *Polylog, Zeitschrift für interkulturelles Philosophieren* 50 (2023), 9–23.

[46] So wird die Tagung „Meine, deine, unsere Vernunft?" im März 2025 in Wien (Kooperation von AIPPh und WiGIP) diese Rationalitätstypen diskutieren.

[47] Vgl Gabriele Münnix, „Logikdidaktik", *Mitteilungen des Fachverbandes Philosophie 2009*, 129–143.

missachtet einen wichtigen Teil der menschlichen Natur: Wir wissen spätestens[48] seit Schelers „Wertfühlen", dass Gefühle einen rationalen Kern haben[49]: Man ist wütend *auf etwas*, hat Angst *vor etwas*, ist enttäuscht *von etwas*. Dieses „Worumwillen" bezeugt Wertgefühle, wie sie für Charles Taylor zu „Quellen des Selbst" werden und *vor* aller rationalen Überformung in den Menschen wirksam seien.[50] Die analytische Philosophie der Emotionen, z. B. bei de Sousa und Döring, ist also zu befragen. Das Verdienst, diese Überlegungen mit der politischen Philosophie verknüpft und aktualisiert zu haben kommt m.E. aber Martha Nussbaum zu: Bereits 2016 hat sie, nicht nur in Bezug auf die amerikanische Situation, über „Anger and Forgiveness, Resentment and Justice"[51] in der Politik geschrieben und das Thema später in einem Buch über „Politische Emotionen" weitergeführt. Eine solche philosophische Reflexion über Emotionalität in der Politik ist unabdingbar und kann zu mehr Verständnis führen. Schließlich können populistische Bewegungen in der heutigen Form mit Stegemann als Indikatoren gesehen werden für das, was in einer Demokratie nicht stimmt und entbehren keinesfalls – jenseits aller Auswüchse – einer inneren Logik.

Nötig und sogar elementar wichtig ist es also auch seitens der Politik, gründlich über Gefühle, vor allem der benachteiligten „Wutbürger" nachzudenken.[52] Die Demokratie ist kein selbstverständliches Gut. Sie ist gefährdet und gerade weil sie durch philosophische Reflexion entstanden ist, haben PhilosophInnen auch die Aufgabe, diesen Gefährdungen etwas entgegenzusetzen.[53] Es gilt daher Strategien zu entwickeln, vielleicht auch unter Einbeziehung von emotiona-

---

[48] Vorher bereits Herder gegen Descartes' *cogito*: „Ich fühle mich: ich bin", in: Johann Gottfried Herder, *Zum Sinn des Gefühls*, Werke Bd. 4, Schriften zur Philosophie, *Kunst und Altertum 1774-1787*, ed. Jürgen Brummack, Martin Bollader, Deutscher Klassiker Verlag: Frankfurt/Main 1994, 235f.

[49] Max Scheler, *Der Formalismus in der Ethik und die materiale Wertethik. Neuer Versuch der Grundlegung eines ethischen Personalismus*, Sarastro: Paderborn 2012, 169–206, 248–259 (seine Kritik an Kants Ethik geht von Kants Gleichsetzung von formal / apriori und material / a posteriori aus); s. aber auch Ronald de Sousa, *Die Rationalität des Gefühls*, Suhrkamp: Frankfurt 1997, und Sabine Döring (ed.) *Philosophie der Gefühle*, Suhrkamp: Frankfurt a.M. 2009.

[50] Charles Taylor, *Quellen des Selbst*, Suhrkamp: Frankfurt a.M. 1996, s. auch das Interview mit Charles Taylor, „Identity, Moral Value and Violence", in: *Europa Forum Philosophie* 64 (2015), 13.

[51] Martha Nussbaum, *Anger and Forgiveness, Resentment and Justice*, Oxford: Oxford University Press 2016. Sowie Martha Nussbaum, *Politische Emotionen*, Suhrkamp: Berlin 2016 (Vielleicht aus heutiger Perspektive neben ihrer Rawls-Kritik im *capability approach* ihre wichtigste Arbeit.)

[52] Vgl Klaus Blesenkemper, "Gefühle geben zu denken", in: *Zeitschrift für Didaktik der Philosophie und Ethik* 4 (1998), 254-265.

[53] Siehe dazu auch die Ausgabe 6/2024 des *Philosophie Magazin*, die das Thema „Die Geister von Amerika. Woher kommt der Trumpismus?" aufgreift.

len Dimensionen in Richtung „Verfassungspatriotismus". Solche Wertebindung hat nichts mit einer Befeuerung von völkischem Nationalismus zu tun, ist aber eine Aufgabe für die philosophische und politische Bildung. Die Demokratie darf gerade von der Philosophie nicht kampflos preisgegeben werden, ihre Wertschätzung muss nicht nur auf allen Ebenen der philosophischen Lehre zum Thema gemacht werden, sondern auch zum öffentlichen Diskurs gehören.

Zum Schluss noch einmal warnend Horkheimer: „Ist einmal die philosophische Grundlage der Demokratie zusammengebrochen, so ist die Feststellung, Diktatur sei schlecht, nur für solche Menschen rational gültig, die nicht ihre Nutznießer sind; und es gibt kein theoretisches Hindernis, diese Feststellung in ihr Gegenteil zu verwandeln."[54] Natürlich ist ein „Populismus", der sich für die Rechte Benachteiligter um ihrer selbst willen einsetzt, zu begrüßen. Andernfalls sollten wir wachsam sein.

[54] Horkheimer, *Kritik der instrumentellen Vernunft*, 37.

*Georgi Kapriev (Sofia, Bulgarien)*

# Die Wurzeln des bulgarischen Populismus

Der Populismus, ein unvermeidbarer Teil des politischen Bildes der Modernität, weist auf dem Balkan, d.h. in den Ländern, deren Sozial- und Kulturgeschichte vom Oströmischen Reich (Byzanz) und dem Osmanischen Reich beeinflusst wurde, einige besondere Merkmale auf. Der bulgarische Populismus mit seiner Spezifik hat seine Genese und Entwicklung in diesem Milieu.

Der Begriff ‚Populismus' wird hier in seinem gängigen Sinn aufgefasst. Gemeint ist ein politisches Verfahren, das sich für das ‚einfache Volk' einsetzt. Der ‚gesunde Verstand' des ‚Volkes' wird dabei einer politischen, wirtschaftlichen und kulturellen Elite gegenübergestellt, die als unanständig, korrupt und ausbeuterisch dargestellt wird. Indem man die Ängste und Komplexe des vermeintlichen ‚einfachen Volkes' schürt, wird dieses für die Umwandlung des ‚volksfremden' Systems angeworben. Diese Anwerbung beruft und stützt sich auf ‚Traditionswerte', die ihrerseits als nationale Werte gedeutet und gegen eine ‚nivellierende Globalisierung' gerichtet werden.

## Das Oströmische Reich

Das Oströmische Reich verstand sich als das Römische Reich schlechthin, dessen Hauptstadt seit dem 4. Jahrhundert Konstantinopel wurde. Das starre monarchische System war alternativlos, und das Zentrum der Macht wurde ausschließlich durch den Kaiser verkörpert. Der Gesetzgebung nach war der Kaiser nicht an die Gesetze gebunden (*princeps legibus solutus est*)[1]: Was dem Kaiser gefällt, hat Gesetzeskraft (*quod principi placuit legis habet vigorem*).[2] Alle anderen waren seine Untertanen: οἱ ὑπὸ χεῖρα – sie waren ganz in seiner Hand. Das Gleiche galt auch für die an der Staatsregierung Beteiligten, einschließlich ihrer Positionen und Privilegien.

Diese Sachlage erklärt eines der sozial-politischen Hauptprinzipien in Byzanz: das Fehlen einer Erbaristokratie. Selbst der kaiserliche Sitz war dem Gesetz nach nicht erblich. Die Worte εὐγένεια, εὐγενής wurden nie zur Bezeichnung irgendeiner Art von Familienaristokratie verwendet. Adel wurde als moralische Tugend angesehen, die der einzelnen Person den Zugang zur politischen

---

[1] Digesta Iustiniani, I, 3, 31, in: *Digesta Iustiniani Augusti*, Bd. 1, ed. T. Momsen, Wiedmann: Berlin 1870, 13.

[2] Digesta Iustiniani, I, 4, 1, in: *Digesta Iustiniani Augusti*, Bd. 1, ed. T. Momsen, Wiedmann: Berlin 1870, 14.

und gesellschaftlichen Elite ermöglichen konnte. Um eine Position in der Staats- oder Kirchenhierarchie zu erreichen, spielte die Abstammung und die ethnische Zugehörigkeit keine erstrangige Rolle. Wenn also von einer Aristokratie in Byzanz gesprochen werden sollte, dann ging es meist um eine Amts- oder Dienstaristokratie. Die ‚aristokratische' Position wurde mit der Amtsstelle erworben bzw. verloren.[3]

Der Reichsideologie nach war die Βασιλεία τῶν Ῥωμαίων die οἰκουμένη, die bewohnte Erde bzw. die zivilisierte Welt. Die Kaiser waren überzeugt, dass sie über die Ökumene Verfügungsgewalt hätten, während die anderen Herrscher durch ihre Gunst regierten. Die Völker außerhalb dieser Welt wurden als Barbaren qualifiziert, die allesamt zu ihrem Wohl zivilisiert werden sollten. Laut der Ideologie war die *pax romana* auch für das Oströmische Reich ein Hauptziel, das als Argument für die politische Dominanz des Zentrums über die Peripherie galt – eine Dominanz, die zunächst als zivilisierende Aktivität und erst dann als politische Hegemonie verstanden werden sollte. Zu diesem Zweck wurde zunächst die Infrastruktur errichtet. Es galt, sozialen Komfort und Möglichkeiten für die wirtschaftliche und kulturelle Realisation der Peripherie im Umfang der Ökumene zu schaffen.[4]

Das Expansionsprogramm, das spätestens im 9. Jahrhundert durch das Missionsprojekt von Kaiser Michael III. und dem Patriarchen Photios umrissen wurde, erzielte die Dursetzung einer einheitlichen politischen, juristischen und kulturellen Ordnung. Der Umfang dieser Maßnahmenfestlegung bzw. die Vorherrschaft dieser Kultur fiel nicht mit den geschichtlich schwankenden Staatsgrenzen von Byzanz zusammen. Es wurde von *Byzantine commonwealth* gesprochen. Damit ist eine Tradition gemeint, die von der byzantinischen Kultur grundlegend beeinflusst wurde, ohne dass die Territorien, in denen sie entfaltet wurde, innerhalb der Reichsgrenzen lagen. Es geht hierbei um ein Paradigma, das sich durch mannigfaltige synchrone Variationen eines komplexen Prozesses behauptete. Auf alle Fälle blieb dieses System mit Konstantinopel und den übrigen großen Kulturzentren des Reiches im Allgemeinen verbunden. Zu diesem System gehörte ebenso das mittelalterliche Bulgarien.[5]

Nach dem Untergang des bulgarischen Staates im Nordosten des Schwarzen Meers erreichte um 679 ein Teil der Bulgaren unter der Führung von Aspa-

[3] Cf. Dimiter Angelov, *Imperial Ideology and Political Thought in Byzantium, 1204-1330*, Cambridge University Press: Cambridge 2007, 217-234.
[4] Cf. Dimitri Obolensky, *The Byzantine Commonwealth: Eastern Europe 500-1453*, Cardinal: London 1971, 69-101.
[5] Cf. Dimitri Obolensky, *The Byzantine Commonwealth: Eastern Europe 500-1453*, Cardinal: London 1971, passim.

ruch, einem Sohn des ehemaligen Herrschers, die Gebiete auf beiden Ufern des östlichen Teils der Donau. Im Sommer 680 zog Kaiser Konstantin IV. an der Spitze eines Heeres gegen die Bulgaren. Das Ergebnis war das Abschließen eines Friedensvertrags im Jahre 681, durch den die Grenzen des neuen Staates und eine Tributpflichtigkeit Konstantinopels vereinbart wurden. Eine Hypothese lautet, dass die neue Staatsbildung auch als Wächter des *limes* des Reiches dienen sollte.

Die Deutung Bulgariens als Reichsperipherie sieht problematisch aus, insofern – mit Ausnahme der Periode zwischen 1018 und 1185 – das Land ein selbständiger Staat war, dessen Herrscher seit 927 den Titel ‚Zar/Kaiser' innehatten. Die beiden Staaten, Bulgarien und Byzanz, führten mehrere Kriege gegeneinander, und es waren bulgarische Herrscher, die Konstantinopel selbst nach der Christianisierung Bulgariens belagerten. Doch selbst die aggressivsten unter ihnen strebten nicht an, die Stadt bzw. den Staat zu vernichten, sondern danach, Konstantinopel einzunehmen, um rhomäische Kaiser zu werden. Die moderne romantisch-nationalistische Geschichtsschreibung verschleiert jedoch durch eine Überbetonnung der militärischen Rivalitäten die Tatsache, dass Bulgarien der eifrigste Nachahmer des byzantinischen politischen und kulturellen Modells war. Der mittelalterliche bulgarische Staat und seine offizielle Politik wurden als Nachbildung des byzantinischen Staates errichtet, und dieser Umstand wurde von ihrem Erbauer als Zeugnis einer besonderen Würde angesehen.

Ein Beispiel für die Art und Weise der Wirkung des byzantinischen ‚Missionsprojekts' ist die Adoption der slawischen Schrift seitens des in den Sechzigerjahren des 9. Jahrhunderts christianisierten Bulgariens. Kernbestandteil der Missionspolitik war das für das Ost-Christentum übliche Verständnis, dass der Gottesdienst in einer für das Volk verständlichen Sprache abgehalten werden soll. Diese Regel wurde im Jahre 867 von Kyrill und Methodius, die seit 863 in Großmähren lehrten, zunächst in Venedig und dann in Rom erfolgreich begründet. Kyrill schuf die erste slawische Schrift, die sog. Glagoliza, und übersetzte mit seinem Bruder Methodius die Evangelien und die wichtigsten liturgischen Texte. Nach einer misslungenen Mission unter den Mähren und nach dem Tod des Methodius (885), der es 884 schaffte, dem Kaiser Basileios I. die slawischen Gottesdienstbücher zu überreichen, wurden 886 einige Schüler von ihm in Bulgarien empfangen. Sie entwickelten eine großartige Lehrtätigkeit. Gegen Ende des 9. Jahrhunderts, mit dem entscheidenden Beitrag des Methodius-Schülers Kliment von Ochrid, wurde die slawische Schrift durch eine Annäherung an das griechische Alphabet modifiziert. Die sog. Kyrilliza wurde später von weiteren slawischsprachigen Völkern übernommen.[6]

Im byzantinischen Missionsprojekt ging es um ein Anbinden an die byzantinische Welt durch das Absichern einer relativen, aber breiten Selbständigkeit. Zeugnis dafür ist z. B. die Eigenart der mittelalterlichen bulgarischen Kunst, die fraglos in der Umlaufbahn der byzantinischen Kunst blieb, indessen sie eigene Züge und eine eigenartige Rezeption (von orientalischen und westchristlichen Kulturen) aufwies.[7] Das Wert- und Sinnzentrum blieb dabei unumstritten. Es wurden in Bulgarien einige byzantinische Universalgeschichtswerke übersetzt, die oft auf eine kuriose Weise ergänzt oder abgeändert wurden. Es erschien aber kein originaler bulgarischer Text. Das unbezweifelbare Universalzentrum, ohne das die Verfassung einer mittelalterlichen Universalgeschichte undenkbar war, war Konstantinopel. Dasselbe war an der Rechtsordnung des mittelalterlichen Bulgariens zu erkennen, die das römische Recht in der Form rezipierte, die in Byzanz entwickelt wurde. Alle schriftlich belegten bulgarischen Gesetze wurden aus dem Griechischen übersetzt. Die einzige Ausnahme stellte die von einem Schüler des Methodius verfasste Adaption des fränkischen *Poenitentiale Merseburgense* dar.[8]

## Das Osmanische Reich

Das bulgarische Selbstverständnis als Reichsperipherie wurde im Rahmen des Osmanischen Reiches (1396-1878) transparent. Die politische Reichsideologie wiederholte die Hauptfiguren des byzantinischen Models. Das Zentrum, Kostantiniyye bzw. Istanbul (slawisch: Zarigrad = Kaiserstadt), übernahm vollauf die politische Verwaltung und die volle Verantwortung für die Wahrung des Friedens (die bulgarische Bevölkerung war fast 400 Jahre lang nicht an Militäraktivitäten beteiligt). Der Mangel an Interesse und Ehrgeiz in diesem Bereich war einfach durch die Zahl der hohen Reichsbeamten bulgarischer Herkunft zu erklären, die eine ganz geringe Anzahl im Vergleich mit der der anderen Nichtmuslime war. Die bulgarischen Eliten fühlten sich auf makro-politischer Ebene verantwortungsfrei und wandten sich angenehmeren und gewinnbringenderen Angelegenheiten zu.[9]

---

6 Cf. Francis Dvornik, *Byzantine Mission among the Slavs: SS. Constantine-Cyril and Methodius*, Rutgers University Press: New Jersey 1970.

7 Cf. Bogdan Filow, *Die altbulgarische Kunst*, Akademische Buchhandlung: Bern 1919.

8 Cf. Ivan Alexandrov Biliarsky, "Law", in *The Routledge Handbook of East Central and Eastern Europe in the Middle Ages, 500-1300*, ed. F. Curta, Routledge: London/New York 2022, 425-442.

9 Cf. e.g. Иван Илчев, Розата на Балканите, т. 1, Colibri: София 2019, 235-269. (Ivan Ilchev,

Diese Sachlage wurde durch das Rechts- und Identifikationssystem des Osmanischen Reiches ermöglicht. Mit Bezugnahme auf den Koran, Sure 5, 45-51, wurde das Millet-System etabliert, das erst im 19. Jahrhundert zerfiel. Es wurden vier ‚Völker' genannt, die über eine eigene Heilige Schrift verfügten: die Muslime, die Armenier, die Juden und die Rum-Millet, die ‚Römer', d. h. die orthodoxen Christen. Die Teilung im Osmanischen Reich verlief nicht nach einem ethnischen, sondern nach einem religiösen Prinzip. Der Patriarch von Konstantinopel wurde auch als *millet başı,* ‚Ethnarch' der orthodoxen Christen im Reich angesehen, durch den rechtliche Befugnisse auf die kirchliche Struktur übertragen wurden. Er und die Kirchenhierarchie waren beauftragt, als Vermittler zwischen der Staatsmacht und der Millet zu agieren.[10]

Sowohl wirtschaftlich als auch kulturell suchten die Osmanen keine Integration der andersgläubigen Bevölkerung. Die osmanische Wirtschaft und Kultur reproduzierten sich durch die Aufbewahrung ihrer Fremdheit, ihrer Andersheit. Die grundlegenden Pflichten der Untertanen beschränkten sich rechtmäßig auf die Zahlung spezifischer Steuern und die Einhaltung der Gesetze unter der Leitung ihrer religiösen und kommunalen Führer. Die Absonderung von Millet-Ortschaften oder -Viertel war ein Ergebnis der Bemühungen, den Marktplatz fast zum einzigen Treffpunkt der verschiedenen Millets zu machen. Die kleineren Städte und die Dörfer bestanden faktisch als selbstverwaltete Gemeinden. Es ist daher keine Überraschung, dass die bulgarische Redewendung „Gott ist hoch und der Kaiser weit weg" Analoge, insofern ich feststellen konnte, nur auf Russisch und Chinesisch hat.

Oft wird dabei vergessen, dass es sich bei diesen Gemeinden nicht um weltliche Verwaltungseinheiten, sondern um Kirchengemeinden handelte. Die Religion spielte die Rolle eines konstitutiven und in hohem Maße regulativen sozialen Prinzips. Die Kirchengemeinde wurde zudem mit weltlichen Aufgaben betraut. Manche Historiker sprechen heute von einer ‚Demokratisierung der Kirche'. Damit betonen sie sowohl den Einzug von Laien in ihre Leitung und eine sensible Aufnahme von Elementen parachristlicher Gewohnheitsweltanschauungen und Rechtsnormen als auch die Übertragung eigentlich kirchenfremder Aufgaben wie die weltliche Rechtspflege innerhalb nicht allzu enger Kompetenzgrenzen.[11] Die relativ weitgehende kommunale Selbstverwaltung

---

*Rozata na Balkanite*, Bd.1, Colibri: Sofia 2019, 235-269).

[10] Cf. e.g. Karen Barkey/George Gavrilis, "The Ottoman *Millet* System: Non-Territorial Autonomy and its Contemporary Legacy", in: *Ethnopolitics* 15/1 (2016), 24-42.

[11] Олга Тодорова, *Православната църква и българите XV-XVIII век*, АИ „Проф. Марин Дринов": София 1997. (Olga Todorova, *Pravoslavnata zarkva i balgarite XV-XVIII vek*, AI Prof. Marin Drinov: Sofia 1997).

wurde von den Bulgaren spezifisch genutzt. Die mangelnde Führungskompetenz im Bereich der ‚großen' Politik förderte den Einsatz des ‚berühmten' bulgarischen Pragmatismus mit seiner Zentrierung auf das Individuum oder allenfalls auf die Familie und deren Nutzen. Das Wesensmerkmal der Bulgaren waren die Produktion und der Handel, und – trotz des populären Gejammers – der agrokulturelle Anbau.

## Diskreditierung der vermögenden Schichten

Sowohl in der Wirtschaft als auch in der Kultur spezialisierte sich die bulgarische kaiserliche (byzantinische und osmanische) Peripherie auf ihre Funktion als Vermittler. Sie übernahm ‚natürlich' die Rolle des ‚Dolmetschers' der Einflüsse, die sowohl aus dem Osten als auch aus dem Westen kamen. Wenn das kulturelle Produkt der Peripherie das Zentrum letztendlich nur am Rande zu beeinflussen vermochte, stand der Stellenwert ihres wirtschaftlichen *Tschorbadshii,* der Produkte nicht in Frage – das Zentrum war direkt davon abhängig. Darin lag die Quelle des besonderen imperialen Selbstbewusstseins der provinziellen Eliten. Unter diesen Bedingungen etablierte sich die Schicht der sogenannten wohlhabenden Bürger und Bauern, die die Elite ihrer Ortschaft bildeten. Im Jahre 1910 berichtete Simeon Radev, dass bereits 1857 die bulgarische Presse darüber schrieb, dass es in Bulgarien offiziell nie Leibeigenschaft gegeben hatte, wie diejenige, welche die von der osmanischen Verwaltung mit Macht ausgestatteten bulgarischen Familien Teilen der bulgarischen Bevölkerung auferlegten.[12] Trotz der anerkannten Präsenz von „würdigen und volksnahen Leuten" aus dieser Schicht, die sich „für das Wohl ihres Volkes einsetzen", setzte die damalige liberale Revolutionspropaganda die Tschorbadshii mit den politischen Vertreterm, also mit den Osmanen, und mit den kulturellen Vertretern, mit den „Griechen", wie die Vertreter der konstantinopolitanischen Kirche hartnäckig genannt wurden, gleich.[13] Die Autorität dieser „Vermittler zwischen dem Volk und der Regierung"[14], d. h. der Produktions- und Handelsschicht, die als korrupt und unmoralisch dargestellt wurde, wurde damals schon gestürzt.

---

[12] Cf. e.g. Иван Илчев, Розата на Балканите, т. 1, София 2019, 263. (Ivan Ilchev, *Rozata na Balkanite*, Bd.1, Colibri: Sofia 2019, 235-269).

[13] Симеон Радев, *Строителите на съвременна България*, т. 1, Български писател: София 1990, 27-29. (Simeon Radev, *Stroitelite na savremenna Balgarija*, T. 1, Balgarski pisatel: Sofia1990, 27-29).

[14] Михаил Арнаудовъ, *Българското възраждане*, Българска мисълъ: София 1941, 107. (Mihail Arnaudov, *Balgarskoto vazrajdane*, Balgarska misal: Sofia 1941, 107).

## Entstehung des Nationalismus

Es wird behauptet, dass bis zum Tod des Wesirs Mehmed Sokolović (Sokollu Mehmed Pascha, †1579) die Bulgaren unter türkischer Herrschaft sicher waren. Die Lage habe sich danach vor allem wegen der Korruption in der Verwaltung und Justiz verschlechtert.[15] Die Debatten um die sogenannte bulgarische Wiedergeburt berücksichtigen jedoch selten ein geschichtliches Ereignis: die Kirdzhalis-Zeit (1781-1812, insb. 1792-1806). Diese Periode von Gewalt und Unruhe stellte wichtigen Privilegen infrage, die sich aus der Zugehörigkeit zum Reich ergaben – die Wahrung des Friedens und die Gewährleistung des sozialen Komforts. Das Zentrum scheiterte daran, dass es seine grundlegende Verpflichtung nicht einhielt. Die bulgarische Bevölkerung sah sich gezwungen, sowohl in die Städte zu ziehen bzw. auszuwandern als auch sich selbst zu verteidigen. Die Zentralmacht tolerierte indessen diesen Zivilschutz und die entsprechende Bewaffnung der nichtmuslimischen Untertanen.[16] Zeitgenossen berichten jedoch darüber, dass das bulgarische Schicksal erneut grausam zuschlug: Nach dem Abzug der russischen Truppen in den Jahren 1829 und 1854 als Folge der Beendigung der Kriege mit dem Osmanischen Reich zogen sich die russischen Truppen von den durch die Bulgaren besiedelten Territorien zurück, ohne sich um die mit ihnen kollaborierende Bevölkerung zu kümmern.[17]

Erst seit Ende des 18. Jahrhunderts begannen die balkanischen Nationalismen in den Vordergrund zu treten. Die Grundformel ‚Blut und Boden' setzte sich durch eine besondere Figur (als Gegenpol zum französischen Begriff der Nation) durch. Das einzige hinreichende Kriterium für die Unterscheidung innerhalb der Christen im Reich konnte nur die Sprache sein, die „das wertvollste Erbe unserer Vorfahren, das Symbol und die Unterstützung unserer Nationalität"[18] darstellte und aufgrund derer eine kulturelle und letztendlich geschichtliche Tradition des jeweiligen Ethnos behauptet werden konnte.

## Die politische Funktionalisierung der Ausbildung

Die ersten bulgarischen Nationalisten, unter denen die meisten an den griechischen Befreiungsbewegungen beteiligt waren, bestimmten die Aufklärung

---

[15] Ibid., 24.

[16] Вера Мутафчиева, *Кърджалисйко време*, Наука и изкуство: София 1993, 383-407. (Vera Mutafchieva, Kardjalijsko vreme, Nauka i Izkiustvo: Sofia 1993, 383-407).

[17] Захари Стояновъ, *Записки по българскитѣ възстания 1870-1876*, 4-то поправено пълно издание, Игнатовъ: София 1940,181-182. (Zahari Stojanov, Zapiski po balgarskite vastanija 1870-1876, vierte vollständig überarbeitete Ausgabe, Ignatov: Sofia 1940, 181-182).

[18] Михаил Арнаудовъ, *Българското възраждане*, Българска мисълъ: София 1941, 13. (Mihail Arnaudov, Balgarskoto vazrajdane, Balgarska misal: Sofia 1941, 13).

als die Ursache der bulgarischen „Wiedergeburt". Der „Aufklärungskampf" wurde als absolute Bedingung für den Revolutionskampf betrachtet: „Ohne die Vorherrschaft des Bewusstseins, das eine bestimmte menschliche Gruppe in eine kollektive Individualität verwandelt, die fähig ist, zu kämpfen und uralte Hindernisse zu überwinden", könne nichts in dieser Hinsicht geschehen.[19] Die Etappen des 1762 von Païssi von Hilendar formulierten Programms fasst Mihail Arnaudov auf diese Weise zusammen: „Sprache und Sitten, Kirche und Schule, politische Rechte und Staatsidee" – dieses sollten die Stufen des Nationalaufstiegs sein.[20]

Der Kampf um die politische Befreiung setzte eine Zurückweisung der durch die Kirche von Konstantinopel auferlegten griechischen Bildung bzw. Kultur voraus. Der Nationalrevolutionär und Chronist der bulgarischen Befreiungsbewegung Zahari Stoyanov erwähnte die Entwicklung der bulgarischen Bildung, Literatur und Presse als eine „vorausgehende Ursache für die bulgarischen Aufstände".[21]

Eine wichtige Rolle spielten dabei die sog. Tschitalista (wörtlich: Lesestuben). Zwischen 1856 und 1876 entstanden 130 solcher Institutionen. Sie wurden von wohlhabenden und aufgeklärten Bürgern gegründet und unterstützt. Dabei ging es nicht nur um eine öffentliche Bibliothek, sondern um ein holistisches Kulturzentrum. Stoyanov hebt hervor, das die Tschitalista nicht zuletzt Versammlungsort der revolutionären Komitees waren.[22] Der Beitrag der Schulen war deshalb umso virulenter.

Vasil Aprilow gründete 1835 in Gabrowo die erste Gesamtschule. Bis 1845 wurden noch zehn weitere solcher Schulen eröffnet. 1868 begann in Plovdiv das erste Gymnasium zu unterrichten. Vor allem aus der Lehrerschicht ging eine immer gewichtigere Gruppe bulgarischer Schriftsteller, Publizisten und Übersetzer hervor. Nach einer intensiven Debatte, die über 30 Jahre dauerte, wurde auch die literarische neue bulgarische Sprache kodifiziert, die durch die orthodoxe Bibelübersetzung, mit einer ersten vollständigen Ausgabe im Jahre 1871, etabliert wurde. Somit wurde jedoch das ganze Bildungssystem auf der Basis alter Netzwerke von Kloster- und Kirchenschulen gegründet, in denen die Priester das Amt des Lehrers bekleideten.

[19] Ibid., 7.
[20] Ibid., 14.
[21] Захари Стояновъ, *Записки по българскитѣ въстания 1870-1876*, Игнатовъ: София 1940, 185. (Zahari Stojanov, *Zapiski po balgarskite vastanija* 1870-1876, vierte vollständig überarbeitete Ausgabe, Ignatov: Sofia 1940, 185).
[22] Ibid.

Der Priester bzw. die Priester bildeten die Hauptautorität insbesondere in den kleineren Gemeinden. Im Jahre 1867 bezeugte Ljuben Karawelow, einer der produktivsten bulgarischen Aufklärer und prominenter Revolutionsanführer, dass die Priesterschaft, die grundsätzlich bulgarischer Herkunft war, durch die slawischen Schulen „von alters her“ das bulgarische Volksbewusstsein unterstützte. Er war jedoch kritisch und so vermerkte er: „Aber im Allgemeinen muss man zugeben, dass der Priester für den Bulgaren alles ist: er ist der Vertreter von allem Nationalen, er ist der erste Feind von allem Nicht-Nationalen, Fremden; er ist der erste Freund, der erste Bruder eines jeden Bulgaren, wo immer er ihm begegnet – im Gotteshaus oder in der Kneipe. [...] Und deshalb steht für den Bulgaren nur der bulgarische Priester über allem. Das Volk ist ihm ergeben, liebt ihn, gehorcht ihm und beginnt nichts, ohne seinen Hirten zu fragen“[23].

**Die selbständige Kirche als politisches Instrument**

Darauf gründete der besondere Weg der bulgarischen Befreiungsbewegung. Zahari Stoyanov erklärt dazu: „Die Kirchenfrage war der erste Faktor, der das bulgarische Volk dazu gebracht hat, einen Schritt in Richtung eines bürgerlichen und politischen Bewusstseins zu tun, zu denken, dass es, nachdem es sich von seinem geistigen Tyrannen befreit hat, eines Tages an der Reihe sein wird, das politische Joch abzuwerfen. Die kirchliche Frage diente zuerst dazu, das bulgarische Volk in einem Ganzen zu vereinen, sie legte das festeste Fundament unserer Nationalität, sie verwirrte die verhärteten Vorstellungen vieler und ließ sie zwischen den Worten ‚bulgarisch‘ und ‚christlich‘ unterscheiden“[24]. Die politische Befreiung begann also mit dem Streben nach kirchlicher Selbständigkeit.

Seit den 1830er Jahren waren jedoch auch Proteste gegen die Schikanen seitens der ‚griechischen‘, d. h. der konstantinopolitanischen Metropoliten festzustellen. Am 3. April 1860 erwähnte Bischof Hilarion, ein ethnischer Bulgare, während der Ostermesse den Namen des Patriarchen nicht. Nach wie vor wird in der ost-orthodoxen Tradition durch die liturgische Nennung des Patriarchen die Zugehörigkeit zu der entsprechenden Kirche erklärt. Doch erst zehn Jahre später schafften es die Bulgaren endlich, ein eigenständiges Exarchat zu erwer-

[23] Любен Каравелов, *Записки за България и българите*, Еделвайс: София 2024, 180-181. (Ljuben Karavelov, *Zapiski za Balgaria i balgarite*, Edelweis: Sofia 2024, 180-181).

[24] Захари Стояновъ, *Записки по българскитѣ възстания 1870-1876*, Игнатовъ: София 1940, 184. (Zahari Stojanov, *Zapiski po balgarskite vastanija* 1870-1876, vierte vollständig überarbeitete Ausgabe, Ignatov: Sofia 1940, 184).

ben. Es wurde durch einen Sultan-Ferman von 27. Februar 1870 erklärt.[25] Die Territorien der dadurch konstituierten *Bulgar Milleti* wurden anhand von Sprachkriterien umrissen. Die von der exarchistischen Ideologie eingeführte Perspektive führte zum Paradox, eine *Millet* hauptsächlich aufgrund einer in einzelnen Gebieten mehrheitlich vertretenen nicht endgültig kodifizierten Sprache zu behaupten. Zudem sollte auch aus dieser Perspektive heraus die Geschichte eines Volkes rekonstruiert werden, die somit den Geltungsbereich des bulgarischen Volkes und nicht die Staatsgrenze definieren sollte. Im Juli 1871 genehmigte der erste bulgarische Volkskirchenrat die Exarchiesatzung. Am 16. September 1872 verurteilte eine Synode der östlichen Patriarchen in Istanbul die neugegründete Kirche für den Ethnophiletismus, d. h. die Gründung einer Kirche aufgrund eines Ethnos und nicht auf eine von orthodoxen Gläubigen bewohnte Region ohne Rücksicht auf ihre ethnische Bestimmung. Die bulgarische Kirche wurde schismatisiert.

Die Exarchie wurde von den meisten Volkskirchenratsteilnehmern als Vorstufe des Nationalstaates betrachtet. Simeon Radev berichtet, dass die „gemäßigten" unter den bulgarischen Ideologen Angst gehabt hätten, dass das Nationalgefühl sich als schwächer als die Treue zur religiösen Tradition erweisen könnte. „Sie ahnten nicht", fügt er hinzu, „wie tief das Nationalgefühl der Bulgaren wirklich war". Die Radikalen unter den Teilnehmenden „dachten nicht daran, die nationale Einheit zu opfern. Sie hingen fanatisch an dem Motto: alle bulgarischen Länder innerhalb der Grenzen eines Bezirks und unter der Herrschaft einer Kirche".[26] Radev fasst zusammen: „Das Schisma hat die Bulgaren in ihrem nationalen Aufbegehren nicht erschüttert und auch keinen besonderen Eindruck auf sie gemacht: Zehn Jahrhunderte lang waren sie gewohnt, die Kirche in erster Linie als politische Organisation zu betrachten".[27]

## Abschwächung der Autorität der Kirche

Die Entstehung des neuen bulgarischen Staates war das Ergebnis des russisch-türkischen Krieges von 1877/78. Als der russisch-türkische Vorvertrag von San Stephano vom 3. März 1878 vorsah, dass Bulgarien als autonomes Fürstentum innerhalb der Grenzen errichtet werden sollte, in denen die Mehrheit der Bevöl-

[25] *Образъ на царскый форманъ за Решеніето на Българскый въпросъ*, Македония: Цариград 1870. (*Obraza na zarskij ferman za reshenieto na balgarskij vapros*, Makedonia: Zarigrad 1870).

[26] Симеон Радев, *Строителите на съвременна България*, т. 1, Български писател: София 1990, 110-111. (Simeon Radev, *Stroitelite na savremenna balgarija*, t.1, Balgarski pisatel: Sofia 1990, 110-111).

[27] Ibid.

kerung bulgarisch war,[28] hatten die Verfasser keinen anderen Maßstab für „bulgarisch" als die Exarchatsdiözesen. Es war klar, dass dieses vorläufige Dokument in der Realpolitik angepasst werden würde. Dies geschah mit dem Berliner Vertrag von 13. Juli 1878. Dabei wurde über die Gründung des Fürstentums Bulgarien und Ostrumelien als autonome Provinz des Osmanischen Reiches entschieden. Die mazedonischen Diözesen blieben innerhalb des Osmanischen Reiches.[29]

Die Erstrangigkeit der politischen Funktion der Kirche wurde eindeutig durch die Entscheidungen der ersten bulgarischen Volksversammlung (Februar-April 1879) umrissen, die die Verfassung und die Struktur des neuen Staates stiften sollte. Die Vorschläge des Klerus, der russischen Berater und der juristisch gebildeten Abgeordneten, die Kompetenzen der Kirche nur auf das Fürstentum und Ostrumelien zu begrenzen, um ihre Autokephalie zu erlangen, wurden abgelehnt. Radev kommentiert: „Wenn dieses Opfer in den harten Jahren der Wiedergeburt von den Volksführern in Istanbul abgelehnt worden war, so war es jetzt, wo ein übersteigerter nationaler Fanatismus für die neu zersplitterte Einheit des großen Bulgariens erwacht war, umso unerträglicher"[30]. Laut Radev spielten die kanonischen Regeln keine Rolle für eine Versammlung, die kein anderes Motiv als ihren Patriotismus agnoszierte. Er zitiert den seit Jahrzehnten anerkannten Volksführer Petko Slaveykov mit seiner Äußerung vor der Versammlung, dass, auch wenn alle bisherigen Kämpfe für eine Volkseinheit waren, „jetzt [...] [aber das Volk] nichts mehr außer [der] kirchlichen Einheit [habe]. Alle unsere Kämpfe waren volksnah und hätten für unsere Einheit sein sollen, aber jetzt haben wir nichts mehr außer unserer kirchlichen Einheit."[31]

Die bulgarische orthodoxe Kirche blieb bis 1953 schismatisch. Sie war in jeder Hinsicht von dem Staat abhängig, den sie bediente. Die Fälle, in denen der hohe Klerus der Staatsobrigkeit widersprach, bildeten eine absolute Ausnahme. Das prominenteste Beispiel darunter war das Verhindern der Deportation der Juden aus den ‚alten' Staatsgrenzen. Mitglieder der Synode standen an der Spitze der Aktion von März-Mai 1943, die auch von Politikern, Intellektu-

---

[28] Сан-Стефанский прелиминарный мирный договор, Статья VI: http://www.hist.msu.ru/ER/Etext/FOREIGN/stefano.htm.

[29] The Treaty of Berlin, July 30th, 1878, in: Gladstone's Speeches, hrsg v. A. T. Bassett, Methuen & Co: London, 1916, 505-552.

[30] Симеон Радев, *Строителите на съвременна България*, т. 1, Български писател: София 1990, 115. (Simeon Radev, *Stroitelite na savremenna balgarija*, Bd..1, Balgarski pisatel: Sofia 1990, 115).

[31] Ibid., 121.

ellen, Gewerkschaften etc. unterstützt wurde und erfolgreich endete.[32] Analogien dieses Ereignisses sind jedoch schwer zu finden. In Zeiten der kommunistischen Diktatur, die die Religion als feindliche Ideologie und die Kirche als historisches Relikt deutete, war die Kirche nicht nur unterdrückt und kontrolliert, sondern auch instrumentalisiert. In den 1990ern Jahren erlebte die Kirche eine weitere politische Spaltung. Trotz des positiven Ausgangs dieses Konflikts und abgesehen davon, dass der Druck seitens des Staates nicht im früheren Umfang ausgeübt wird, wird die soziale Autorität der bulgarischen orthodoxen Kirche weiterhin untergraben.

**Bloßstellung der Intellektuellen**

Die erste Volksversammlung im Jahre 1879 bereitete jedoch die Zerstörung der letzten bisher unbestrittenen Autorität vor. „Der Bulgare von damals hatte großen Respekt vor der Wissenschaft, die ihn wieder zum Leben erweckt hatte", erklärt Radev.[33] Damit bezeugte Zahari Stoyanov, dass unter den Anführern des Aufstandes von April 1876 nur Panayot Wolov eine mehr oder weniger systematische Bildung besaß.[34] Das heroische Tun der Befreiung, erklärte er im Jahre 1884, ist den „gelehrten Häuptern, schweren Kaufleuten, einflussreichen Geldmännern" fremd; es sei ein Werk der „einfachen und gemeinen Leute, alle vom unteren Stand"[35]. Diese Äußerung entsprach zwar nicht der tatsächlichen Lage, sie wurde aber unisono mit der Position verteidigt, die von den liberalen Abgeordneten im Jahre 1879 vertreten wurde.

Das Ziel der liberalen Volksvertreter war, das Projekt für die Verfassung maximal populistisch umzuformen. Sie haben z. B. Ideen für einen Senat und für eine Wahlhürde (für bestimmte Volksgruppen) verworfen. Zu diesem Zweck sollten die konservativen Abgeordneten bloßgestellt werden, zu denen die besser Gebildeten, inklusive die an mitteleuropäischen Universitäten promovierten Personen, zählten. Hauptmerkmal der Liberalen war der Glaube an die Tugenden des Volkes. Ihre Führer hatten mit der Masse gekämpft, hatten aus ihrem festen Willen Mut geschöpft, und sie hielten es für ein Sakrileg, ihre Vollkommenheit infrage zu stellen. Sie stützten sich auf die die Mehrheit immer beste-

[32] Cf. e.g. Tzvetan Todorov, *The Fragility of Goodness. Why Bulgaria's Jews Survived the Holocaust*, Weidenfeld & Nicolson: London 2001; M. Bar-Zohar, *Beyond Hitler's Grasp. The Heroic Rescue of Bulgaria's Jews,* Adams Media Corporation: Holbrook, Minnesota 1998.

[33] Симеон Радев, *Строителите на съвременна България*, т. 1, София 1990, 83 (Simeon Radev, *Stroitelite na savremenna balgarija*, Bd.1, Balgarski pisatel: Sofia 1990, 83).

[34] Захари Стояновъ, *Записки по българскитѣ въстания 1870-1876*, Игнатовъ: София 1940, 187. (Zahari Stojanov, *Zapiski po balgarskite vastanija 1870-1876*, vierte vollständig überarbeitete Ausgabe, Ignatov: Sofia 1940, 187).

[35] Ibid., 18-19.

chende Gleichheitsidee, die durch den Mangel von geschlossenen oder erblichen Eliten getragen wurde. Das bulgarische Volk hat niemals die Gültigkeit von Standesunterschieden anerkannt, bemerkt Simeon Radev und fasst zusammen: „Der Bulgare ist ein Feind der Hierarchie, sei sie nun sozial oder politisch“[36]. Die Fachkompetenz und die daraus folgenden Ansprüche wurden erfolgreich kompromittiert.

Der treuherzige Zahari Stoyanov schließt sein Vorwort mit einem Vorwurf gegen die „gelehrten Köpfe und die Saureichen“. Und bringt seine Überlegung auf den Punkt: „Vorwärts, Brüder! Schämt euch nicht eurer Einfachheit [...]. Sagt nicht, dass Lernen etwas Schlechtes ist. Gott bewahre! Es sind gelehrte Männer, die die Menschheit aus den Klauen des Tyrannen befreit haben; aber es ist sehr schade, dass wir noch keine solchen gelehrten Männer haben. Von nun an ist Gott gut [...]“[37]. Und der alte Dichter Grigor Parlitschev kommt 1884 zum folgenden Schluss: „Die elende Selbstverachtung ist ein Zeichen des Bulgarentums“[38] – ein Zeichen, das seine Gültigkeit bis heute nicht verloren hat.

## Der neue bulgarische Staat

1879 mussten die Bulgaren die Früchte ihrer über Jahrhunderte gewachsenen makropolitischen Unerfahrenheit auskosten. Die Zuversicht bezogen auf ‚Großvater Iwan‘ ist Ausdruck der Hoffnung, dass das Russische Reich das ‚Transdanubische Gouvernement‘ als seine Peripherie anerkennen wird. Doch das tat es nicht. Die bulgarische Elite sah sich bald gezwungen, politisch aktiv zu werden – und sie wurde es, mit zunächst ermutigendem, wenn auch zaghaftem Erfolg. Vor dem Hintergrund der durch die Vorarbeit der bulgarischen Diplomatie gesicherten Neutralität der Großmächte errang Bulgarien auf eigene Faust sowohl die ‚Wiedervereinigung‘ (der Anschluss von Ostrumelien an das Fürstentum erfolgte 1885) als auch die volle Unabhängigkeit des Staates: 1908 wurde Bulgarien zum Königreich erklärt. Die Periode der relativen Unabhängigkeit von

---

[36] Симеон Радев, *Строителите на съвременна България*, т. 1, Български писател: София 1990, 27 und 82-83. (Simeon Radev, *Stroitelite na savremenna balgarija*, t.1, Balgarski pisatel: Sofia 1990, 27, 82-83).

[37] Захари Стояновъ, *Записки по българскитѣ възстания 1870-1876*, Игнатовъ: София 1940, 26. (Zahari Stojanov, *Zapiski po balgarskite vastanija 1870-1876*, vierte vollständig überarbeitete Ausgabe, Ignatov: Sofia 1940, 26).

[38] Григор Пърличев: Автобиография, в: *Сборник за народни умотворения, наука и книжнина*, 11, 1894: http://macedonia.kroraina.com/gp/avtob_12.html. (Grigor Parlichev: Avtobiografija, in: *Sbornik za narodni umotvorenija,* nauka i knijnina, 11, 1894). http://macedonia.kroraina.com/gp/avtob_12.html.

einer Großmacht endete mit dem Beginn des Ersten Weltkriegs, als Bulgarien sich auf die Seite des Dreibundes stellte.[39]

Von der Gründung des unabhängigen Staates Bulgarien bis heute sehen die Bulgar:innen den Staat nicht als ‚Mutter', sondern als ‚böse Stiefmutter' an. Die Masse verhält sich ihm gegenüber entfremdet und feindselig. Die Politiker werden ausnahmslos als sich profilierende Diebe betrachtet. Das hat auch eine Berechtigung. Politische Ämter werden meist als Quelle der persönlichen und familiären Bereicherung wahrgenommen und innegehabt. Sie werden so ausgeübt, als ob ein großmächtiges Zentrum immer noch in den makropolitischen Prozess involviert ist und ihn garantiert. Aus dieser Perspektive lässt sich die gesamte politische Geschichte Bulgariens in den letzten 145 Jahren beschreiben. Ein Boris III., Zar der Bulgaren, Prinz von Sachsen-Koburg-Gotha und Herzog von Sachsen, zugeschriebener Aphorismus lautet, dass er der einzige Bulgarophile unter germanophilen, frankophilen, anglophilen und russophilen Politikern sei. Dem ‚Volks-Zaren' und den Regierungen im Laufe seines autoritären Regimes (1935-1943) war Populismus durchaus nicht fremd.[40]

Die Sehnsucht nach der Zugehörigkeit zu einem Reich (Russland) oder zu den ihm nachfolgenden Pseudo-Reich (UdSSR) übertraf in ihrer Tragikomik das Verlangen nach einer peripheren Eingliederung in das zunächst siegreiche ‚Dritte Reich', mit dem Bulgarien am 1. März 1941 einen Pakt schloss. Auch nach dem Krieg versuchten die bulgarischen Machthaber, Aufgaben unter einen Hut zu bringen, die schwer zu vereinbaren waren, da weder das ‚Dritte Reich' noch die UdSSR wie klassische Imperien funktionierten und sich weigerten, die Verpflichtungen des Zentrums vollständig zu übernehmen.

## Das kommunistische Regime

Als groteskeste Gestalt dieses Begehrens gelten die von Todor Schiwkow, dem Generalsekretär der Kommunistischen Partei, und ihrem Zentralkomitee formulierten Vorschläge, Bulgarien durch vollständigen Verzicht auf die formale nationale Souveränität an die UdSSR als sechszehnte Republik anzugliedern. Das erste Angebot wurde 1964 von der sowjetischen Regierung abgelehnt. Durch die Worte: „Diese Schlaumeier in Sofia möchten sich gerne an unserem Tisch

[39] *Българската армия в Световната война 1915-1918 г.*, т. 1-12, Щаб на войската – Военно-историческа комисия, Държавна печатница. София, 1939-1940. (*Balgarskata armija v Svetovnata vojna* 1915-1918, Bd. 1-12, Shtab na vojskata -Voenno-istoricheska komisija, darjavna pechatniza: Sofia, 1939-1940).

[40] Cf. *Словото на Богдан Филов. Речи на 28-ия български министър-председател*, Еделвайс: София 2022, passim, insb. 109-163. (*Slovoto na Bogdan Filov, Rechi na 28-ija balgarski minister-predsedatel*, Edelweis: Sofia 2022).

setzen" habe Nikita Chruschtschow in seinem Stil das Verdikt ausgesprochen. Die Sowjetunion sollte dadurch nicht nur freier Rohstoffspender werden, sondern auch die Zahlung der bulgarischen Nachkriegsreparationen vornehmen. Die erstmalige Absage störte Schiwkow und seinen Parteigenossen nicht, 1973 und 1978 das Angebot erneut zu unterbreiten. Doch auch Breschnew lehnte es ab.[41]

Das kommunistische Bulgarien nannte sich „Volksrepublik" und der ständig wiederholte Slogan lautete: „Alles im Namen des Menschen, alles zum Wohle des Menschen". Vor dem Hintergrund einer Politik der beschleunigten Industrialisierung und Urbanisierung verherrlichte die extrem populistische offizielle Propaganda das Dorf mit seiner (inzwischen ideologisch stilisierten) Folklore, das patriarchalische Verhalten, die ‚Volksweisheit'. Die kommunistischen Führer waren überzeugt, dass das ‚gemeine Volk', der ‚einfache Mensch', definitiv vorzüglicher als die ‚Anspruchsvollen' seien. Selbst der Dokumentarfilm von 1981, der das Leben und Werk von Schiwkow hochpreisen musste, hieß *Ein Mensch aus dem Volk.*[42] Das öffentliche Benehmen des Parteiführers war entsprechend einfältig und rüpelhaft. Die Arbeiter:innen und die Bauern wurden als die Triebkraft der Gesellschaft postuliert. Die Künstler:innen und die Akademiker:innen sollten unbedingt zu der ‚Arbeiter-und-Bauern-Intelligenzia' zählen. Ihre Ergeb-

---

[41] *1963 - отричането от България. Стенограма от Пленума на ЦК на БКП от 4.XII.1963 г. за присъединяването на България към Съветския съюз*, Огледало: София 1994. (1963 – otrichaneto ot Balgarija. Stenogra,a ot plenuma na ZK na BKP ot 4.XII.1963 za prisaedinjavameto na Balgarija kam Savetstkija sajuz, Ogreladalo: Sofia, 1994); Искра Баева/Евгения Калинова, *16-а република ли? Изследвания и документи за българо-съветските отношения след Втората световна война*, Изток-Запад: 2017. (Iskra Baeva/Evgenija Kalinova, 16-a republika li? Izledvanija i dokumenti za balgaro-savetskite otnoshenija sled vtorata svetovna vojna, Iztok-Zapad: 2017); Николай Киров, Най-голямото предателство в българската история, в: DW, 21.12.2018,
https://www.dw.com/bg/най-голямото-предателство-в-българската-история/a-46815221/.
(Nikolaj Kirov, Naj-goljamoto predatelstvo v balgarskata istorija, in: DW, 21.12.2018), https://www.dw.com/bg/най-голямото-предателство-в-българската-история/a-46815221/.

[42] *1963 - отричането от България. Стенограма от Пленума на ЦК на БКП от 4.XII.1963 г. за присъединяването на България към Съветския съюз*, Огледало: София, 1994. (1963 – otrichaneto ot Balgarija. Stenogra,a ot plenuma na ZK na BKP ot 4.XII.1963 za prisaedinjavameto na Balgarija kam Savetstkija sajuz, Ogreladalo: Sofia, 1994); Искра Баева/Евгения Калинова, *16-а република ли? Изследвания и документи за българо-съветските отношения след Втората световна война*, Изток-Запад: 2017. (Iskra Baeva/Evgenija Kalinova, 16-a republika li? Izledvanija i dokumenti za balgaro-savetskite otnoshenija sled vtorata svetovna vojna, Iztok-Zapad: 2017); Николай Киров, Най-голямото предателство в българската история, в: DW, 21.12.2018,
https://www.dw.com/bg/най-голямото-предателство-в-българската-история/a-46815221/.
(Nikolaj Kirov, Naj-goljamoto predatelstvo v balgarskata istorija, in: DW, 21.12.2018,
https://www.dw.com/bg/най-голямото-предателство-в-българската-история/a-46815221/).

nisse wurden aufgrund der Befolgung der ‚einzig wahren Parteilinie' beurteilt und bewertet. Die Strafen für die Abweichungen variierten von streng bis grausam.

Während das System einerseits soziale Gleichheit förderte, bildete sich simultan eine Staats- und Parteihierarchie, deren Mitglieder allerlei Privilegien, je nach Rang, erhielten. Diese Schicht schaffte es jedoch in der Realität nicht, sich als wahre Elite zu etablieren, weil die Teilhabe daran eine Funktion der politischen Konjunktur war. Andererseits wurden alle vorkommunistischen einflussreichen Figuren und Gruppen systematisch beseitigt. Direkt nach der Machtergreifung ermordeten die von der Sowjetunion installierten kommunistischen Gebieter zwischen 20.000 und 30.000 Industrielle, Landwirt:innen, Intellektuelle, Kleriker:innen, Politiker:innen, Offiziere oder einfach gebildete und reichere Personen. Die Überlebenden und ihre Nachfahren wurden offiziell während der gesamten kommunistischen Zeit als ‚Feinde des Volkes' und ‚ehemalige Leute' tituliert und gänzlich marginalisiert. Die Tatsache, dass etwa 80 % der ersten kommunistischen Machthaber, von denen einige bis zum Ende des Regimes regierten, schlecht oder gar nicht ausgebildet waren, und der Umstand, dass die wichtigste Voraussetzung für eine Karriere die Loyalität zur Partei war, erklären das unerträgliche Ausmaß des Populismus in dieser Zeit. Der Zusammenbruch der kommunistischen Diktatur hat daran nichts Entscheidendes geändert.

## Die gegenwärtige Situation

Die politische Selbsteinschätzung als imperiale Peripherie, die früher das Dritte Reich und die Sowjetunion als Imperium zu identifizieren gesucht hat, deutet nun auf diese Weise die Europäische Union aus. Bulgarien ist gleichberechtigtes Mitglied der EU seit 2007. Nichtsdestotrotz verbreiten sowohl die populäre wie auch die offizielle politische Rhetorik, dass ‚Brüssel' bzw. die EU verordnen, fordern, erlauben oder zuteilen, wodurch sie die Außen- und Innerpolitik Bulgariens gänzlich bestimmen würden. Die Masse der Bulgar:innen und ihre Politiker:innen wollen keine Freiheit, weil sie Angst haben, Verantwortung zu übernehmen. Die Rechtsstaatlichkeit und die wirksame Bekämpfung der Korruption sind dabei nach wie vor äußerst problematisch.

Vor dem Hintergrund einer seit mehr als 25 Jahren laufenden negativen Personalauswahl in den politischen Parteien, die meist sogenannte ‚Führerparteien' sind, prosperiert eine sich zu einem ‚Traditionalismus' als Grundwert bekennende ‚Volkselite'. Sie wird aufgrund ihrer Finanzkraft oder einer durch die Massenmedien geschaffenen Popularität etabliert und keinesfalls aufgrund intellektueller Überlegenheit. Die Intellektuellen werden weiterhin aus dem öffentlichen Leben verdrängt. Die Arbeit und die Leistungen im Bereich der Künste und der Wissenschaften bleiben eine persönliche Angelegenheit, die mit einer blassen Wahrnehmung erst nach einer Anerkennung ‚im Ausland' rechnen darf. Das ‚Volk' wird offiziell einer intellektuellen Minderheit gegenübergestellt. Der Mangel an einem Wertesystem ist ‚glücklich' mit der Wirkung der sozialen Medien kombiniert, in denen die Kompetenz kein Kriterium darstellt. Diese Mentalität ist zunehmend typisch für das gesamte Medienumfeld, das ‚natürlich' zu einer Bühne für Fehlinformationen wird. Die ‚öffentliche Meinung' lässt sich mit populistischen Parolen und Beschwörungsformeln sehr leicht manipulieren.

Man erkennt als notwendige Faktoren für die Entfaltung populistischer Strömungen die strukturelle Deklassierung wesentlicher Teile der Bevölkerung, die Legitimationskrise der bestehenden Ordnung und das Bestehen von realen oder angeblichen Krisenereignissen.[43] Alle diese Faktoren sind heute in Bulgarien vorhanden. Es gibt keine Partei, die als durchaus nichtpopulistisch zu bestimmen ist. Immer größer ist die Zahl der ‚Retter', die sich bereitstellen, ‚die Würde der Bulgaren wiederherzustellen' und ‚Bulgarien wieder groß zu machen', wobei manche unter den extremsten Populisten dieses ‚Wiedergroßmachen' groteskerweise mit einer Russlandstreue verbinden. Offensichtlich wächst die Lust auf das Anführen von ‚bürgerlich-patriotisch-konservativen' Bewegungen, die sich ‚auf die nationale Würde, christliche Ethik und traditionelle bulgarische Werte' stützen. Die Hauptparole lautet dabei: ‚traditionelle Religion, Traditionswerte, traditionelle Familie', wobei diese ‚Pfeiler' aus einer mythologisierenden und verfälschenden Erzählung abstammen, die durch die Verbreitung von einem nationalistischen und religiösen Kitsch getragen wird, der zudem staatspolitisch stimuliert wird.

Diese Parole weist auch den besonderen Antieuropäismus auf, der in Bulgarien teilweise verbreitet ist. Gegen eine falschverstandene europäische ‚Zivilisation' wurde noch im 19 Jahrhundert argumentiert. Der sich gegen eine Affenimitation des abendländischen Lebensstils erklärende Karawelow schreibt: „Ich werde euch sagen, dass der europäische Einfluss unserem Volk mehr geschadet als genützt hat. [...] Gebt dem bulgarischen Volk eine Bewegung und einen Ausweg, zeigt ihm, wo der Übergang ist, belebt seine Bräuche, und ein neuer Weg wird sich vor ihm auftun, eine *glückliche* Zukunft, ehrliche Tätigkeit und ein

[43] Cf. Cornelia Koppetsch, *Die Gesellschaft des Zorns – Rechtspopulismus im globalen Zeitalter*, Transcript: Bielefeld 2019, 42.

mächtiges historisches Leben“[44]. Der nichtgenannte Adressat sind hier die liberalen und innovativen Nationalisten des 19. Jahrhunderts. Der heutige konservative Nationalismus erschaudert jedoch auch beim Wort ‚Innovation‘. Er ist nicht so sehr auf Europa oder die Europäische Union wütend, sondern ebenso auf die eigenen tatsächlichen wirtschaftlichen und intellektuellen Eliten, die im Globalnetz mitwirken. Die Angst vor einer Zukunft, die eine verantwortungsvolle Selbstbestätigung verlangt, erzeugt die Sehnsucht nach einem imaginären in der Peripherie irgendeines Reiches selbstgenügenden bulgarischen Dasein, das die heutigen Populisten bewerben.

Die starken Wurzeln des bulgarischen Populismus und seine solide gesellschaftspolitische Basis zeigen, dass es ein unbegründeter Optimismus wäre, seinen baldigen Untergang vorherzusagen.

[44] Любен Каравелов, *Записки за България и българите*, Българска история: София 2024, 98. (Ljuben Karawelow, *Zapiski za Balgarija i balgarite*, Balgarska istorija Sofia 2024, 98).

*Mohamed Turki*
*(Tunis, Tunesien / Recklinghausen, Deutschland)*

# Von der Revolution zum Populismus in Tunesien

## Einleitung

Vor 15 Jahren fand am 17. Dezember 2010 in Tunesien ein Ereignis statt, das die gesamte Bevölkerung erschütterte und das herrschende Regime zu Fall brachte. Es war der Tag an dem Mohamed Bouazizi, ein Straßenhändler aus der Stadt Kasserine, sich mit Benzine schüttete und anzündete aus Verzweiflung vor dem ihm zugefügten Unrecht seitens der staatlichen Behörden. Dieser Fall löste Unmut im ganzen Lande aus und entfachte Demonstrationen in den größten Städten, die zum Sturz des Regimes führten. Das war der Anfang des sog. „Arabischen Frühlings", der fast alle arabischen Völker von Tunesien über Ägypten, Bahrain, Jemen, Libyen, Marokko bis hin zu Syrien erfasste und den Beginn der Revolution ebnete, die alle absoluten Herrscher in der arabischen Welt in Schrecken versetzte.

Nach der Flucht des Machthabers Ben Ali am 14. Januar 2011 nach Saudi-Arabien erlebte Tunesien eine bewegte politische Übergangsphase, die von einem ungewissen Umbruch gekennzeichnet war. Dennoch konnten bestimmte Gremien konstituiert werden, die für einen demokratischen Wandel sorgten. So wurde zunächst eine Übergangsregierung berufen, deren Aufgabe die Vorbereitung von freien Wahlen zu einer verfassungsgebenden Versammlung und die Durchführung von Parlamentswahlen war. Diese fanden am 23 Oktober 2011 statt, aus denen die islamistische Partei *Ennahdha* als Siegerin hervorging.

Seitdem erlebte Tunesien eine wechselhafte politische Entwicklung, die das Land von der Revolution über die Konstituierung demokratischer Strukturen und Haltung freier Wahlen bis hin zur Auflösung des Parlaments katapultierte. Der zuletzt 2019 gewählte Präsident Kais Said löste im Zuge der ideologisch geführten Auseinandersetzungen innerhalb des Parlaments zwischen den politischen Fraktionen der Islamisten und der säkularen Kräften am 25. Juli 2021 das Parlament auf, setzte die Verfassung außer Kraft und rief zu einer Volksabstimmung über die Verabschiedung einer neuen Verfassung, die ihm größere Befugnisse ermöglichte. Damit begann eine weitere Phase der politischen Herrschaft, die von populistischen Diskursen legitimiert und durch eigene Entscheidungen des Präsidenten per Dekret geführt wird.

Die Verfestigung dieser populistischen Macht wurde mit der Wahl eines neuen Parlaments zementiert, zu dem keine Parteien zugelassen wurden, sondern nur Personen, deren Legitimität von den Wählern in den jeweiligen Kommunen gesegnet wurde. Diese Tendenz zur Basisdemokratie sollte nach außen den Schein geben, gegen Nepotismus und Korruption vorzugehen. In Wirklichkeit aber verfolgt sie das Ziel, keine demokratischen Strukturen und politischen Parteien konstituieren zu lassen und ein autokratisches Regime zu etablieren.

Im Folgenden Beitrag wird in einem ersten Schritt einen Rückblick auf den Verlauf der Revolution in Tunesien geben. Dabei werden die Träger dieses Volksaufstands eruiert und die Ziele sowie Auswirkungen ihrer Handlungen dargestellt. In einem zweiten Schritt werden die Versäumnisse der demokratischen Entwicklung nachgezeichnet und die Gründe genannt, die zu einem Aufstieg des Populismus geführt haben. Besonders nennenswert sind die ideologischen Querelen zwischen den Parteien im Parlament, die zur Verhinderung der Etablierung eines Verfassungsgerichts führten, welches zur Konsolidierung des Rechtsstaates beigetragen hätte. Zum Schluss werden die Mechanismen populistischer Ideologie offengelegt und analysiert. Diese kommen vor allem in den Diskursen der politischen Träger deutlich zum Ausdruck, denn darin werden ihre Widersacher mit demagogischen Parolen verleumdet und irgendwelchen Vorwürfen beschuldigt, um sie gerichtlich zu verfolgen. Ziel dieser Strategie soll in erster Linie die Ausschaltung der politischen Gegner dienen und folglich die Opposition mundtot machen. Als konkretes Ergebnis dieser populistischen Strategie kann die Präsidentschaftswahl vom 6. Oktober 2024 genannt werden, in deren Folge der bisherige Präsident Kais Said mit geringer Wahlbeteiligung für ein zweites Mandat gewählt wurde.

## 1. Der ‚Arabische Frühling' und seine Auswirkung

### *1.1. Der Aufbruch der Revolution*

Ein Gespenst ging um in der arabischen Welt, das Gespenst der Revolution. So konnte man in Anlehnung an Marx die Lage beschreiben, in der sich dieser Raum seit Januar 2011 befand. Dabei darf der Begriff der ‚Revolution' nicht bloß politisch verstanden, sondern eher in seinem ursprünglichen Sinne betrachtet werden, d. h. als „kopernikanische Wende der Denkungsart", wie sie Kant formuliert hat. Die Umwälzungen, die in Tunesien ihren Ausgang fanden und dann über mehrere arabischen Länder erstreckten, zeigten, dass es sich hier nicht einfach um einen politischen Wechsel an der Spitze des Staates ging, sondern vielmehr um grundlegende Veränderungen in den Herrschaftsstrukturen, die diese Gesellschaften betrafen. Die in den erwähnten Ländern entstandenen Volkserhebungen machten deutlich, wie sich ein radikaler Wandel vollzog, der durch klare Forderungen der Demonstranten artikuliert wurde und in den folgenden Parolen seinen genauen Ausdruck fand, nämlich *Freiheit, Gerechtigkeit, Demokratie* und *Menschenwürde*.

Natürlich scheinen diese Begriffe als Erbe der Moderne auf den ersten Blick wie ein Import aus dem Westen zu sein und manche Beobachter gingen soweit zu behaupten, dass die geistigen Väter dieser Revolution wohl im Westen zu suchen seien, namentlich bei Denkern wie Gene Sharp mit seinem Buch *Von der Diktatur zur Demokratie*[1] oder bei Stephan Hessel und seiner viel zitierten Streitschrift *Empört Euch.*[2] Aber solche Behauptungen implizieren von vornherein, dass die arabischen Völker kein eigenständiges Denken besitzen bzw. über keine kulturelle Tradition verfügen, die ihnen den Weg zur Revolution weisen könnte. Dagegen spricht jedoch vieles, was durch die Medien und die Stellungnahmen namhafter Denker aus diesen Ländern bestätigt wird. Allein einen Blick auf die Liste der arabischen Intellektuellen zu werfen, die sich seit Jahrzehnten mit den Ursachen der bisher herrschenden Gesellschaftsstrukturen und Machtmechanismen beschäftigt haben, reicht um solche Behauptungen entschieden zu widerlegen.[3] So schrieb z. B. der 2010 verstorbene marokkanische Philosoph Mohammed Abid al-Jabri in der Einführung zu seinem Werk *Kritik der arabischen Vernunft* „Rationalität und Demokratie sind keine Importartikel, sondern konkrete Praktiken, die sich nach Regeln richten“ und fügt hinzu: „solange wir allerdings die Rationalität nicht auf unsere Tradition anwenden und in ihr die Quellen des Despotismus aufdecken und dessen Äußerungen anprangern, werden wir nicht in der Lage sein, eine uns eigene Moderne hervorzubringen, durch die wir uns als Handelnde und nicht länger als Behandelte in die ‚globale Moderne‘ einbringen“.[4]

Ausgehend von diesem theoretischen Ansatz können wir nun die bisher abgelaufenen Ereignisse, die zu einer revolutionären Wende in Tunesien geführt haben, genauer betrachten und versuchen, die Dynamik ihrer Entwicklung etwas besser zu verstehen, denn sie erlauben einige Merkmale dieser Umwäl-

---

[1] Gene Sharp, *Von der Diktatur zur Demokratie*, Beck: München 2008.

[2] Stephan Hessel, *Empört Euch*, Ullstein: Hamburg 2011.

[3] Eine ganze Reihe von arabischen Denkern wie die Philosophen Mohammed Abid al-Jabri, Sadek Jalal al- Azm, Taieb Tizini und Hisham Sharabi befasst sich mit dieser Thematik. Siehe hierzu: *Islam, Demokratie, Moderne, Aktuelle Antworten arabischer Denker*, hrsg. v. Edmute Heller und Hassouna Mosbahi, Verlag C.H.Beck, München 1998 und Mohamed Turki, Kritik, „Menschenrechte und Revolution, Paradigmen aus der aus der arabisch-islamischen Philosophie“, in: ders.: *Rationalitätsdebatten im arabisch-islamischen Diskurs der Gegenwart,* Wissenschaftsverlag: Leipzig 2022, 288-305.

3 Mohammed Abid al-Jabri, *Kritik der arabischen Vernunft, Naqd al-`aql al-`arabi, Die Einführung*, Perlen: Berlin 2009, 59.

zung zu erfassen. Schon der Anlass für die Selbstverbrennung von Mohamed Bouazizi am 17. Dezember 2010, der zum Auslöser der Revolution wurde, stellt eine klare Anklage gegen die verschiedenen Praktiken der Unterdrückung im Lande dar: Von der Arbeitslosigkeit über die Schikanen der Polizei bei der Ausübung irgendwelcher Nebentätigkeiten bis hin zur Demütigung der Bürger beim Einreichen von Beschwerden an die betreffenden Behörden. All diese Fakten stehen in eklatantem Widerspruch zu den Menschenrechten, die der autokratische Herrscher Ben Ali formal gern nach außen zu seinem Vorteil propagierte, sie aber in Wirklichkeit einfach missachtete.

Aus der Sicht von Mohammed Abid al-Jabri leidet die arabische Welt bisher an der Hegemonie einer bestimmten Art von Irrationalität. „Es handelt sich um eine mittelalterliche Irrationalität mit all ihren Konsequenzen, insbesondere dem Fortbestehen eines Verhältnisses zwischen Regierenden und Regierten, in dem letztere auf den Status einer Herde reduziert, im intellektuellen und sozialen Leben unter dem Stab des Hirten vorangetrieben werden.“[5] Gerade gegen dieses irrationale und patriarchalische Verhältnis hat sich das tunesische Volk erhoben. Es wurde bei seiner Auflehnung besonders von der Jugend als derjenigen Gruppe geführt, die nichts zu verlieren hatte. Diese Jugend, die mittlerweile eine Art ‚akademisches Proletariat‘ bildet und ihre Rechte aufgrund ihrer Ausbildung genau kennt, hat sich der neuesten Informationsmedien wie Internet, Twitter und Facebook zur Verbreitung ihrer Forderungen und zur Organisation ihrer Demonstrationen bestens bedient. Dadurch wurde das Volk unerwartet auf einmal in das dritte Millennium katapultiert, und zwar nicht nur technologisch und mediengerecht, sondern auch gesellschaftspolitisch. Es hat sich im echten Sinne des Wortes ein grundlegender Wandel vollzogen und war, um mit Kant zu sprechen, das Signal für den „Ausgang aus der selbst verschuldeten Unmündigkeit“[6].

So beteiligten sich an den täglichen Treffen und Demonstrationen Tausende von Menschen aus allen Schichten der Gesellschaft, ungeachtet ihres Alters und ihres Geschlechts, was ein Novum für eine orientalische Gesellschaft darstellt. Vor allem dic Teilnahme der Frauen an diesen Märchen war bemerkenswert. Das zeigte, dass diese „Hälfte des Himmels“, um den chinesischen Spruch zu nutzen, sich ihrer Rolle bei diesem Umwälzungsprozess bewusst war und sich an der Zersetzung der patriarchalischen Machtstrukturen aktiv teilnehmen wollte.

---

[5] Ibid., 62.

[6] Immanuel Kant, *Was ist Aufklärung?*, in: ders.: *Schriften zur Anthropologie*, Wissenschaftliche Buchgesellschaft: Darmstadt, 1975, Bd. 9, 51-61.

Die Philosophin Seyla Benhabib fasst in ihrem Artikel in den *New York Times* 2011 zum *Arabischen Frühling* die Situation folgendermaßen zusammen: „Ce à quoi nous avons assisté est véritablement révolutionnaire, au sens où un nouvel ordre de liberté – a novo ordo saeclorum – est en train d'émerger transnationalement dans le monde arabe“[7], d.h. was wir mitverfolgt haben, ist wirklich revolutionär, und zwar in dem Sinne, wie eine neue Freiheitsordnung – a novo ordo saeclorum – transnational in der arabischen Welt entsteht.

In der Tat war die erste Forderung der Demonstranten gegenüber der herrschenden Macht nichts anders als der Ruf nach *Freiheit* und *Menschenwürde*, begleitet später mit der Forderung nach *Gerechtigkeit* und *Arbeit*. Die in der Charta der Vereinten Nationen verankerten Grundrechte tauchten zum ersten Mal als Bedingungen für eine Veränderung der sozialen und politischen Situation auf. Sie wurden nicht mehr als gegeben und rechtlich in der Verfassung verankert betrachtet. Das tunesische Volk verlangt die Einhaltung dieser Rechte konkret im Alltag und ihre Umsetzung in die Realität.

Zu den weiteren politischen Forderungen gehörten ebenfalls der *Absturz des Regimes* und die *Abschaffung des herrschenden* Systems als Modell neopatriarchalischer Herrschaft sowie die *Wahl einer Verfassungsgebenden Versammlung*, die eine neue Verfassung erarbeiten soll. Darin sollte eine klare Trennung der jeweiligen Gewalten festgelegt und die Unabhängigkeit der Gerichte gewährleitet werden. Hinzu bedarf es der Einrichtung eines Verfassungsgerichts, das über die Vereinbarkeit der Gesetze entscheidet und ihre Einhaltung kontrolliert. Schließlich müssen die Zulassung von politischen Parteien zu freien Wahlen gewährt, der Kampf gegen Nepotismus und Korruption geführt und die Verantwortlichen für die Ermordung von Demonstranten während des Aufstandes zur Rechenschaft gezogen werden. Diese Maßnahmen bildeten den Rahmen für ein politisches Programm, das von den Komitees zur Überwachung der Errungenschaften der Revolution in Tunis verabschiedet wurde.[8]

### *1.2. Das Unbehagen im demokratischen Wandel*

Wirft man heute einen kritischen Blick auf die politische Lage in Tunesien, so stellt man mit Bedauern fest, dass die Aussicht auf ein Gelingen der Revolution und einen friedlichen Übergang zu einer echten Demokratie eher gedämpft und mit Unbehagen begleitet wird. Eine gewisse Skepsis trat inzwischen anstelle der Zuversicht bei der Berichterstattung und in den Medien auf. Die Fragen, die in

---

[7] Seyla Benhabib, „Le printemps arabe: religion, révolution et place publique“, in: https://raison-publique.fr/2203/ [17.11.2024].

[8] Für eine weitere Analyse des revolutionären Wandels in Tunesien siehe Fethi Meskini, „Zur Identität der Revolution“, in: *polylog* 28 (2012), 5-25.

den Kommentaren geäußert wurden, lauteten: Sind die bisherigen Ereignisse tatsächlich die Boten eines revolutionären Wandels oder die Vorzeichen einer Götterdämmerung? Triumphiert im Laufe dieser Entwicklung der Islamismus statt der Demokratie? Bedroht die fanatische Gewalt den eingeleiteten Prozess zu einer Rechts- und Zivilgesellschaft? Welche Erwartungen können noch mit diesem Wandel geknüpft werden?

Nach dem Verlauf der Wahlen zur verfassungsgebenden Versammlung am 23. Oktober 2011, aus der die islamistische Partei „*En-Nahdha*", was Renaissance bedeutet, mit 42% der Stimmen siegreich hervorging, wurde sowohl in Tunesien als auch in Europa über den künftigen Kurs heftig diskutiert. Das Land, das sich bisher von den arabischen Staaten am meisten weltoffen war und von den Errungenschaften der Moderne profitiert hat, stand auf einmal durch das starke Auftreten der islamistischen Partei auf die politische Bühne vor einem Scheideweg: Entweder Stärkung der säkularen Institutionen des Staates und ihre Anbindung an die Moderne oder Rückwendung zur islamischen Rechtsprechung, „Scharia" genannt. Sicherlich war das gute Abschneiden der Islamisten bei den Wahlen überraschend, da man mit einem solchen Ergebnis nicht gerechnet hat, zumal die Islamisten so gut wie keine Rolle bei der revolutionären Wende gespielt haben. Dennoch sollte die Situation vorerst nicht dramatisiert werden. Es müssen vielmehr die Gesellschafts- und politischen Strukturen näher betrachtet werden, um die Lage besser zu verstehen.

Tatsächlich ist nach dem Fall der Diktatur in Tunesien ein Kulturkampf entbrannt worden. Wie Charlotte Wiedemann in ihrem Artikel in der Wochenzeitung *Die Zeit* feststellte, trug die Gesellschaft zwei Impulse in sich: „Das Bedürfnis nach einem modernen Rechtstaat und nach einer religiös gefärbten Identitätspolitik".[9] Sie fügte hinzu: „Die Tunesier, so hat eine Studie ergeben, denken ‚politisch progressiv und sozial konservativ'. Progressiv heißt: eine große Mehrheit verlangt härtere demokratische Kontrollinstrumente als sie die meisten Parteien in ihren Programmen anbieten. Doch eine ebenso große Mehrheit will dem Staat die Befugnis geben, Kunst und Ausdrucksfreiheit zum Schutz der Moral einzuschränken. Moins de voleurs et plus de valeurs, ‚weniger Diebe und mehr Werte', so übersetzt sich der Volksmund".[10] Es schien also, als ob der Bruch mit dem alten korrupten Regime der Wunsch nach einer „arabisch-islamischen Kulturidentität" einhergeht, die den Bürgern ihre Würde wiedergibt.

Zunächst zeigte der Verlauf der Wahlen zur verfassungsgebenden Versammlung, dass die Demokratie in Tunesien ihre erste Probe gut bestanden

---

[9] Charlotte Wiedemann, „Triumphiert der Islam?", in: *Die Zeit* Nr. 44 vom 27.10.2011, 3.
[10] Ibid.

hat. Die Beobachter stellten keine groben Verletzungen bei der Durchführung der Wahlen fest und die Ergebnisse wurden ohne nennenswerte Proteste angenommen. In seinem Kommentar zur Frage nach der Chance der Demokratie in Tunesien merkt der frühere deutsche Botschafter in Tunis Horst-Wolfram Kerll in der Zeitschrift *Inamo* nach der Verabschiedung der Verfassung am 7.02.2014, dass „es Tunesien gelungen ist, eine quasi konsensuale neue und moderne Verfassung zu verabschieden. Sie kann mit Fug und Recht als die bisher demokratischste und liberalste Verfassung in einem arabischen Land bezeichnet werden. Alle wichtigsten Prinzipien einer Demokratie und vor allem Grund-, Freiheits- und Menschenrechte wurden festgeschrieben und bekommen nun eine echte Chance, beachtet zu werden“[11]. Doch zur gleichen Zeit schreibt Kamel Jendoubi, der frühere Leiter der Wahlkommission zur verfassungsgebenden Versammlung, in einem Artikel der französischen Zeitung *Le Monde* vom 19. Januar 2014, dass die neue tunesische Verfassung keine Garantie für die Verwirklichung der Demokratie in Tunesien darstelle. Er verwies auf die Gefahren, die den Prozess der Demokratisierung seitens der islamistischen Kräfte im Lande bedrohen und rief zur Wachsamkeit auf, allen voran vor der islamistischen Partei *En-Nahdha*. Er fügt hinzu: „Die Erfahrung hat gezeigt, dass man sich vor dem doppelten Diskurs der Islamisten in Acht nehmen muss. Die Verfassung ist eine wichtige Errungenschaft, aber sie wird selber den Gang der Ereignisse nicht bestimmen“[12].

Diese Angst vor dem Islamismus war in der Tat berechtigt, denn im Zuge der Wahlen zur verfassungsgebenden Versammlung am 23. Oktober 2011, aus denen die Islamisten die Mehrheit der Sitze im Übergangsparlament erhielt, übernahmen sie auch die Regierung durch die Bildung einer dreier Koalition mit der sozialdemokratischen Partei *Attakattul* und dem *Congrès pour la Republique*. Damit erlangten sie auch die Kontrolle über Polizei und Armee. Die Sicherheit im Lande wurde jedoch dadurch nicht gewährleistet, sondern das Gegenteil war der Fall. Sowohl die Salafisten, d. h. Anhänger eines traditionalistischen Islams, als auch Mitglieder der Al-Qaida im Maghreb konnten sich neben anderen islamistischen Gruppen wie die Partei der Befreiung (*Hizb at-Tahrīr*) überall frei bewegen und ihre Militärübungen in den Bergen durchführen. In einigen Vororten der Hauptstadt Tunis gründeten sie sogar eigene Emirate, die sie nach islamischem Recht verwalteten. So machte sich eine Stimmung der Unsicherheit und

[11] Horst Wolfram Kerll, „Wie steht um die Chancen einer echten Demokratie in Tunesien?“, in: *Inamo* 77 (2014), 3.

[12] Kamel Jendoubi, „Espoirs fragiles en Tunisie“, in: *Le Monde* vom 19. Januar 2014.

der Angst in der Bevölkerung breit, als die Regierung auf deren Warnung und die der Opposition nicht reagierte.

Mit der Ermordung des Führers der linken Oppositionspartei Chokri Belaid am 6. Februar 2013 durch Islamisten erreichte die Gewalt einen Höhepunkt, der eine Welle des Protests und der Entrüstung auslöste. Der Ruf nach einem Rücktritt der Regierung und die Forderung nach einer Ahndung der Mörder wurde immer lauter, was zu einem Rücktritt des Premierministers und zu einer Umbildung der Regierung mit der Ernennung des vorherigen Innenministers an der Spitze führte. Dennoch wurden keine ernsthaften Maßnahmen zur Eindämmung der Gewalt im Lande getroffen. Erst nach dem Angriff islamistischer Gruppen auf die amerikanische Botschaft in der Umgebung von Tunis und dem Mord an den Abgeordneten Mohamed Brahmi am 25.Juli 2013, in dessen Folgen die Opposition ihre Arbeit im Parlament einstellte, entschied die Regierung, gegen illegale Organisationen der Islamisten vorzugehen und sie zu verbieten. Doch der Preis für diese Wende der Politik der islamistischen Partei *Ennahdha* war zu hoch. Über fünfzig Tote waren allein bei Armee und Sicherheitskräften zu beklagen, die im Kampf gegen die islamistischen Gruppierungen fielen.

Das Paradox an der Politik dieser Partei war, dass sie eine doppelte Strategie verfolgte und sich entsprechend eines ambivalenten Diskurses bediente. Diese Ambivalenz zeigte sich gerade in der Diskussion um die neue Verfassung. Das Auslavieren zwischen einem Festhalten an der Scharia als Quelle des Rechts und der Anpassung an das moderne Zivilrecht hat bei der Verhandlung über den Kurs der Verfassung viel Zeit in Anspruch genommen. Nur der Druck der Opposition innerhalb der verfassungsgebenden Versammlung und die breite Aktivität der Zivilgesellschaft außerhalb des Parlaments sowie der Medien zwangen die Islamisten zur Aufgabe ihrer Haltung und zur Akzeptanz bestimmter Kompromisse.

Nach der Verabschiedung der neuen Verfassung und der Wahl des neuen Parlaments sowie des Präsidenten Beji Kaid Essebsi von der säkularen Partei *Nidaa Tunis* (der Ruf Tunesiens) am 31. Dezember 2014 konnte der Vormarsch der Islamisten gestoppt werden. Dennoch bedrohten sie weiterhin die Errungenschaften der Revolution und drängten die Bürger auf eine Rückbesinnung zur alten islamischen Tradition. Der „Krieg der Götter“, um Max Weber zu zitieren, bezüglich der Werte und Normen, fand nun auf der kulturellen Ebene statt und war im Begriff die Gesellschaft in zwei Lagern zu spalten: in Traditionalisten, die an den festen Säulen des Islam hielten auf der einen Seite, und Säkularen, die eine klare Trennung von Staat und Religion befürworteten auf der anderen. Für Mohammed Haddad, der die islamistischen Bewegungen seit ihrer Entstehung kritisch verfolgt, bleibt die Vertrauenskrise gegenüber den Islamisten bestehen, weil ihr politisches Programm mehr nach rückwärts orientiert ist und keine klare Philosophie für die Zukunft bietet.[13] Den Islamisten fehlte in der Tat an konkreten politökonomischen Perspektiven, mit deren Hilfe sie das Land aus der wirtschaftlichen Krise herausholen konnten. Es reicht nicht, das Modell der Türkei als Alternative zu zeigen, da jedes Land seine eigenen Besonderheiten hat. Außerdem setzte die Türkei zunächst auf Laizität, bevor sie ihre ökonomischen Reformen durchführte.

## 2. Der Aufstieg des Populismus in Tunesien

Im Allgemeinen zeichnet sich der Populismus durch verschiedene Konstellationen und Erscheinungen ab, die von mehreren Faktoren und Ursachen abhängig sind. Häufig erscheint er als Bestandteil politischer Ideologien, die sowohl auf der rechten als auch auf der linken Seite des politischen Spektrums entstehen. Meistens benutzen die Populisten einfache Botschaften, um komplexe Zusammenhänge politischer, sozialer und wirtschaftlicher Natur zu erklären. Sie agitieren vor allem gegen bestehende Verhältnisse und bieten eigene Alternativen zu den etablierten Institutionen und Parteien. Dabei setzen sie in ihrer Rhetorik auf *Polarisierung* und *Moralisierung*, um möglichst breitere Interessengruppen zu erreichen. In Tunesien scheint der Populismus eigene Formen zu besitzen, die eine besondere Betrachtung verlangen.

### *2.1. Der Islamismus und seine populistische Ideologie*

Ein der Aspekte des Populismus in Tunesien nach der Revolution bestand zunächst in den Versuch, die „Islamisierung“ der Gesellschaft und besonders der Hochschule während der Übernahme der Übergangsregierung von der islamistischen Partei *Ennahdha*. In dieser Übergangsphase ließ die Regierung verschiedene islamistische Gruppierungen wie die *Salafisten* und *Hisb at-tahrir* (die Partei der Befreiung) die Moscheen mit radikalen Imamen, d. h. Leitpredigern besetzten, die mit ihren Freitagsreden und Predigen die Gläubigen auf ihre Seite zu gewinnen versuchen. Vor allem die Verschleierung der Frauen in der Öffentlichkeit stand auf dem Programm. Freiheit, Gleichberechtigung und Würde spielten indessen keine Rolle. Für sie war der Islam die Losung. Außerdem stürmten sie kulturelle Ausstellungen und zerstörten ihre Exponate mit der Begründung, sie widersprechen den Lehren des Islams.

[13] Mohammed Haddad, „Al-Islam as-siyyasi ba`da Thawret al-Yāsamīn“ (der politische Islam nach der Jasmin-Revolution), in: *Min Qabdhat Ben Ali ilā thawret al-Yāsamīn, al-Islām as-siyyāsī fī Tūnis* (Vom Würgegriff Ben Alis zur Jasmin-Revolution. Der politische Islam in Tunesien), Dubai 2011, 89.

Auf der Ebene der Hochschulen und Universitäten fand eine schleichende Islamisierung statt, bei der der designierte Minister für Hochschule und Forschung einen Reformkurs nach dem Modell der Türkei unter Ministerpräsident Erdogan einschlug. Auf einer internationalen Konferenz kündigte er „die Einrichtung von spezialisierten Masterstudiengängen im Bereich der Wirtschaft und Finanzen an; ferner teilte er mit, er wolle den Banksektor im selbigen Sinne fördern, sodass er den Prinzipien der Scharia adäquater entspräche und dass sich die konventionelle Wirtschaft in eine islamische umwandele“[14].

Neben diesen Entscheidungen bemühte sich der Minister, die Studentenschaft auf einen ‚islamistischen' Kurs zu bringen, in dem er die Kontroverse um das Tragen des *Niqab*, d.h. der Ganzkörperverschleierung, an den Universitäten freien Lauf gab. Er stellte sich damit indirekt auf die Seite der radikalen Salafisten, die nicht nur das Tragen des *Niqab* in den Hörsälen und bei den Prüfungen forderten, sondern auch die Trennung der Studenten nach ihrem Geschlecht und die Bereitstellung eines Gebetsraums innerhalb der Fakultäten. Diese Forderungen wurden vom wissenschaftlichen Rat aus pädagogischen Gründen abgelehnt. Sie sahen darin eine versteckte ‚Afghanisierung' der Hochschule und folglich der Gesellschaft. Diese Kontroverse führte zu einem dramatischen Konflikt zwischen dem Lehrkörper mit dem Dekan der Fakultät La Manouba an der Spitze und den Salafisten, die das Hauptgebäude besetzten, den Dekan in seinem Büro gefangen hielten und den Studierenden der Zutritt zu ihren Seminaren hinderten. Ein Rechtsbeistand fand indessen weder vom Innen- noch vom Hochschulministerium statt, was die Opposition und die Zivilgesellschaft scharf kritisierten.

### *2.2. Die politischen Debatten im Parlament und ihre Folgen*

Die ideologischen Auseinandersetzungen zwischen Islamisten und säkularen Kräften wurden nicht nur in der Öffentlichkeit und über die Medien getragen, sondern auch im neu gewählten Parlament heftig geführt. Zwar beteiligte sich die islamistische Partei *Ennahdha* mit kurzer Unterbrechung an den Regierungen zwischen 2011 und 2019, hielt sie aber trotz gewisser Kompromisse an ihr Islamorientiertes Programm fest. Sie konnte vor allem ihr Profil in den Auseinandersetzungen mit linken Bewegungen und Gewerkschaften schärfen, denn sie „stand in direkter Konkurrenz zu Gewerkschaften und Berufsverbänden, die für die Rechte von Arbeitern und Bürgerrechte kämpften“[15]. Sie bildete sogar

---

[14] Khaled Chaabane, „Der misslungene Versuch der Islamisierung der Hochschulen“, in: *Inamo* 77 (2014), 26.

[15] Rainer Hermann, „Welche Rolle haben die islamistischen Parteien bei der Entwicklung des ‚Arabischen Frühlings' bisher gespielt? Wie sind die westlichen Akteure, insbesondere die Euro-

eigene Gewerkschaftsorganisation OTT (Organisation Tunisienne du Travail), um die religiös orientierten Arbeiter auf ihre Seite zu ziehen und ihre Forderungen in ihrem Sinne zu vertreten.

Schon während der ersten Wahlkampagnen auf der Grundlage der neuen Verfassung im Jahre 2014 hatte die islamistische Partei die wesentlichen Forderungen der Revolution – Arbeit, Freiheit und Würde – einfach vergessen und reduzierte den gesamten Wahlkampf auf die Dichotomie Modernismus versus Islamismus bzw. Säkularismus versus islamischer Identität. Kaum aber gewählt, begann sie in der Koalition mit der säkularistischen Partei *Nidaa Tuni*s zu streiten. Probleme und Querelen um Posten standen auf einmal im Mittelpunkt. Die Verteidigung von Privilegien hatte nun den Vorrang vor echten Reformen. Programmatische Debatten fanden im Grunde nicht statt, dafür aber leere Rhetorik und gegenseitige Beschuldigungen und Beschimpfungen seitens der Abgeordneten im Parlament.

Symptomatisch für diese Stimmung war das Verzögern einer Aufstellung der Richter zum Verfassungsgericht, das als oberste Instanz die Vereinbarkeit der Gesetze und die Kontrolle der Exekutive beaufsichtigen soll. Das Parlament hatte es nicht geschafft, eine konsensuale Entscheidung diesbezüglich zu treffen. Angesichts dieser verwirrenden Lage und der negativen Erfahrungen, war es nicht verwunderlich, dass sich die Bürger Tunesiens emotional immer mehr von der Politik und besonders von der repräsentativen Demokratie abwandten. Es herrschte inzwischen eine Skepsis bezüglich der Glaubwürdigkeit der Parteien und vor allem der Islamisten, die falsche Versprechen hinsichtlich der Einhaltung demokratischer Prinzipien machten und doch nicht hielten. Die Folge zeigte sich bei der Präsidentschaftswahl von 2019, die nach dem Tod des ersten demokratisch gewählten Präsidenten Beji Kaid Essebsi gehalten wurde. Bei dieser Wahl gewann Kais Saied, ein parteiloser und dezidierter Anti-Establishment-Kandidat, der bei der Wahlkampagne mit einem populistischen Narrativ auftrat, in dem er die Bekämpfung der Korruption und eine Neuorientierung der Wirtschaftspolitik versprach. Doch vom Hoffnungsträger wurde er zur größten Gefahr für die tunesische Demokratie, denn er hat die Parteiendemokratie zugunsten einer Autokratie abgeschafft und die Befugnisse des Präsidenten noch weiter verstärkt.

## 3. Die neue Phase des Populismus

päer, mit dieser Situation umgegangen?", in: *Der „arabische Frühling" im Wandel. Zukunft und Perspektiven*, hrsg. v. Abdallah Saaf u. a., Tunis 2022, 28.

Neben der Variante des islamistischen Populismus, der sich im letzten Jahrzehnt nach dem Aufbruch der Revolution in Tunesien ausbreitete, tauchte eine neue Form des Populismus auf, die mit der Wahl des Präsidenten Kais Saied 2019 entstanden ist. Diese Art von Populismus profitierte zunächst von der Unzufriedenheit in der Bevölkerung wegen der prekären Wirtschaftslage im Lande und der hohen Arbeitslosigkeit aufgrund des Fehlens der Touristen nach den Terroranschlägen auf Hotels und Museen in der letzten Dekade, aber auch von der politischen Lethargie, die das Volk infolge der Parteienzerschrittenheit heimsuchte.

Nach dem Bericht des *German Institut for Global and Arie Studies (GIGA)* in Hamburg erfolgte dieser Populismus im Zuge folgender Tatsachen :

- „Kais Saied wurde von marginalisierten und desillusionierten Bevölkerungsschichten gewählt, nachdem die Regierungen der letzten zehn Jahre keine entscheidenden sozial- und wirtschaftspolitischen Fortschritte vorwiesen konnten. Er versprach eine Neuausrichtung der Wirtschaftspolitik sowie einen entschlossenen Kampf gegen die Korruption.
- Saieds zentrales Interesse ist die dauerhafte Zerschlagung der bestehenden Machtzentren. Dies wird flankiert von Repressionsmaßnahmen gegen Politikerinnen und Politiker der Ennahda-Partei, Medienschaffende, Juristinnen und Juristen sowie Aktivistinnen und Aktivisten. Dabei ist fraglich, inwiefern die Bevölkerung von dem gegenwärtigen Elitenumbau profitiert.
- Die rasche Autokratisierung der tunesischen Institutionen ist begleitet von kompromisslosen populistischen Narrativen. Als Sündenböcke beschuldigte Saied im Februar 2023 afrikanische Migrantinnen und Migranten und löste eine rassistische Verfolgungswelle aus.
- Einige politische Parteien und zivilgesellschaftliche Organisationen protestieren gegen die Autokratisierung, sind aber untereinander sowie intern gespalten. Dies ist ein Resultat der erfolgreichen Polarisierung durch den Präsidenten“[16].

### *3.1. Strategie und Diskurs des neuen Populismus*

In der Tat präsentierte sich Kais Saied zu den Präsidentschaftswahlen von 2019 als Outsider ohne Parteibasis, die ihn unterstützte und als der ‚saubere Mann', der gegen das inkompetente Establishment und die Korruption in der Bürokratie vorgehen wollte, was ihm viel Sympathie bei der Bevölkerung bescherte. Um seine Volksnähe zu unterstreichen bereiste er das Land und besonders die

[16] Kressen Thyen/ Maria Josua, „Tunesiens Präsident Kais Saied: vom Hoffnungsträger zum Autokraten“, in: *GIGA Fokus Nahost*, Nr.4, Hamburg 2023, 1-12.

unterentwickelten Regionen des Zentrums und Süden. Hierbei sprach er mit den Armen und arbeitslosen Akademikern, die seit langem auf eine Beschäftigung hofften, aber nichts bekamen. Er nahm ihre Frustration wahr und versprach ihnen Hilfe zu leisten, was seine Glaubwürdigkeit in der Wählergunst steigerte.

Bei der Stichwahl am 13. Oktober 2019 gewann er die zweite Runde haushoch mit 72% der Stimmen gegenüber seinem Gegenkandidaten Nabil Karoui, der wegen Korruption und Geldwäsche gerichtlich geahndet wurde. Anfang Januar 2020 trat der neue Präsident, Kais Saied, sein Amt an in einer von Corona-Pandemie und wirtschaftlicher Stagnation verschärften Situation. Diese führte zu Protestaktionen seitens der Bevölkerung und zu Demonstrationen, die von der Polizei mit Gewalt zerschlagen wurden. Hinzu spitzten sich die Auseinandersetzungen zwischen den regierenden Parteien zu, die von den Abgeordneten im Parlament heftig durchgeführt wurden. Diese Faktoren schufen eine untragbare politische Atmosphäre. Zuletzt kam das Fehlen des vorgesehenen Verfassungsgerichts dem Präsidenten zugute, der seinen Machtanspruch auszuweiten und sich juristisch abzusichern versuchte. Mit Berufung auf den Artikel 81 der Verfassung führte er einen Putsch durch, indem er am 25. Juli 2021 das Parlament suspendierte und somit die Volksvertretung entmachtete. Mit Einsetzung des Militärs vor dem Parlamentsgebäude verweigerte er den Abgeordneten den Zugang und ließ danach einige Vertreter der Ennahdha-Partei wie auch der liberalen Destour-Partei sowie Aktivisten und Journalisten verhaften.

Das Vorgehen des Präsidenten blieb nicht bei diesen Schritten. Im Januar 2022 rief Kais Saied eine Kommission zum Entwurf einer neuen Verfassung, die alle Errungenschaften der Verfassung von 2014 zurücknahm und die Kompetenz des Parlaments einschränkte. Diese Abwertung des Parlaments erfolgte vor allem durch die Schwächung seiner Kompetenzen und Einführung eines Wahlrechts, nach dem die Abgeordneten in allgemeiner und direkter Wahl und nicht über Parteilisten gewählt werden. So wurde die neue Verfassung am 25. Juli 2022 den Wählern per Volksentscheid vorgelegt, ist sie aber wegen des Rufes zum Boykott seitens der Opposition nur mit einer geringeren Beteiligung der Bevölkerung (11%) angenommen. Dadurch wurde ihr im Grunde jegliche Legitimität entzogen. Im Anschluss darauf ließ der Präsident ein neues Parlament wählen, das wiederum von der Opposition boykottiert wurde.

### *3.2. Der Populismus und die Dekonstruktion der Demokratie*

Angesichts der zunehmenden Machtkonzentration in den Händen des Präsidenten sowie der Repression und Verhaftung der Opposition konnten die neuen geschaffenen demokratischen Strukturen dem Angriff des Autokraten nicht standhalten. Im Gegenteil, es kam eher zu einer langsam geschlichenen Dekonstruktion der Demokratie. Die Strategie von Kais Saied folgte in diesem Fall dem Programm vieler populistischer Politiker. Sie bediente sich Narrativen mit nationalistischen, religiös-konservativen und antipluralistischen Elementen, um die Gegner zu verunglimpfen oder sie als Feinde des Staates zu beschuldigen. Außerdem setzte sie auf eine Polarisierung, die den politischen Oppositionellen oder Andersdenkenden des Staatsverrats bezichtigt. Zuletzt greift sie auf Verschwörungsansätzen und juristischen Maßnahmen zurück, um die Widersacher zum Schweigen zu bringen. So nutzte der Präsident z. B. das Gesetz zur Bekämpfung der Cyberkriminalität, das hauptsächlich gegen falsche Berichterstattung oder ‚fake-News' angewendet werden sollte, um Journalisten und Dissidenten wegen Verbreitung von Nachrichten oder Meinungen strafrechtlich zu verfolgen. Dadurch sind die bis dahin lebhaft geführten Debatten über die Entwicklung und Zukunftsperspektiven des Landes verstummt und Tunesien sank laut Reporter ohne Grenzen in der Rangliste der Pressefreiheit von Platz 73 auf Platz 121.

Die Fortsetzung populistischer Propaganda erreichte einen Höhepunkt, als der Präsident sein Narrativ mit einem rassistischen Diskurs gegen afrikanische Migranten südlich der Sahara ergänzte. Im Februar 2023 nannte er sie in einer Rede „Horden illegaler Einwanderer", die Gewalt und Kriminalität ins Lande bringen und Lebensmittelpreise in die Höhe treiben. Diese Rede schürte Ressentiments und eine rassistische Hasswelle in der Bevölkerung, die zu Übergriffen sowohl von Sicherheitskräften als auch von Privatpersonen gegen die Migranten führten. Manche Aktionen endeten sogar mit willkürlichen Deportationen von Afrikanern seitens der Sicherheitskräfte bis an die Grenze des libyschen Gebiets, ohne Gewährung humanitärer Hilfe wie Wasser und Nahrung.[17]

Doch der letzte Akt dieser Dekonstruktion der Demokratie und des Aufbaus der Autokratie zeichnete sich durch die gerade durchgeführte Wahl zur Präsidentschaftswahl am 6. Oktober 2024 ab, bei der Kais Saied mit 90,70% der angegebenen Stimmen ein zweites Mandat erhielt. Diese Wahl wurde jedoch nur von 28% der Wähler wahrgenommen im Vergleich zu 56% 2019, d.h. 72% der Wähler blieben den Urnen fern, was die Legitimität des wieder gewählten Präsidenten stark beeinträchtigte. Unabhängige Beobachter sprachen von einer maßgeschneiderten Wahl, nachdem viele Kandidaten von der Wahlbehörde aus

[17] Siehe https://www.hrw.org/news/2023/10/10/tunisia-african-migrants-intercepted-sea-expelled [17.11.2024].

dem Wettlauf ausgeschlossen und nur zwei zugelassen wurden, von denen einer kurz vor dem Wahltermin festgenommen und zu vierzehn Jahren Haft wegen Urkundenfälschung verurteilt wurde.[18]

Zusammenfassend kann das Ergebnis der Präsidentschaftswahlen als ein weiterer Schritt in der Regression des demokratischen Wandels und der Zunahme der Autokratie in Tunesien bezeichnet werden. Diese gefährliche Entwicklung scheint den Partnern in Europa, die eine privilegierte Beziehung zu Tunesien unternehmen, leider nicht zu stören, denn die Europäische Union hat bereits mit Kais Saied ein Abkommen zur Eindämmung der illegalen Migration unterzeichnet, was sich schon im Rückgang der Zahlen der Migranten von Tunesien nach Italien widerspiegelte. Vor allem mit der faschistischen Regierung in Italien führt der Präsident eine ähnliche populistische Politik, die sie ebenso ideologisch wie machtpolitisch verbindet. Deshalb herrscht in Europa gegenwärtig ein Schweigen bezüglich der Ereignisse in Tunesien, was seine Glaubwürdigkeit hinsichtlich der demokratischen Regression in Frage stellt.

[18] „Tunesiens Staatschef Saied wiedergewählt", in: *Der Spiegel* vom 7.102024.

# 3. Practical-philosophical Transformations / Praktisch-philosophische Umsetzungen / Transformations pratico-philosophiques

*Johannes Balle (Köln, Deutschland)*

## SICH-ZEIGEN-LASSEN. Phänomenologisches Lernen zur Einübung einer philosophischen Haltung jenseits von Dogmatismus und Populismus

### 1. Zeigen-Lassen im Philosophieunterricht

Wenn die Phänomenologie eine Philosophie der Erfahrung darstellt, die sich der Husserlschen Losung „zu den Sachen selbst" verschreibt, könnte diese mit Blick auf den Unterricht als Haltung und Praxis des Sich-Zeigen-Lassens[1] von lebensweltlichen Phänomenen aufgefasst werden. „Sehen lernen" wäre entsprechend der Slogan einer phänomenologisch orientierten Philosophiedidaktik, was gleichzusetzen ist mit dem Versuch, die Phänomene der Welt auf voraussetzungsfreie Weise zu erfassen. Sofern „Phänomene" im Mittelpunkt der Bemühungen stehen, könnte man diese mit Martin Heidegger als das bezeichnen, was sich von sich her zeigt.[2] Und entsprechend wäre die Aufmerksamkeit ge-

---

[1] Ich entlehne den Titel meiner Überlegungen einer Formulierung von Malte Brinkmann („Sich-Zeigen-Lassen) in: ders., „Phänomenologische Methodologie und Empirie in der Pädagogik. Ein systematischer Entwurf für die Rekonstruktion pädagogischer Erfahrungen", in: *Pädagogische Erfahrung. Theoretische und empirische Perspektiven*, hrsg. v. Malte Brinkmann, Richard Kubac, Severin Sales Rödel, Severin Sales, Springer: Wiesbaden 2015, 32-60. Brinkmann führt in seinen Schriften den ganzen Reichtum und die Originalität phänomenologischer Pädagogik inspirierend vor Augen. Hier kann nur eine kleine Auswahl genannt werden: Malte Brinkmann (Hrsg.), *Erziehung. Phänomenologische Perspektiven*. Königshausen & Neumann: Würzburg 2010; ders. (Hrsg.), *Phänomenologische Erziehungswissenschaften von ihren Anfängen bis heute. Eine Anthologie* [Phänomenologische Erziehungswissenschaften Bd. 4]. Springer: Wiesbaden 2018; ders., „Phänomenologische Pädagogik", in: *Zeitschrift für Didaktik der Philosophie und Ethik* 3 (2018), 19-27. Überdies sei verwiesen auf die wertvolle phänomenologische Forschungsarbeit von Käte Meyer-Drawe, z. B. *Leiblichkeit und Sozialität. Phänomenologische Beiträge zu einer pädagogischen Theorie der Inter-Subjektivität*. Wilhelm Fink: München: Fink 2001 [1984]; dies., „Lernen als Erfahrung", in: *Zeitschrift für Erziehungswissenschaften* 6 (2003), 505-514.

[2] Vgl. Heidegger zur „phänomenologischen Methode" und über das „phainomenon" (§7) in: *Sein und Zeit*, (18. Aufl.). Niemeyer: Tübingen 2001 (18. Aufl.).

genüber dem, was sich zeigt, der erste Schritt hin zu dem, was man als Praxis des Sich-Zeigen-Lassens im Rahmen einer Pädagogik des Sehen-Lernens bezeichnen könnte: Statt hinter den Erscheinungen ein verborgenes Wesen, eine versteckte Interpretation zu erwarten und gefangen zu sein in Vorverurteilungen, wäre es mit Husserl und Heidegger angebracht, sich von Vorurteilen zu befreien und das Sich-Zeigen-Lassen der Phänomene selbst in den Mittelpunkt des Unterrichtes zu rücken.[3]

Diese Haltung, die sich dem Gegenstand unbefangen und vorurteilsfrei nähert, nannte Edmund Husserl *„Epoché"*. Alle Vor-Interpretationen werden eingeklammert, so dass nur die Erfahrung der Sache selbst zum Tragen kommt. Indem man sich jeder Deutung enthält und sich auf das Schauen verlässt, nähert man sich einem schwebenden Zustand, als betrachte man die Sache zum ersten Mal. Diese phänomenologische Fähigkeit des sehenden Zeigen-Lassens kann man durchaus einüben. Erforderlich ist Geduld, Interesse am Phänomen und Genauigkeit der Beschreibung, um eine kontemplative Praxis zu entwickeln, deren phänomenologischer Blick sich den Phänomenen jenseits der alten Denkgewohnheiten öffnet.

Eine solche phänomenologische Haltung gegenüber Welt und Mitmensch stellt gerade in Zeiten gesellschaftspolitischer Radikalisierungen ein heilsames Mittel gegen Dogmatismus, Willkürlichkeit und Populismus dar. Hier ist Phänomenologie insofern eine gewinnbringende Praxis, als ihr Wesenskern eine zeigen-lassende Offenheit gegenüber den Phänomenen darstellt. Dasselbe gilt für die Thematisierung der Fremdheitserfahrung jeder menschlichen Existenz: In Gesellschaften, die zunehmend dem Gift der populistischen Fremdenfeindlichkeit anheimfallen, erweisen sich phänomenologische Übungen als pädagogisch sinnvolles Gegengift.

Im Folgenden sollen zunächst zentrale Aspekte eines phänomenologisch orientierten Unterrichtes skizziert werden: *Epoché*, das Konzept des dichten Sehens und Eidetik; die atmosphärische Resonanz des leiblichen In-der-Welt-Seins; die individuelle Dimensionierung durch variierende Gestaltung einer figu-

---

[3] Martin Heidegger äußert sich zu dieser phänomenologischen Vorgehensweise folgendermaßen: „Faktisch ist es [...] so, dass unsere schlichtesten Wahrnehmungen und Verfassungen schon *ausgedrückte*, mehr noch, in bestimmter Weise *interpretierte* sind. Wir sehen nicht so sehr primär und ursprünglich die Gegenstände und Dinge, sondern zunächst sprechen wir darüber, genauer sprechen wir nicht das aus, was wir sehen, sondern umgekehrt, wir sehen, was man über die Sache spricht." (Martin Heidegger, *Prolegomena zur Geschichte des Zeitbegriffs*, hrsg. v. Petra Jaeger [Gesamtausgabe Bd. 20, II. Abteilung, Vorlesungen 1923-1944], Vittorio Klostermann: Frankfurt a.M. [3]1994 , 75.

rierenden *Poiesis*, die sich in personalen Narrativen äußert. Abschließend wird ein phänomenologisches Unterrichtskonzept (EIDOS-Modell) vorgestellt.

## 2. Vom Sehen-Als zum Sehen-Von

„Sehen" steht hier für die Inhalte intentionaler Erfahrungen, auf deren Grundlage sich, allgemein gesprochen, individuelle Fürwahrhaltungen ausbilden. Phänomenologisches Sehen weist einen komplexen, dichten Charakter auf: Wenn wir etwas auf bestimmte Weise erfahren, erfassen wir nicht nur seinen propositionalen Gehalt, der durch Wahrheitsbedingungen von Aussagesätzen abgebildet werden kann. Sehen als Konzept dieses komplexen Erfahrungsbegriffes impliziert Aspekte, die den qualitativen und existentiellen Tiefencharakter unserer Existenzgefühle abbilden: Als verkörperte und praktische situierte Wesen erfahren wir Gegenstände und Ereignisse unserer Lebenswelt auf qualitative Weise. Die Objekte der Wahrnehmung und des Denkens sind uns nicht nur begrifflich gegeben, sondern auch in phänomenalen Modi. Es ist hier nicht der Ort, die unterschiedlichen Thesen über das Phänomen begrifflicher Qualia in differenzierter Weise darzustellen. Es soll genügen, den intuitiven Grundgedanken der essentiellen kognitiven Phänomenologie[4] zu umreißen: Im Rahmen von kognitiven Lernprozessen haben wir es immer auch mit einer individuellen Phänomenologie des Verstehens zu tun, die unsere Erfahrungen qualitativ und narrativ dimensioniert und das Konzept des „dichten Sehens" fundiert.[5]

Um das, was hier individuell-qualitative Dimensionierung genannt wird, zu erfassen, denke man etwa an Situationen, die Menschen als bedeutsam erfahren: Empörung, Scham, Angst oder Ekel, um einige Erlebnisformen zu nennen. Urteile, die sich im Zusammenhang mit solchen und anderen affektiven Erfahrungen bilden, können zwar propositional rekonstruiert werden; doch die entsprechenden Begriffe und damit die Urteile selbst sind durch individuelle Dimensionierungen unterbestimmt, da sie ihrerseits qualitativ erlebt werden. Daher genügt es nicht, den begrifflichen Gehalt zu identifizieren, um adäquat zu verstehen, was für Lernende bedeutsam ist.

---

[4] Einen guten Überblick über das Forschungsfeld der kognitiven Phänomenologie bietet *Phenomenology of Thinking. Philosophical Investigations into the Character of Cognitive Experience*, hrsg. v. Thiemo Breyer u. Christopher Gutland, Routledge: London/New York 2016.

[5] „Dimensionierung", wie unten zu sehen sein wird, bezeichnet den individuellen Erlebnishorizont, der im Sinne von Gestaltqualitäten und begrifflichen Qualia den narrativen Charakter unserer Welterfahrungen zentriert. Dies bildet den Kern dessen, was für die individuelle Persönlichkeit mit ihrer besonderen Lebensgeschichte bedeutsam ist sowie die damit verbundenen Fürwahrhaltungen, Werthaltungen, Schemata und praktischen Fähigkeiten.

Propositionale und intentionale Einstellungen nun werden üblicherweise durch das Schema des „Sehens-Als“ charakterisiert: Wir denken stets an etwas als etwas. Wir erfassen Gegenstände auf bestimmte Weise, und dieses hermeneutische ‚Als‘, das hier als komplexes dichtes Sehen aufgefasst wird, spiegelt sich in individuellen Narrativen wider und lässt sich durch diese besser interpretieren.

Wenn wir also Erfahrungen und Urteile in diesem dimensionierten Modus beschreiben, entspricht dies *grosso modo* auch Husserls Auffassung, der betont, dass die phänomenologische Erklärung des Sehens-Als stets im Rückgang auf das Sich-Zeigende selbst erfolge, das sich in einer unendlichen Reihe von Erscheinungsweisen in der Zeit manifestiert und jede Auffassungsweise desselben transzendiert. Husserls Antwort auf die Frage, wie wir dieser transzendenten Sache näherkommen, lautet: durch das Verfahren der Eidetik.[6] Die oben erwähnte Enthaltung von vorgefassten Urteilen führt über die phänomenologische Deskription zur eidetischen Variation oder Wesensschau, wodurch habitualisierte Formen des Sehens-Als überwunden werden können, um die mannigfachen Formen des Sehen-Als mit Blick auf ein „Sehen-Von“ (des Gegenstandes) zu überschreiten.

Der hier verwendete Ausdruck „Sehen-Von“ dient mithin als Zielvorstellung, um des thematisierten Gegenstandes approximativ, frei von Vormeinungen, inne zu werden. Indem ausgeklammert wird, wie und als was der Gegenstand üblicherweise bewertet wird, zeigt er sich sukzessive jenseits eingespielter Deutungsweisen, indem die ihm zuerkannten Eigenschaften frei variiert werden. Diese eidetische Herangehensweise dient, in aufklärerischer Absicht, als Befreiung von dogmatischen und radikal-einseitigen Sichtweisen. Um der Sache auf den Grund zu gehen, sind also keine weiteren Interpretationen erforderlich, sondern jenes eidetische Zeigen-Lassen, das eine möglichst genaue und erfahrungsgetreue Beschreibung dessen erfordert, was sich am Phänomen von selbst zeigt, um auf dieser Grundlage die Sache immer besser zu erkennen. Die dem Objekt zugeschriebenen Eigenschaften werden hierzu variiert, Merkmale hinzugefügt oder weggelassen, um zu verstehen, welche Attribute dem Objekt notwendigerweise zukommen. So besteht das Ziel der Eidetik darin, das Wesentliche aus dem Phänomen herauszuschauen. Im Rahmen des unterrichtlichen EIDOS-Modells, so werden wir sehen, wird Husserls Eidetik modifiziert, in-

[6] Eidetik wird ausführlich erläutert in Edmund Husserls *Phänomenologische Psychologie*, Nijhoff: Den Haag 1962, 72-87, sowie in ders., *Erfahrung und Urteil*, Springer: Berlin 2017, §§ 86-89.

dem perspektivische Narrative ausgestaltet werden, um eine individuelle Tiefe im Zuge handlungsorientierten Philosophierens zu bewirken.

### 3. Leibliche Resonanz und praktisches In-der-Welt-Sein

Philosophieunterricht ist keine rein begriffliche Beschäftigung mit abstrakten Gegenständen. Verhandelt werden existentiell bedeutsame Phänomene, auf die wir uns im Alltag vermeintlich praktisch verstehen. Dieser praktisch gestaltende und kreative Umgang mit der Welt ist ein fundamentaler Modus menschlichen Verstehens.[7] In diesem Sinne ist der menschliche Geist als ausgedehnt, praktisch-enaktiv, eingebettet und verkörpert[8] zu betrachten. Wie wir die Welt sehen, ist nicht das Ergebnis der Aktivität eines cartesianischen Cogito, das einer Objekt-Welt gegenübersteht, sondern eine enaktiv-individuelle Dimensionierung der Lebenswelt. Dieser Gedanke einer leiblich-praktischen Welthaftigkeit ist in pädagogischer Hinsicht richtungsweisend: Menschen lernen nicht als abstrakte Subjekte, sondern als leibliche und affektive, praktisch-gestaltende und narrative Wesen, weshalb Lernen durch den einseitigen Rekurs auf kognitiv-propositionale Subjekt-Objekt-Relationen kaum zufriedenstellend erklärbar ist. Man könnte vielmehr sagen, als leiblich-affektive Wesen stehen Menschen stets in atmosphärischen Resonanzverhältnissen zu ihrer Welt, die sie in dichter Weise erfahren und die sich durch komplexe nichtbegriffliche, dichte Inhalte auszeichnen. Man denke an Scham-, Schuld-, Ekelgefühle oder an Atmosphären der Heiterkeit, Freude oder Hochstimmung. Diese atmosphärisch erlebten Unverfügbarkeitserfahrungen wollen wir als Resonanzerlebnisse fassen. Ein positiv gestaltender Zugang zu diesen Erfahrungen nimmt seinen Anfang in einer mitschwingenden Haltung, um die Welt als eine sich zugleich offenbarende und sich entziehende Realität zu erfahren. Es ist eine Herausforderung, sich der Welt in dieser resonanten Weise zu öffnen, statt sie mittels fertiger Interpretationsmuster und Vorurteilen zu erklären. In diesem Sinne sollte ein phänomenologisch inspirierter Philosophieunterricht zu einem Ort des Resonanzgeschehens werden, in dem die Lernenden in einem kontemplativen Raum das nicht-

---

[7] Heidegger eröffnet (spätestens in *Sein und Zeit*, Max Niemeyer: Tübingen 1953) der Phänomenologie in Auseinandersetzung mit Aristoteles die praktische Dimension der Existenz: Menschen verstehen sich auf die konkreten Begebenheiten ihrer Lebenswelt und sind kraft dieser Faktizität praktisch vertraut mit den Phänomenen.

[8] Einer solchen phänomenologischen Vorstellung des Geistes begegnet man bei Heidegger oder auch Maurice Merleau-Ponty, *Phänomenologie der Wahrnehmung*, De Gruyter: Berlin 1966. In dieser Traditionslinie wird Kognition gegenwärtig im Rahmen einer 4E-Theorie erforscht. Für eine Darstellung der Theorie eingebetteter Kognition vgl. z. B. Evan Thompson, *Mind in Life. Biology, Phenomenology, and the Sciences of Mind*, Harvard University Press: Cambridge 2007.

begriffliche Mitschwingen einüben, statt sich ohne Übergang sofort in argumentative Diskurse zu begeben.[9]

## 4. Gestaltqualität, Poiesis und Narrativität

Dichtes Sehen wird als „Aspekt- oder Gestaltsehen"[10] betrachtet, da Phänomene nicht auf ihre Komponenten reduziert erlebt werden. Ihre Bedeutsamkeit wird vielmehr im Nu erfasst. Wertwahrnehmungen, die sich auf bedeutsame Situationen beziehen, folgen diesem Schema: Wir erleben nicht situative Komponenten und addieren diese zu einer evaluativen Gesamtinterpretation. Im Gegenteil, wir erkennen ihre Signifikanz direkt. Hierbei weisen Wertwahrnehmungen im Kern narrative Strukturen auf, da in ihnen autobiografische Erzählungen konserviert sind, die den Sinnzusammenhang der Situation individuell dimensionieren. Gestaltqualitäten sind zwar selbst keine Geschichten, aber in ihnen schlummern evaluative Narrative, die Hinweise auf individuelle Signifikanz beinhalten. So kommt dem evaluativen Narrativ eine integrative Funktion mit Blick auf die vielfältigen Sehens-Aspekte zu, wodurch ein individueller Sinnzusammenhang konstituiert wird. Diese individuellen Erzählungen dienen als Grundlage unserer Erfahrung von Bedeutsamkeit, die im Gestaltsehen erfasst wird. Daher ist im Unterricht der Rückgriff auf narrative Inhalte ausdrücklich erwünscht, da er der philosophischen Auseinandersetzung ihre individuelle Tiefe verleiht. Evaluative Narrative bilden hilfreiche Strukturelemente, um dem auf die Spur zu kommen, was wir persönlich für wichtig halten. Wenn man diese Narrative sofort in abstrakte Thesensätze übersetzt, kann die spezifisch individuelle Qualität verloren gehen, die ihrerseits ein Motor des Philosophierens ist.

Wir sehen: Die Gestaltwahrnehmungen, die Bedeutsamkeiten anzeigen, enthalten Mikro-Narrative, die Hinweise darauf geben, wie wir die Welt deuten, bewerten und unsere Zwecke in ihr verwirklichen. Diese evaluativen Narrative

---

[9] Vgl. für diesen Zusammenhang Bernhard Waldenfels, *Antwortregister*, Suhrkamp: Frankfurt a.M. 2000 sowie ders., *Grundmotive einer Phänomenologie des Fremden*, Suhrkamp: Frankfurt a.M. 2018, aber auch Hartmut Rosa: *Resonanz. Eine Soziologie der Weltbeziehung*, Suhrkamp: Berlin 2016. Rosa spricht von „Resonanz" als Mitschwingen mit dem Unverfügbaren der Welt. Dadurch setzt sich Rosa ebenso wie Waldenfels und andere Vertreter der Phänomenologie gegen den Impuls zur Wehr, Phänomene mit vorschnellen Interpretationen zu versehen und Neues in habitualisierte doxastische Systeme zu integrieren. Stattdessen soll das Phänomen in der Schwebe der qualitativen Nicht-Verbegrifflichung belassen werden, damit es in seiner Unverfügbarkeit erlebbar wird als das, was sich zeigt.

[10] Die Konzeption einer evaluativen Gestaltwahrnehmung wird entwickelt bei Sabine Döring, *Gründe und Gefühle: Zur Lösung ›des‹ Problems der Moral,* De Gruyter: Berlin/New York 2011, und Robert Roberts, *Emotions: An Essay in Aid of Moral Psychology*, Cambridge University Press: Cambridge 2003, sowie Jan Slaby, *Gefühl und Weltbezug: Die menschliche Affektivität im Kontext einer neo-existentialistischen Konzeption von Personalität,* Mentis: Paderborn 2008.

offenbaren zugleich individuelle Gestaltungsweisen, denn die Geschichten, die wir erzählen, bringen ans Tagelicht, wie wir das, was für uns bedeutsam ist, individuell-praktisch gestalten. Daher liegt in ihnen ein wertvolles pädagogisches Potential: In unseren Narrativen begegnen wir uns selbst. Das Profil unserer Gestaltungen bildet die individuelle *Poiesis*, mittels der wir uns gestaltend auf die Phänomene der Welt verstehen.

Nun sahen wir, dass in Husserls eidetischer Variation ein gedachtes Objekt im Geiste mittels Variationen möglicher Prädikate modelliert wird. Indem verschiedene Eigenschaften ausgetauscht werden, werden diejenigen herausgeschaut, die dem Gegenstand wesensmäßig zukommen. Begreift man Personen als praktisch-gestaltende und narrative Wesen, folgt dem aus unterrichtlicher Perspektive das Erfordernis einer figurierenden *Poiesis*, die individuelle Gestaltungsweisen abbildet, die wir durch unsere Erzählungen darstellen. Im Unterricht wird diese individuelle Dimensionierung durch Figuration der betreffenden Phänomene im Zuge kreativen Um- und Weitererzählens handlungsorientiert modelliert. Es erfordert Fantasie, wenn die genau beschriebene Sache im Fortgang gestaltend variiert wird, um durch Perspektivwechsel und andere kreative Erzähltechniken den individuell bedeutsamen Zusammenhang auszuleuchten.[11] Wir werden abschließend nun sehen, wie diese figurierende *Poiesis* im Rahmen des EIDOS-Modells ins Werk zu setzen ist.[12]

## 5. EIDOS-Modell[13]

EIDOS ist ein Konzept des problemorientierten Philosophieunterrichtes, das den Lernenden üblicherweise nicht vorgibt, welches philosophische Problem erarbeitet wird. Stattdessen entwickeln sie ihre eigenen Ideen, um damit zu lernen, philosophische Themen in der eigenen Lebenswelt selbstständig zu sehen. EIDOS ist ein Akronym aus Begriffen, die lose Phasen des Unterrichtes abbilden, die je nach Anforderung auch in ihrer Abfolge getauscht werden können: E

---

[11] Peter Bieri 2001, S. 377. Dies entspricht dem, was Bieri treffend als eigentliche phänomenologische Arbeit bezeichnete, die ihm zufolge narrativen Charakter aufweist: „Erzählerische Genauigkeit ist phänomenologische Genauigkeit."

[12] Das Konzept des narrativen Philosophierens kann im Unterricht durch unterschiedliche Methoden eingeübt werden, vgl. Johannes Balle, „Erzählte Philosophie. Fünf Methoden des narrativen Philosophierens im Unterricht", 2024, URL: https://www.pedocs.de/volltexte/2024/29031/pdf/Balle_2024_Erzaehlte_Philosophie.pdf [17.10.2024].

[13] Zu einer ausführlichen unterrichtspraktischen Ausarbeitung des EIDOS-Modells vgl. Johannes Balle, „Eidos: Ein Modell des problemorientierten Philosophieunterrichtes", URL: https://www.pedocs.de/volltexte/2024/29032/pdf/Balle_2024_Das_EIDOS-Modell.pdf [17.10.2024].

= Enthaltung/Epoché, I = Idee, D = Individuelle Dimensionierung, O = Organisation, S = Sinn. Eine EIDOS-Stunde startet mit der Aufforderung, ein Phänomen als Anlass des Philosophierens zu finden. Anlass kann eine alltägliche Begebenheit oder Geschichte sein oder ein Foto oder ein Gegenstand im Klassenraum oder der Lebenswelt. Entscheidend ist, dass keine Thematik vorgegeben wird, so dass die Lernenden den Anlass ihres Philosophierens selbstständig finden.

Ist dies geschehen, beginnt der Unterricht, indem die Phase ‚E' für die Urteils-Enthaltung erfolgt. Wie oben dargestellt, ist hier nicht zu *urteilen*, sondern sich jeder Beurteilung des Gegenstandes oder der Situation zu *enthalten*, indem die Sache ohne Vorurteile *beschrieben* wird. Diese Phase impliziert keine sozialen Interaktionen: Die Lernenden beschreiben kontemplativ, was sie sehen, hören etc.

Dem folgt die Phase der Idee. Die Lernenden überlegen auf Grundlage ihrer Beschreibungen, worum es ihrer Ansicht nach mit Blick auf die Sache geht. Sie bedienen das, was im klassischen Unterricht die Lehrkraft vorgibt. Sie entscheiden frei aufgrund ihrer Deskription, was Thema oder Problem ist und finden eine Forschungsfrage. Diese Ideen müssen noch nicht notwendigerweise in begrifflicher Form formuliert sein.

Dann beginnt die Phase der Dimensionierung, die gleichsam eine individuelle Ventilation des Phänomens bewirkt: Die Lernenden *variieren narrativ* gestaltend aus unterschiedlichen Perspektiven das Phänomen. Ziel dieser narrativen Variation ist das Heraussehen dessen, was für die Lernenden individuell an dem entsprechenden Alltagsphänomen bedeutsam ist. Man kann dies mit Husserls Wesensschau vergleichen: Indem man Eigenschaften des Phänomens so variiert, dass einzelne Merkmale versuchsweise abstrahiert werden, entsteht sukzessive ein Bild, welche Eigenschaften wesentlich bzw. unwesentlich sind. Vergleichbar damit ist die narrative Variation: Indem die Lernenden im Prozess des gestaltenden Erzählens perspektivische Variationen ins Werk setzen, wird klarer, was für sie an der Sache bedeutsam ist.

Nun folgt die zweite Phase der Dimensionierung in Form einer *fachlich-vertiefenden Ventilation*. Zunächst prüfen die Lernenden, ob das zuvor in der IDEE-Phase erkannte Problem noch gültig ist. Hier sollte die Lehrkraft nun individuell als beratschlagende Expertin fungieren: Im Dialog wird geklärt, wie die individuelle Forschungsproblematik durch fachliche Positionen, etwa Ideen, Zitate, Texte etc. vertiefend reflektiert werden kann.

Dann erfolgt die Phase der logisch-begrifflichen Organisation. Die Lernenden haben die Aufgabe, ihre Gedanken und Ergebnisse aus Deskription und

Dimensionierung mit philosophischem Material in Beziehung zu setzen und rational argumentativ aufzubereiten.

Zuletzt folgt die Sinn-Phase, in welcher die Lernenden reflektieren, welche Bedeutung das von ihnen entwickelte Thema für ihr Leben hat, wobei sie zugleich nach philosophischen Begründungen hierfür suchen. Abschließend erarbeiten sie ein Statement zu ihrer Forschungsarbeit, stellen dieses vor und kommen miteinander in die Diskussion.

*Edwige Chirouter (Nantes, France)*

# Reconnaissance, émancipation, résonnance: Enjeux éthiques et politiques de la philosophie avec les enfants

## Introduction. Des « ateliers de philosophie » à une « école philosophique »

L'éveil à la philosophie dès le plus jeune âge dépasse largement la seule nécessité de démocratiser l'accès à une discipline scolaire mais interroge profondément les conditions d'une éducation émancipatrice. Les ateliers de philosophie avec les enfants (dès 5 ans) pourraient préfigurer ce que devrait être l'école au quotidien et lui servir de paradigme pour être pleinement une oasis de pensée, c'est-à-dire un lieu de reconnaissance de l'enfant comme sujet, un lieu de déploiement de l'esprit critique et de coopération intellectuelle, un lieu d'émancipation où se forgent, se nouent, se tissent des formes de résonnance profonde à soi, aux autres et au monde. La philosophie avec les enfants pourrait ainsi servir de modèle à ce que nous nommons ici « une école philosophique ».

Dire que les processus de reconnaissance et d'émancipation devraient être au cœur de l'éducation est une évidence de principe mais rappeler haut et fort cette mission éthique et politique est cependant nécessaire alors que la tension est particulièrement saillante aujourd'hui entre les valeurs de l'institution scolaire - qui restent fondée sur l'idéal émancipateur des Lumières - et une société en crise(s) où la transmission de la culture humaniste ne va plus de soi. Entre la montée des fanatismes, des populismes, des fake-news, les crises écologiques et sanitaires, la guerre au cœur de l'Europe, l'accélération générale de nos existences et la multiplication des réseaux d'informations, tout concoure à réaffirmer cet idéal et à rendre nécessaire des temps de suspension pour prendre le temps de penser.

La philosophe américaine M. Nussbaum dénonce dès 2011 dans *Les émotions démocratiques* une crise silencieuse de l'éducation qui se traduit par une transformation de fond des politiques (et donc des philosophies) de l'école. Ces politiques délaissent les Humanités et la nécessité de former des citoyens critiques, lucides, et développent *a contrario* une vision techniciste des savoirs et des compétences au seul service de l'adaptation de l'individu à la vie professionnelle et surtout à l'idéologie ultralibérale et à ses valeurs de compétition et de rentabilité. Les systèmes éducatifs ont ainsi profondément changé de nature et les effets de cette transformation sur la vie démocratique n'ont pas été assez analysés : « Avides de profit national, les États et les systèmes éducatifs bradent avec insouciance des atouts indispensables à la survie des démocraties »[1]. Méprisant et dévalorisant les Humanités (perte de temps inutile et non rentable), les États-nations ne produiront bientôt plus que des générations de machines efficaces, et non des citoyen(ne)s éclairé(e)s, capables de penser par eux-mêmes, de déployer leur esprit critique au moment du vote, de résister aux visions les plus manichéennes et populistes du monde, incapables de prendre de la distance par rapport aux affects, d'envisager l'intérêt général, et sourds aux valeurs humanistes issues de l'idéal universaliste des Lumières. Et M. Nussbaum de souligner que « l'avenir des démocraties mondiales est en jeu »[2].

Les expérimentations et recherches autour des pratiques philosophiques avec les enfants - qui se développent partout dans le monde depuis plus de cinquante ans - s'inscrivent dans cette préoccupation politique de démocratiser l'apprentissage de la pensée critique, de réhabiliter les valeurs et la culture humaniste. L'enseignement de la philosophie en France par exemple reste cantonné à l'année de Terminale dans les lycées d'enseignement généraux et techniques - mais pas dans les lycées professionnels qui n'y ont toujours pas droit, excluant de fait une grande partie des enfants des classes populaires. Or les pratiques expérimentales dès l'école maternelle se développent depuis les années 1970 – sous l'impulsion notamment de l'injonction de Jacques Derrida et du G.R.E.P.H. à « Philosopher hors les murs »[3]. Bouleversant radicalement les représentations traditionnelles de l'enseignement de la philosophie, ces pratiques à l'école primaire, au collège et dans les lycées professionnels se développent selon des dispositifs très divers et répondent à des enjeux pluriels mais complémentaires :

- Un premier enjeu *éthique de reconnaissance* car elles permettent de reconnaître derrière l'*élève* (même le plus en difficulté ou en situation de handicap) un *sujet* digne d'écoute, de respect, de parole et de pensée ;
- un second enjeu d'ordre politique car ces pratiques - fondées sur les principes de la discussion démocratique, coopérative et de l'intelligence collective - sont l'occasion de s'exercer à la délibération, à l'écoute critique des désaccords et à la pensée complexe ;
- enfin, un enjeu pédagogique puisqu'il s'agit aussi de démocratiser l'accès à une discipline scolaire réputée hermétique et élitiste et encore réservée à quelques un(e)s.

---

[1] Martha Nussbaum, *Les émotions démocratiques. Comment former le citoyen du XXIe siècle*, Climats, Flammarion: Paris 2011, 10.

[2] Ibid.

[3] GREPH, *Qui a peur de la philosophie?*, Flammarion: Paris 1979.

Ces trois enjeux sont évidemment complémentaires. Faire de la philosophie avec les enfants nécessite à la fois de poser les bases d'une relation éthique avec eux, de faire le pari de leur éducabilité, d'être aussi convaincu de l'urgence politique de former des citoyen(e)s éclairé(e)s et enfin souhaiter la démocratisation de la discipline. Tout est lié. Dans les pratiques observées en classe, les enseignant.es s'inspirent de ces différents courants pour inventer des dispositifs qui correspondent à leurs objectifs spécifiques et à leur contexte d'exercice particulier.

Le sens même d'introduire la philosophie dès le plus jeune âge dépasse ainsi largement la seule nécessité de démocratiser l'accès à cette discipline scolaire et donc les questions de didactique. Ces pratiques expérimentales interrogent le sens même de la transmission des savoirs et la définition profonde des missions de l'école. La « Communauté de Recherche Philosophique » peut ainsi nous donner le paradigme de ce que devrait être l'école au quotidien : une « école de la pensée » (pour reprendre le titre de l'ouvrage de Matthew Lipman[4]), ou ce que nous appellerons donc plutôt ici une « école philosophique ».

## 1. Pour une « école philosophique », un projet politique

Au-delà des enjeux de démocratisation de la discipline scolaire, les pratiques de la philosophie avec les enfants ouvrent des perspectives de réflexion plus générale sur les missions de l'école dans une démocratie. Elles nous permettent de penser pourquoi et comment cette institution peut véritablement être une « oasis » d'apprentissage d'une citoyenneté éclairée.

Une démocratie exige de ses citoyens rigueur de pensée, bienveillance et ouverture d'esprit, qualités qui ne peuvent être obtenues que par une pratique intellectuelle exigeante, formatrice par la diversité et l'intensité des expériences de l'alliance de la raison et de la sensibilité. C'est à l'école que les futurs citoyen(ne)s) peuvent construire patiemment ces habilités de pensée et cette éthique de relation à soi et aux autres. Pourtant, la philosophe américaine M. Nussbaum, dans *Les émotions démocratiques*, constate que le discours capitaliste a déteint inexorablement sur la sphère éducative contemporaine. Elle décrit le développement de plus en plus prégnant dans un monde globalisé d'une éducation entièrement « tournée vers le profit », visant prioritairement à doter les « apprenants » d'une quantité de « compétences » qui leur permettront d'évoluer dans un monde de concurrence économique mondialisée. Cette éducation « pour le profit » sape les conditions mêmes du fonctionnement ordinaire de

---

[4] Matthew Lipman, *A l'école de la pensée. Enseigner une pensée holistique*, De Broeck: Paris 2011.

nos sociétés démocratiques. A cette « éducation pour le profit », Martha Nussbaum oppose un modèle d'éducation pour la démocratie et l'égalité. Les capacités citoyennes sont essentiellement développées, cultivées, par les Arts et les Humanités, ou plus exactement par une certaine pratique des Humanités : non pas seulement la transmission de contenus caractéristiques d'une culture (la transmission passive de connaissances), mais par une pratique intellectuelle collective, par une appropriation vivante et incarnée des savoirs et des héritages. Dans le contexte de l'économie libérale mondialisée, soumis aux impératifs d'une compétition économique effrénée, à une accélération folle du temps et des échanges, l'essor des réseaux dit « sociaux » et par une disparition des grandes idéologies politiques, la capacité à déployer malgré tout un esprit citrique, une pensée complexe, mais aussi une certaine forme d'empathie et de distance affective est essentielle. Seules ces capacités permettent aux démocraties de survivre aux crises politiques, économiques, écologiques, sanitaires, et existentielles du monde contemporain.

Une authentique éducation démocratique devrait nous rendre plus ouverts en exposant notre sensibilité à la différence et à la reconnaissance de notre insuffisance, de notre vulnérabilité. Car, en plus de rendre libre et lucide, la philosophie nous apprend aussi à être plus humble devant nos propres convictions et visions du monde : accepter de ne pas savoir, accepter le doute, l'incertitude et la complexité mais savoir aussi se (re)construire de façon autonome des repères stables pour agir dans le monde.

La philosophie avec les enfants s'appuie dès son origine sur des enjeux profondément politiques. Les recherches et les expérimentions sur la philosophie avec les enfants débutent dans les années 1970 à l'Université de Montclair aux États-Unis avec les travaux des philosophes M. Lipman et A-M. Sharp, disciples de J. Dewey. Dewey récusait une vision techniciste de la démocratie (comme seul mécanisme formel) et il la considère plutôt comme un mode de vie : c'est-à-dire comme un ensemble dynamique d'habiletés et d'habitudes à se conduire, à se parler et à délibérer les uns avec les autres. Nous avons trop tendance à focaliser la vie démocratique sur une activité politique qui n'a lieu que tous les 5 ans – le vote par exemple - au lieu de mettre en avant ce qui a besoin d'être travaillé tous les jours dans nos interactions sociales quotidiennes. D'où l'idée chez Lipman et Sharp de créer dans les classes avec de très jeunes enfants ce qu'ils appellent des « Communautés de Recherche Philosophique » qui seraient une mise en acte de cette conception de la démocratie. Dans ces ateliers, comme à l'intérieur d'un laboratoire, les enfants - assis tous ensemble en cercle, sous la forme d'une agora - vont formuler des questions et évaluer les idées émises. A partir d'une problématique philosophique (« *qu'est-ce qu'une loi juste ?* » ou « *A-t-on le droit de mentir ?* »), les enfants sont invités à formuler des hypothèses, à déduire des présupposés et des conséquences, à justifier leurs opinions, à évaluer collectivement la validité rationnelle et éthique des différentes propositions. Cette ambition d'élaborer et de construire une école de la maternelle à l'Université sur ce modèle socratique n'est pas une utopie irréaliste, mais elle est l'objet d'un programme, d'une volonté et d'une lutte politique : L'ONU et l'UNESCO préconisent d'inclure la philosophie avec les enfants dans les systèmes éducatifs à l'horizon 2030.[5]

Un des grands défis de l'éducation démocratique contemporaine est de lutter contre les écueils du dogmatisme et du relativisme. Elle doit permettre aux futurs citoyens de développer des défenses intellectuelles qui évitent de tomber dans ces deux dangers qui, selon la formule de Michel Fabre, sont « les deux maladies séniles de notre modernité tardive »[6]. Alors que le dogmatisme (religieux, politique, économique) reste crispé sur des réponses fermées, révélées, non critiquables et que le relativisme, à l'inverse, renonce à donner des repères fiables, seule une approche herméneutique du monde, fondée sur l'interprétation rigoureuse, réflexive des phénomènes, peut permettre un éclairage pertinent de la complexité du réel et de l'existence. Le monde est comme un texte à interpréter et comme toute interprétation littéraire, les lectures en sont plurielles mais reposent aussi sur des données stables. Interpréter un texte complexe, implicite, poétique, subtil n'est pas délirer et lui faire dire tout et n'importe quoi et ce n'est pas non plus être figé dans une seule lecture littérale. Ainsi pour lutter contre les dérives dogmatiques et relativistes, le modèle interprétatif, incarné dans la pratique de la lecture philosophique de récits, nous semble extrêmement porteur. En participant régulièrement aux Communautés de Recherche, les enfants comprennent progressivement qu'en philosophie non seulement il ne faut pas craindre de ne pas savoir mais que l'incertitude y est même nécessaire, salutaire, normale. Sans tomber dans le relativisme et du tout se vaut, l'atelier de philosophie - d'autant plus s'il s'appuie sur la lecture de récits complexes - permet de développer une posture interprétative sur des questions humaines fondamentales. Face à ces grandes questions universelles et atemporelles, il ne peut exister qu'une seule réponse possible mais toujours une plura-

---

[5] Edwige Chirouter, „Infusing philosophy in education from early learning onward", in *Humanistic Futures of Learning. Perspectives from UNESCO Chairs and UNITWIN Networks*, ed. UNESCO: Paris 2020, 186-197.

[6] Michel Fabre, *Éduquer pour un monde problématique. La carte et la boussole*, PUF: Paris 2011, 108.

lité d'idées et de convictions qui feront toujours objets de discussion et de controverses complexes.

Le fanatisme se fonde ainsi sur l'impossibilité à la fois de remettre en cause ses propres croyances ou convictions particulières (et de les reconnaitre épistémologiquement comme telles), mais aussi d'aller fraternellement, comme le dirait H. Arendt, « à la rencontre de l'autre »[7]. Dans les ateliers de philosophie, les élèves apprennent patiemment à accepter l'incertitude nécessaire face à de grandes questions universelles et intemporelles pour lesquelles il ne peut y avoir « une » seule réponse définitive. Face aux questions soulevées par les concepts de Liberté, du Bonheur, de l'Amour ou de la Morale, il faut accepter le principe d'incertitude. Cette démarche intellectuelle aide à lutter contre la rancœur et le sentiment de toute puissance à la source des dogmatismes. Affronter collectivement les grandes questions qui traversent l'existence – la liberté, la justice, le bonheur, l'altérité, l'identité - et apprendre patiemment à les examiner de façon raisonnable, minutieuse, rigoureuse, distanciée, constitue un monde à part, loin de la tendance encore trop fortement présente dans le système éducatif à transmettre des connaissances absolues et faisant autorité. Les enfants y apprennent ainsi à la fois à accepter leur vulnérabilité, mais aussi à se (re)construire des repères stables, grâce à la rencontre avec les autres et les œuvres (littérature, peintures, cinéma, etc.). La reconstruction de repères stables et rationnels est aussi une étape indispensable dans le processus philosophique : ce n'est pas parce qu'il n'y a pas une seule et définitive réponse qu'il n'y pas pour autant des idées ou des convictions qui nous permettent de configurer notre expérience du monde pour mieux y agir. Telle est l'urgence politique de mettre en œuvre au cœur même de l'école une pédagogie de l'interprétation du monde.

## 2. La littérature (de jeunesse) comme médiation pour apprendre à philosopher

Une des fonctions essentielles de la littérature est de nous aider à penser le monde, à l'éclairer pour s'y orienter et donner sens à notre expérience. Les grands dilemmes soulevés par les récits invitent à la réflexion, bouleversent les évidences, apportent de la complexité à notre vision du monde. Le détour par la fiction permet ainsi d'aborder avec subtilité des questions délicates à la fois universelles et intimes (comme la mort, l'amour le bien et le mal, le bonheur, etc.). Il n'y a d'ailleurs pas de civilisation sans récits qui permettent justement cette plus grande intelligibilité du monde et de la condition humaine. Comme l'écrit Roland Barthes:

[7] Hannah Arendt, *La vie de l'esprit* PUF: Paris 1975, 17.

> « De plus, sous ces formes presque infinies, le récit commence avec l'histoire même de l'humanité ; il n'y a pas, il n'y a jamais eu nulle part aucun peuple sans récit ; toutes les classes, tous les groupes humains ont leurs récits et bien souvent ces récits sont goûtés en commun, par des hommes de culture différente, voir opposée : le récit se moque de la bonne et de la mauvaise littérature : international, transhistorique, transculturel, le récit est là, comme la vie ».[8]

Pour Paul Ricœur, tout comme le discours philosophique - plus conceptuel, argumentatif et rationnel - le récit nous permet d'interroger le réel et le penser. Parce qu'il représente la possibilité démultipliée d'expériences exemplaires et signifiantes sur la ou les vérité(s) du monde, il constitue un espace autonome de pensée. La littérature constitue à ce titre une expérience authentique, singulière et universelle à la fois, par laquelle les lecteurs et lectrices vont pouvoir appréhender le réel. Elle est un immense laboratoire où nous pouvons redessiner à l'infini les situations, les dilemmes, les problèmes qui nous travaillent. « Les expériences de pensée que nous conduisons dans le grand laboratoire de l'imaginaire sont aussi des explorations menées dans le royaume du bien et du mal »[9], écrit ainsi Paul Ricœur. Dégagée des contraintes du réel empirique, des lois de la physique, et des lois de la morale, la fiction nous permet de vivre par procuration ce que le réel, seul, ne nous permettra jamais de vivre : en tant que lecteur, je peux commettre un crime et expérimenter par procuration les tourments du remord ; je peux aussi devenir invisible (tel le berger Gygès dans le mythe de Platon) et expérimenter les limites du Bien et du Mal (« Et si j'étais à la place de Gygès… »). Les enfants adorent cette expérience de pensée…[10]

La littérature procède ainsi d'un recueillement c'est-à-dire d'un retour à soi par l'intermédiaire de l'œuvre. La littérature ne vise donc pas à adapter l'enfant par exemple à la société et à la culture particulière dans laquelle il est immergé. Elle ne cherche pas à lui transmettre des valeurs morales particulières. Elle n'est pas purement descriptive et fonctionnelle. Un texte littéraire est un texte avec lequel je peux vivre une rencontre initiatique, fondamentale. Il peut m'aider à me comprendre, à mettre de l'ordre dans mes sentiments, dans mes angoisses, dans mes doutes, dans mes espérances. Il bouleverse et me construit en même temps. La littérature dépasse ainsi largement la distraction, l'évasion, le divertissement. Elle ne nous permet donc pas seulement de nous « évader »

---

[8] Roland Barthes, « Introduction à l'analyse structurale du récit », *Communications* 8 (1966), 1-27 (p. 1).

[9] Paul Ricœur, *Soi-même comme un autre*, Seuil: Paris 1990, 194.

[10] Pour les propos d'enfants dans des ateliers à partir de « L'anneau de Gygès » voir : Edwige Chirouter, « Platon au programme. Des ateliers de philosophie à l'école primaire à partir de ‚L'anneau de Gygès'. Un exemple de laboratoire de pensée », *Spirale* 62 (2018), 39-50.

du réel mais bien au contraire – après cette échappée dans l'imaginaire – de le rendre plus intelligible. Quand je me demande ce que j'aurai fait à la place d'Antigone, je m'oblige à questionner ma définition de la Justice ; quand je juge Cyrano, je clarifie ma définition de ce qu'est l'amour (car Cyrano aime-t-il vraiment Roxanne, peut-on aimer sans être jaloux, peut-on aimer dans le mensonge et sans laisser l'autre libre de choix éclairés ?).

La littérature est donc une médiation particulièrement féconde pour apprendre à philosopher à de très jeunes élèves. La fiction ouvre des possibilités démultipliées d'expérimentations des relations humaines. À hauteur de notre seule expérience personnelle et sensible du monde, notre connaissance de la réalité est forcément très limitée : je suis né(e) dans un espace et un temps déterminés et je n'ai exploré qu'un infime de tous les possibles d'une existence. La fiction crée, elle, à l'infini des mondes possibles où se disent les vérités du monde. Elle élargit à l'infini les représentations de la réalité et de l'existence humaine en les transfigurant. La fiction me permet de vivre par procuration ce que le réel seul ne me permettra jamais de vivre. Et pour l'enfant, dont la capacité d'abstraction est en cours d'élaboration, les fictions jouent un rôle de médiation nécessaire et donnent forme à des problématiques éthiques ou existentielles encore confuses. Plus on est jeune et plus notre expérience du monde est limitée : je ne connais que ce que je vis dans ma famille, mon quartier, mon époque, ma culture. La littérature ouvre sur l'altérité et multiplie les expériences possibles. Même si je n'ai jamais été dans la situation d'Antigone ou du jeune africain dans le célèbre album *Yakouba* de Thierry Dedieu par exemple,[11] je peux m'interroger sur ce que j'aurais fait dans cette situation, je peux émettre des jugements moraux sur les décisions des personnages et par là mettre à jour une vision du monde et un système de valeur jusque-là implicites. Les expériences de pensée vécues par procuration grâce aux récits favorisent une vision complexe des notions travaillées en philosophie.[12]

Parce que les grands récits sont à la fois proches de nos préoccupations internes et suffisamment éloignés pour ne pas nous obliger à les affronter di-

[11] L'album - construit comme un conte africain - soulève un profond dilemme moral : pour intégrer la tribu des guerriers, les jeunes de la tribu doivent s'aventurer dans la savane et tuer un lion. Mais le jeune Yakouba ne rencontre qu'un lion blessé et mourant : faut-il qu'il le tue (pour revenir glorieux au village) ou qu'il lui laisse la vie sauve (honoré à ses propres yeux par cette clémence mais à jamais banni de la communauté des Hommes) ? Par quel geste Yakouba va-t-il devenir un homme ? Les programmes de littérature au cycle 3 encouragent une exploitation philosophique de l'album.

[12] Pour aller plus loin sur la façon dont les enfants s'emparent de la littérature pour philosopher, voir notamment Edwige Chirouter & Nathalie Prince (dir.), *Lumières de la fiction. Philosophie (avec les enfants) et littérature (de jeunesse)*, Raison publique: Paris 2019.

rectement, ils sont une médiation nécessaire pour oser penser. L'imaginaire est donc bien pour les enfants un immense laboratoire où ils peuvent commencer à penser leur condition humaine et leur rapport aux autres et au monde.

### 3. La philosophie avec les enfants comme « oasis de pensée »

La philosophie avec les enfants est une philosophie de l'éducation et donc une philosophie politique. Les ateliers de philosophie avec les enfants nous permettent de penser la fonction de l'école dans une société démocratique. A. M. Sharp, dans un article tissant les liens entre les philosophies de M. Lipman et de H. Arendt, synthétise tous les objectifs politiques de la Communauté de Recherche :

> « Amener les enfants à avoir une pensée créative, critique et vigilante ; les aider à maitriser les outils leur permettant de réfléchir, de dialoguer et de chercher ensemble ; les aider à devenir sensibles à la dimension logique, où éduquer leurs émotions et où pratiquer un mode de vie qui soit, par nature, à la fois pluraliste, multiculturel et démocratique, les rendre conscients de la dimension philosophique de l'expérience humaine. »[13]

Un des enjeux les plus essentiels de notre postmodernité est de penser et d'inventer une éducation qui englobe la personne, une éducation qui se soucie autant de l'éthique et des valeurs que des connaissances et des compétences et qui pour cela ne fasse pas l'impasse sur l'imagination, les émotions, l'éthique de la discussion et de la relation à l'autre. D'où l'importance d'associer constamment pensée critique, pensée créative et pensée vigilante.

Dans les ateliers, les enfants apprennent par le dialogue à prendre en considération la pluralité des points de vue, à raconter le récit de ce dialogue qui, dans un espace public sécurisant, a rendu accessible à chacun la diversité des convictions. Dans ces espaces de pensée sur des questions universelles et intemporelles - où le doute, l'acceptation de sa propre vulnérabilité, de son ignorance, est condition même de l'exercice – les enfants apprennent patiemment à construire des idées, à proposer des contre-exemples, à déceler les présupposés et les conséquences des opinions ou des idées toutes faites, à décrypter les cohérences et incohérences des discours, à mettre en lumière les systèmes de valeurs, à construire des passerelles entre leur vision du monde et celles des autres. Tout en restant soi-même – et en se donnant aussi la possibilité de se transformer et de changer d'avis - la communauté de recherche permet de jeter des ponts entre les visions du monde, d'éprouver parfois un sentiment de fra-

---

[13] In Marie-Pierre Grosjean (dir.), *La philosophie au cœur de l'éducation. Autour de Matthew Lipman*, Vrin: Paris 2014, 21.

ternité envers des semblables qui ne pensent pourtant pas comme eux, d'envisager des désaccords à l'amiable, mais aussi de se positionner sur ce qui leur parait intolérable (certaines idées peuvent être considérées comme intenables du point de vue des valeurs).

En ce sens, la Communauté de Recherche Philosophique donne bien corps à ce que H. Arendt appelait les « oasis », c'est-à-dire la création d'un temps et d'un espace coupés de l'affairement du monde où chacun peut prendre de la distance pour penser et trouver sa place dans une agora délibérative qui instaure l'égalité de la parole dans le respect des différentes opinons (tant que les idées sont certes fondées le plus rationnellement possible).

Et c'est bien toute l'école dans son ensemble qui doit être un « oasis » de pensée et non le seul moment déconnecté de l'atelier de philosophie. La philosophie avec les enfants peut avoir non seulement un rôle propédeutique à l'enseignement de la philosophie, mais elle peut servir de modèle à l'école dans son ensemble pour abolir l'empilement encyclopédique d'une culture patrimoniale devenue instrument de reproduction sociale et la froideur sèche et désincarnée des compétences, des techniques et des méthodologies vides de tout contenu.

Ce projet de penser une école philosophique au cœur de la postmodernité rejoint également les travaux de l'école de Francfort et en particulier les travaux d'Axel Honneth ou d'Hartmut Rosa – qui est le parrain de la Chaire Unesco « Pratiques de la philosophie avec les enfants ». L'école philosophique, portée par le paradigme de la communauté de recherche, répond aussi à l'impératif de la lutte pour une vraie reconnaissance, de la lutte contre l'aliénation et la dictature de l'accélération du temps. H. Rosa, dans *Aliénation et accélération*, soutient la thèse que notre modernité tardive est surtout caractérisée par une pression constante d'un rythme effréné où les individus, adultes et enfants confondus, font désormais face au monde sans pouvoir l'habiter et se l'approprier. Le sentiment d'avoir en permanence à se hâter (« dépêche-toi » serait la phrase la plus entendue par les enfants au quotidien ...), à être constamment débordé, l'intériorisation des valeurs de compétition, de performance et d'individualisme effréné génèrent une angoisse, une culpabilité diffuse et un sentiment de perte de sens et de prise sur la réalité et son existence. Saturés d'informations et de sollicitations parfois (souvent) contradictoires (comme dans les publicités : il faut être « soi-même » mais en répondant à une norme bien précise), nous devenons étrangers à nous-mêmes et étranger au monde. Cette tension sape les fondements même de l'espoir des Lumières : la promesse d'un monde fondé sur l'autonomie de la raison. Il est donc urgent de reconstruire un autre rapport au temps où chacun puisse se réapproprier son histoire, son récit, retisser les liens qui feront la trame de son existence. L'enjeu, nous l'avons souligné, n'est pas seulement *existentiel* (lutter contre la « fatigue d'être soi »), mais aussi *politique* car H. Rosa démontre que cette accélération hystérique du temps provoque une crise démocratique et humaniste (la même que dénonce M. Nussbaum) en portant au pouvoir au mieux le plus fort en communication au pire les plus populistes. Il souligne ainsi :

> « Comme Benjamin l'avait prédit, nous devenons de plus en plus riches d'épisodes d'expérience, mais de plus en plus pauvres en expériences vécues. Il en résulte que le temps semble « se consumer par les deux bouts », il passe vite et disparaît de la mémoire. Ceci pourrait même être en fait l'explication centrale de notre sens de la vitesse rapide du temps dans la modernité tardive. [...]. Un manque d'appropriation de nos propres actions et de nos propres expériences, cependant, ne peut que mener à des formes plus – plutôt que moins – sévères d'autoaliénation ».[14]

Ainsi, ce qui se joue et se pratique dans ces ateliers - l'éthique de relation aux enfants, le rapport au savoir, l'exigence unie à la bienveillance, la posture de l'enseignant - doit servir de modèle pour mettre en œuvre au quotidien à l'école cinq types de pédagogie :

- Une « pédagogie de l'enquête », du problème, de l'interprétation et non de la transmission passive et froide des résultats ;
- Une « pédagogie du sens », de l'expérience, de la sensibilité, de la résonnance, qui sait dévoiler et faire éprouver aux élèves comment les savoirs font écho à leurs préoccupations et leur volonté de donner sens au monde ;
- Une « pédagogie de l'intelligence collective » - pour cultiver l'esprit de coopération. Lorsque les enfants sont effectivement invités à réfléchir aux grandes questions universelles, ils font ensemble l'épreuve d'une commune vulnérabilité face à la complexité de ces questions qui ne trouvent pas de réponse unique et définitive. Ils se rendent alors compte qu'ils ne vont pas pouvoir prendre en charge seuls la difficulté de ces questions qui nécessitent de fait une coopération de toutes les intelligences.
- Une « pédagogie critique des valeurs » qui instaure un rapport réflexif à la loi, aux normes et aux conflits (« Y-a-t-il des violences légitimes ? », « faut-il toujours obéir ? ») - au-delà d'une obéissance aveugle aux règles et aux inutiles et contre-productives injonctions morales.

[14] Hartmut Rosa, *Aliénation et accélération*. La Découverte: Paris 2012, 132.

- Enfin une « pédagogie de la lenteur » qui prenne le temps - loin des injonctions à l'urgence permanente – d'apprendre patiemment à grandir et penser.

## Conclusion

Les ateliers de philosophie, en offrant aux enfants des oasis de pensée et de décélération pour prendre le temps de rentrer de résonance avec soi, les autres et le monde sont un des leviers pour reprendre part au processus d'émancipation. Ils nous imposent ce temps de suspension nécessaire pour penser en nous obligeant à prendre de la distance face à l'urgence du monde. Si l'émancipation principale aujourd'hui se situe dans une réappropriation du temps et d'une nouvelle résonnance au monde, alors effectivement la philosophie avec les enfants participe pleinement de ce projet politique.

*Griet Galle (Leuven, Belgium)*

# Classroom Detection of Fallacies in Political Debates

This paper presents a structured learning path aimed at enabling students to recognise, analyse, and refute fallacies within political debates and populist discourse. Before introducing the learning path (§ 2), I will outline the rationale for incorporating fallacy detection in populist discourse as an educational goal (§ 1).

## 1. Detecting Fallacies in Political Discourse as an Educational Aim

In this section, I argue that education should empower students to identify and critically challenge fallacies in political discourse, with a particular emphasis on populist rhetoric (§ 1.4.). To substantiate this claim, I will introduce populism (§ 1.1), fallacies (§ 1.2), and the relation between them (§ 1.3).

### *1.1. Populism as Ideology and Style*

How might populism be defined? Stefan Rummens highlights the need to distinguish between populism as an ideology and populism as a style.[1] Populism as an *ideological view* on the essence of democracy and the nature of the democratic people refers to 'hard' populism found in both right- and left-wing parties, such as Front National (France), the Vlaams Belang (Belgium), the FPÖ (Austria), Nigel Farage's UKIP (UK), Geert Wilders' PVV (Freedom Party in the Netherlands), the Alternative für Deutschland (Germany), Viktor Orbán's Fidesz (Hungary), the Polish PiS (Law and Justice in Poland), the Lega and the Movimento 5 Stelle (Italy), Podemos (Spain), and Syriza (Greece).[2] Cas Mudde's influential definition, frequently quoted in philosophical discussions on populism,[3] characterises populism as "an ideology that considers society to be ultimately separated into two homogenous and antagonistic groups, 'the pure people' versus the 'corrupt elite', and which argues that politics should be an expression of the *volonté générale* (general will) of the people."[4] According to

---

[1] Stefan Rummens, Wat een theater! Politiek in tijden van populisme en technocratie, Pelckmans Pro: Kalmthout 2016, 135.

[2] Stefan Rummens, "Populism," in: Mortimer Sellars/Stephan Kirste (eds.), Encyclopedia of the Philosophy of Law and Social Philosophy, Springer: Dordrecht 2023, 2743-2751 (p. 2744), doi: 10.1007/978-94-007-6730-0_1016-1

[3] Rummens, Wat een theater!, 144.

[4] Cas Mudde, "The Populist Zeitgeist," in: Government and Opposition 39, no. 4 (2004), 541-563 (p. 543).

Rummens, populism as an ideology poses a significant threat to democracy, as it denies fundamental values of the democratic constitutional state.

Populism as a political *style* involves employing rhetorical techniques and electoral strategies to influence public opinion. It is a widespread phenomenon, present not only in ideologically populist parties but across (nearly) all political parties. In Rummens' view, populism as a style is not inherently problematic and is closely linked to the mediatization of politics.[5]

The following table, based on Rummens' work, outlines characteristics of populism as a style (left column), alongside the hard and ideological form of these style characteristics (right columns). The middle column explains how the media democracy, which has supplanted the former pillarized party democracy, fosters an environment in which the use of populist style elements is attractive for politicians.[6] The table can support classroom instruction, enabling students to differentiate between populist style elements and populism as an ideology, as well as to examine the connections between populism and the use of fallacies (cf. infra, § 2.3, 2.4 and 2.6).

| Populism as a style | Mediatization of democracy | Populism as an ideology |
|---|---|---|
| An anti-establishment discourse characterised by a stark opposition between 'the people' and (political, economic, and cultural) elites, whom politicians portray as alienated from the public. Politicians align themselves with 'the people' while distancing themselves from elites. | Use of catch-all terms like 'the people' or 'the citizens' to appeal to a wide electorate. | A delegitimization of the political elite and institutions, depicting the establishment as a corrupt clique and betrayer of the people. |
| Promotion of a strong, charismatic, and voluntaristic leader in whom voters recognize themselves and who claims to express the true desires | The personalization of politics: voters choose a person who represents a certain ideology and whom they trust. | The leader identifies with and embodies 'the people.' He positions himself as the sole representative of 'the people' and can speak on |

[5] Rummens, Wat een theater!, 136, 143-144.

[6] The information in this scheme is based on Rummens, Wat een theater!, 136-139, 145-146; Stefan Rummens, Politieke Filosofie, Acco: Leuven 2020-21, 185-188.

| | | |
|---|---|---|
| and thoughts of the people. | | behalf of the people without representative mediation or deliberations. He becomes an authoritarian figure. |
| Presentation of simplistic analyses and solutions (framed as common-sense responses) to complex issues. | Direct media communication with voters favours short, impactful slogans that are often oversimplified. | Promotion of a binary, simplistic worldview, distinguishing between good 'own people' and bad 'enemies of the people.' They create enemy stereotypes (such as the Muslim, the foreigner, the capitalist, or the intellectual). |

### *1.2. Fallacies*

The theoretical framework regarding fallacies in this paper is based on the pragma-dialectical theory of argumentation, pioneered by Frans H. van Eemeren and Rob Grootendorst, and further developed with Francisca Snoeck Henkemans. This theory establishes ten rules for critical discussion, which must be adhered to in order to resolve a difference of opinion or disagreement.[7] Fallacies, within this framework, are understood as argumentative moves that violate these ten rules,[8] but are "incorrectly presented as complying with the rules."[9] For instance, the freedom rule specifies that "parties must not prevent each other from putting forward standpoints or casting doubt on standpoints."[10] The fallacy *argumentum ad hominem* or personal attack is a violation of this rule.[11]

Moreover, the pragma-dialectical theory posits that arguers, when making an argumentative move, should adopt a strategic approach that balances convincingness (i.e., effectiveness in achieving rhetorical goals) with reasonableness.[12] Fallacies are thus conceptualised as "derailments of strategic manoeu-

[7] Francis H. van Eemeren/A. Francisca Snoeck Henkemans, Argumentation. Analysis and Evaluation, second edition, Routledge: New York 2017, 96.
[8] Van Eemeren/Snoeck Henkemans, Argumentation, 96.
[9] Van Eemeren/Snoeck Henkemans, Argumentation, 142-143.
[10] Van Eemeren/Snoeck Henkemans, Argumentation, 97.
[11] Van Eemeren/Snoeck Henkemans, Argumentation, 98.
[12] Van Eemeren/Snoeck Henkemans, Argumentation, 136-137.

vring," occurring when arguers overemphasise effectiveness and neglect reasonableness.[13]

The pragma-dialectical theory also contends that fallacies are particularly challenging to detect due to their deceptive nature. Fallacies often have a misleading appearance, as arguers presenting fallacious arguments strive to conceal any unreasonableness, adhering closely to the legitimate forms of argument. This obfuscation is facilitated by the fact that "fallacious and sound manifestations of the same mode of strategic manoeuvring look the same," and for arguments positioned in the middle of the fallacious-sound spectrum, it may be unclear whether they are indeed fallacious.[14] Additionally, the classification of an argumentative move as sound or fallacious ultimately depends on the context of the communicative activity type (such as a criminal trial or a political debate).

### *1.3. The Relationship between Fallacies and Populism*

Politicians frequently employ fallacious arguments as rhetorical tools to persuade audiences of their views.[15] Populist actors, in particular, tend to rely heavily on such fallacies. Empirical research by Blassnig, Büchel, Ernst, and Engesser indicates that populist politicians generally employ informal fallacies extensively and that these fallacies "occur overwhelmingly in combination with populist key messages."[16]

When these fallacies are left unchallenged, the public may be misled and disinformed, which could have far-reaching consequences on issues such as the decision to initiate a war.[17] Fallacies in political discourse contribute not only

---

[13] Van Eemeren/Snoeck Henkemans, Argumentation, 142.

[14] Van Eemeren/Snoeck Henkemans, Argumentation, 143-144.

[15] Valentino Zurloni/Luigi Anolli, "Fallacies as Argumentative Devices in Political Debates," in: Multimodal Communication in Political Speech. Shaping Minds and Social Action: International Workshop, Political Speech 2010, Revised Selected Papers, ed. Isabella Poggi et al., Lecture Notes in Artificial Intelligence 7688, Berlin: Springer 2013, 245-257.

[16] Sina Blassnig et al., "Populism and Informal Fallacies. An Analysis of Right-Wing Populist Rhetoric in Election Campaigns," in: Argumentation 33 (2019), 107-136, doi: 10.1007/s10503-018-9461-2. The researchers investigated the use of informal fallacies by right-wing populist parties in both their self-presentation through press releases and their representation within the print media during the 2015 elections in Switzerland and the United Kingdom. Their empirical research indicates that nearly one-third of the analysed texts contain at least one informal fallacy, leading them to conclude that populist politicians generally employ fallacies extensively. However, they note that it remains unexplored whether populist actors use fallacies more frequently than other politicians, as a comparative analysis between populist and non-populist parties has not yet been conducted (133).

[17] Blassnig et al., "Populism and Informal Fallacies," 108. John Wilson/Ahmed Sahlane/Ian Somerville, "Argumentation and Fallacy in Newspaper Op/Ed Coverage of the Prelude to the Invasion of Iraq," in: Journal of Language and Politics 11, no. 1 (2012), 1-30, doi: 10.1075/jlp.11.1.01wil.

to the spread of misleading or false information but also to the promotion of populist ideology. Given that populist ideology poses a potential threat to democratic principles, the use of fallacious arguments by populists can be considered especially concerning and even dangerous.

### *1.4. The Importance of Learning to Detect Fallacies in Political Discourse*

Education should equip students to uphold and defend democratic values and principles, fostering their ability to participate actively and critically in democratic processes.[18] Furthermore, it should develop students' capacity to distinguish between rational and irrational, as well as truthful and false, assertions. Given that populist rhetoric often spreads misinformation and promotes ideologies that may undermine democracy, education should empower students to identify and critically analyse fallacious arguments within political discourse, especially those prevalent in populist narratives.

## 2. Learning Path for Detecting Fallacies in Political Discourse

I have designed a learning path aimed at equipping my first-year Philosophy students at KU Leuven's Institute of Philosophy with the knowledge and skills to identify fallacies, including those frequently found in political discourse. This learning path, which can be adapted for advanced secondary school students, aligns with the central theme of this volume by integrating an analysis of populist rhetoric.

The learning path begins with foundational knowledge acquisition and gradually introduces increasingly complex exercises to develop the ability to recognise and analyse fallacies in various contexts. It concludes with a reflective component on the presence and implications of fallacies within political discourse, particularly populist rhetoric.

### *2.1. Foundational Knowledge of Fallacies and Populism*

The initial phase focuses on acquiring basic knowledge and understanding of argumentation theory and fallacies, primarily through independent study. My coursebook, grounded in pragma-dialectical argumentation theory, includes over thirty fallacies. These include those identified by van Eemeren and Snoeck Hen-

[18] According to the "Council of Europe Charter on Education for Democratic Citizenship and Human Rights Education" education should empower learners to "exercise and defend their democratic rights and responsibilities in society, [...] and to play an active part in democratic life, with a view to the promotion and protection of democracy and the rule of law." Recommendation CM/Rec (2010)7 of the Committee of Ministers to member states on the Council of Europe Charter on Education for Democratic Citizenship and Human Rights Education (11.05.2010), Section 1, § 2a.

kemans,[19] along with additional fallacies I deem relevant, such as the is-ought fallacy and the false dilemma. For each fallacy, I provide examples drawn from various contexts. Alongside the coursebook, students receive a reference guide summarising each fallacy, allowing them to quickly identify and apply the theory in practice.

Adopting the pragma-dialectical framework provides students with a sophisticated understanding of fallacies for several reasons: (1) By linking fallacies to the ten rules for critical discussion, students move beyond rote memorisation of a fallacies list and gain insight by contextualising fallacies within a theoretical structure. (2) The pragma-dialectical approach highlights the persuasive function of fallacies, which prepares students to understand why these errors commonly appear in political discourse, where the aim is often to persuade. (3) Pragma-dialectical theory emphasises that fallacies can be challenging to detect due to their often misleading presentation, encouraging students to remain vigilant when analysing contemporary debates. (4) The approach promotes a nuanced perspective on fallacy detection, noting that the context of an argument can sometimes make it difficult to determine whether it is truly fallacious.

In a lesson series focused on fallacies in populistic discourse, students should also gain foundational knowledge and understanding of populism, for example using the theoretical framework discussed in § 1.1 as a basis.

### *2.2. Recognizing Fallacies in Brief Online Multiple-Choice Exercises*

After gaining foundational knowledge of fallacies and populism, students begin practising the identification of fallacies. Initially, they work on recognising fallacies in brief texts and cartoons sourced from diverse fields through online multiple-choice exercises. Each question set contains ten exercises covering a selection of ten fallacies from a larger set of thirty. Following this introductory series, subsequent question sets gradually increase in difficulty. For each set, an additional set of comparable exercises is available for students who either did not achieve a satisfactory score or wish for further practice.

[19] Van Eemeren/Snoeck Henkemans, Argumentation for the basics of argumentation theory and fallacies. For a more detailed explanation of fallacies, Frans Van Eemeren/Rob Grootendorst, Dat heeft u mij niet horen zeggen...: Drogredenen van A tot Z, Rozenberg: Amsterdam 2002.

Below is an example of a question in the first series of exercises:

It is not a big deal to take a beer glass home from a pub. Most students have done that before.
O post hoc ergo propter hoc
O reversal of cause and effect
O slippery slope
O argumentum ad consequentiam
O argumentum ad verecundiam
O argumentum ad populum / consensus gentium Correct answer
O false analogy
O argumentum ad ignorantiam
O affirming the consequent
O denying the antecedent

To reinforce fallacy recognition throughout the academic year, students complete these exercises at intervals (in line with the didactic principle of repetition). Should they disagree with the solution to any exercise, they are encouraged to contact me, as the identification of fallacies is inherently interpretative rather than exact.

### *2.3. Recognising and Analysing Fallacies in Delimited Exercises from Political Discourse*

Secondly, students engage in the practice of recognising fallacies during class through selected examples derived from the realm of political discourse. These examples may include political advertisements, video clips addressing political topics, or text excerpts from political party flyers, news articles, or opinion pieces pertaining to current political issues. The examples encompass a diverse array of political parties, not solely those representing extreme views.

The fallacies are examined in dialogue with the students, taking into account the context and striving for nuance in interpretation. It is important to note that an argument may simultaneously exhibit multiple fallacies, or it may be ambiguous as to whether a particular argument is fallacious. In a series of lessons focused on populism, each example could be explored in relation to the connections between the identified fallacies and the defining characteristics of populism as an ideology or a style. Below are two illustrative examples.

*Example 1*

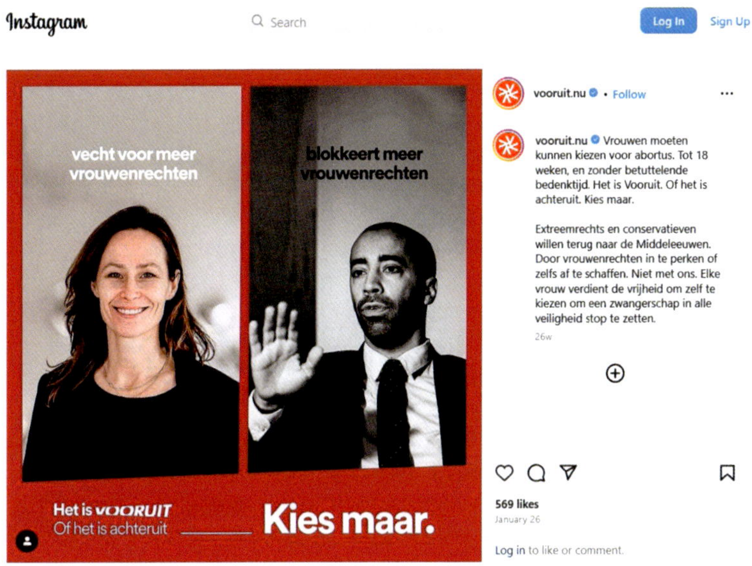


*Fig. 1: Political advertisement of the party 'Vooruit' on Instagram in January 2024.*[20]

This political advertisement for the Flemish socialistic party 'Vooruit' (meaning 'Forward') was posted on Instagram in January 2024, in anticipation of the Flemish, Belgian and European elections scheduled for June 2024. Their slogan for these elections, "It is FORWARD. Or it is backward – Take your choice.", which appears at the bottom of the poster, is an allusion to the party's name.

The background of both the poster and the accompanying Instagram message pertains to ongoing discussions in the Belgian Parliament regarding whether to extend the current abortion period of 12 weeks and whether to abolish the six-day reflection period following an initial consultation with a doctor. All majority parties, including the socialist party, supported an extension of the abortion period to 18 to 20 weeks, except for the CD&V (Flemish Christian Democrats), who proposed a maximum extension of 14 weeks.[21] In contrast, the extreme-right, Flemish nationalist party 'Vlaams Belang' opposes any extension.

---

[20] Instagram, "Vooruit.nu," 26.01.24, https://www.instagram.com/p/C2kjnSltQvc/. [All translations from the Dutch in this article are mine].

[21] VRT NWS, Rik Arnoudt, "Meerderheidspartijen volgen advies om abortustermijn tot 18 à 20

The poster features Freya Van den Bossche, a Flemish member of parliament for 'Vooruit', on the left, with the text: "fights for more women's rights." On the right side, a picture of Sammy Mahdi, a federal member of parliament and president of CD&V, is accompanied by the text: "blocks more women's rights." The right-hand text asserts: "Women should be able to choose abortion. Up to 18 weeks, and without a patronising reflection period. It is Forward. Or it is backwards. Take your choice. // The extreme right [i.e., Vlaams Belang] and conservatives [i.e., CD&V] want to return to the Middle Ages. By restricting or even abolishing women's rights. Not with us. Every woman deserves the freedom to choose to terminate a pregnancy in complete safety."

This message contains the fallacy of the straw man, employing two techniques.[22] First, 'Vooruit' exaggerates, simplifies, and misrepresents the position of the Christian Democrats. While the Christian Democrats do agree with a modest extension of the abortion period, the advertisement suggests that they support the curtailment of abortion rights. Second, the advertisement conflates the position of the Christian Democrats with that of the extreme-right party, Vlaams Belang, which rejects any extension of the abortion term.[23]

Moreover, the text employs the fallacy of false analogy, comparing the CD&V's position with a medieval stance. Additionally, the combination of the poster and text creates a false dilemma, contrasting the extension of the abortion period (which is equated with more women's rights) with the abolition or curtailment of abortion rights (which is equated with fewer women's rights), while overlooking alternative options, such as maintaining the existing abortion period of 12 weeks.

These fallacies exhibit characteristics of a populist style, as the position of the Christian Democrats is overly simplified.

*Example 2*

Another more complex example pertains to the ongoing discussion regarding the period during which abortion is permitted. A scientific committee, comprising experts from diverse backgrounds, reached a consensus recommending the extension of the abortion period to a minimum of 18 weeks of gestation.[24] This

---

weken te verlengen, CD&V staat op de rem," 18.04.23, https://www.vrt.be/vrtnws/nl/2023/04/18/meerderheidspartijen-volgen-advies-om-abortustermijn-tot-18-weke/.

[22] On these techniques, see Van Eeemeren, Argumentation, 103-104.

[23] Vlaams Belang, "Uitbreiding abortustermijn onbespreekbaar," 24.01.24, https://www.vlaamsbelang.org/nieuws/uitbreiding-abortustermijn-onbespreekbaar.

[24] Interuniversitair, multidisciplinair en onafhankelijk comité belast met de studie en de evaluatie

recommendation prompted the following statements from members of parliament representing 'Vooruit', as reported by a news website. The members assert that the scientific consensus indicates the necessity of extending the abortion period:

> Karin Jiroflée [Vooruit]: "There is a scientific consensus here that stems from a study commissioned by CD&V. [...] What more is there to discuss here?"[25]
>
> Melissa Depraetere [Vooruit] is firmly committed to the 18-week term. "Experts have been calling for this for some time, there is growing support among the public. At some point, we need to take steps forward." According to her, CD&V is unwilling to engage in a discussion about what constitutes a unanimous scientific consensus.[26]

This argument exemplifies a subtle form of the is-ought fallacy. It contains the implicit premise that one can derive ethical or political directives from expert opinions or scientific findings. Most philosophers argue that normative conclusions cannot be drawn from descriptive premises, such as scientific statements; in essence, facts do not imply values.[27] The question surrounding the abortion period is fundamentally an ethical issue rather than a scientific one. While scientific information is pertinent to this discussion, the ethical dilemma cannot be resolved solely on the basis of scientific data, as it requires a balancing of values that belongs to the ethical and political domains.[28]

---

van de praktijk en de wetgeving inzake vrijwillige zwangerschapsafbreking, "Studie en evaluatie van de abortuswet en -praktijk in België: Academisch rapport op verzoek van de "Vivaldi" meerderheid op federaal niveau," April 2023, https://vlir.be/wp-content/uploads/2023/03/230411-Abortion-law-and-practice-in-Belgium-uitgebreid-rapport_NL.pdf, 20.

[25] Rik Arnout, "Meerderheidspartijen volgen advies om abortustermijn tot 18 à 20 weken te verlengen, CD&V staat op de rem," VRT NWS, 18.04.23, https://www.vrt.be/vrtnws/nl/2023/04/18/meerderheidspartijen-volgen-advies-om-abortustermijn-tot-18-weke/: "Karin Jiroflée: 'Er is hier een wetenschappelijke consensus die uit een studie komt die CD&V heeft gevraagd. [...] Waarover gaan we hier nog discussiëren?'"

[26] Kathleen Heylen, "Verbolgen Sammy Mahdi over 'totaal onsmakelijke' Vooruit-campagne. 'Dit is kopiëren van Vlaams Belang'", VRT NWS, 28.01.24, https://www.vrt.be/vrtnws/nl/2024/01/28/sammy-mahdi-cd-v-noemt-vooruit-campagne-rond-abortus-wansmake/: "Melissa Depraetere houdt absoluut vast aan de termijn van 18 weken. 'Experts vragen daar al langer om, er is een groeiend draagvlak onder de bevolking. Op een bepaald moment moeten we stappen vooruit zetten.' Volgens haar is CD&V niet bereid om te praten over wat een unanieme wetenschappelijke consensus is."

[27] Benjamin De Mesel, "Moraalfilosofie: Is-Ought," Onder wijsgeren, 08.09.23, https://hiw.kuleuven.be/nl/studeren/toekomstigestudenten/video/onder-wijsgeren/ethiek#section-5.

[28] See the radio-interview with political philosopher Stefan Rummens on Radio 1, De Wereld Vandaag, "Moeten politici het expertenadvies over abortus volgen? 'Abortus is een morele kwestie, geen wetenschappelijke,'" 18.04.23, https://radio1.be/luister/select/de-wereld-

In this specific case, the complexity is further compounded by the fact that the scientists' consensus already implies a value judgement. The Scientific Committee itself acknowledged that "the choice of a specific term [i.e., time limit] is always the result of seeking a delicate balance between various interests and values, and that any proposed term is subject to criticism for being arbitrary."[29] In my classes, I discuss this is-ought fallacy within the broader context of the is-ought problem in philosophy, providing numerous examples of the is-ought fallacy, as it is a mistake that students often make spontaneously during debates.

*2.4. Detecting and Analysing Fallacies in a Political Debate and Populist Discourse*

In the subsequent stage of the learning pathway concerning fallacies, we watch and analyse a segment from a televised political debate on a contemporary issue during class. Students are required to identify the fallacies present in the debate, which we subsequently discuss while considering the context. Additionally, we focus on various other aspects of the debate, such as compelling arguments, points of contention regarding factual claims, verbal and non-verbal communication (including body language and vocal delivery), and rhetorical strategies. We view the debate twice and address different aspects after each viewing.

As an illustrative example, I will analyse segments from a debate regarding the crisis of asylum seeker reception in 2023.[30] Due to the significant influx of individuals seeking asylum in Belgium, the number of available reception places has been insufficient. State Secretary for Asylum and Migration, Nicole de Moor (CD&V), made the decision to deny access to asylum reception for 'single men' (i.e., men without families). In the debate, the chairpersons of five different political parties address the reception crisis. The chairperson of Groen (the Green party) proposes distributing asylum places across Belgian cities and towns. Below is the response from Tom Van Grieken, chairman of Vlaams Belang:

---

vandaag/moeten-politici-het-expertenadvies-over-abortus-volgen-abortus-is-een-morele-kwestie-geen-wetenschappelijke.

[29] Interuniversitair, multidisciplinair en onafhankelijk comité , "Studie en evaluatie van de abortuswet en -praktijk in België," 21: "Het Wetenschappelijk Comité is zich bewust van het feit dat de keuze voor een bepaalde termijn altijd het resultaat is van het zoeken naar een delicaat evenwicht tussen verschillende belangen en verschillende waarden, en dat elke voorgestelde termijn onderhevig is aan de kritiek van willekeur."
I would like to thank my colleague Benjamin De Mesel, moral philosopher, for his advice on the is-ought fallacy in this debate on the abortion term.

[30] Zevende dag, "Opvangcrisis verdeelt Groen en CD&V," 3.09.23, https://www.youtube.com/watch?v=fu_utRlnbuM.

> Tom Van Grieken: "We must finally make the choice. Those who enter our territory illegally lose their right to stay. That is the first measure to take. Second, we know that of all those asylum seekers, six out of ten are asylum cheats. Shorten that procedure and remove those people from the asylum centres, then you will have more space. And third, last but not least, put effort into an effective return policy. When asked where those people should go who have exhausted all legal remedies: back to their own country. Procedure is over. You are ordered to leave the territory, then you must obey it. That is what the public wants. No spreading plans. That is, if your street floods [due to] a breach in the dike, they say: everyone must have an equal amount of water in their basement. No Fleming is asking for that."[31]

When Van Grieken asserts that "We know that of all those asylum seekers, six out of ten are asylum cheats," he commits the fallacy of evading the burden of proof by presenting his standpoint as if it were self-evident. Through statements such as "That is what the public wants" and "No Fleming is asking for that," he again evades the burden of proof. In addition, these statements involve hasty generalisation (*secundum quid*), as he extrapolates the views of a few individuals to represent the entire population. He also commits the *argumentum ad populum* fallacy, claiming that his standpoint should be accepted because it is popular. Lastly, his analogy comparing the equitable distribution of asylum seekers across cities to the dispersal of floodwater into basements is a false analogy: it implies asylum seekers are akin to disruptive water, with the influx resembling a flood. Yet asylum seekers differ significantly from water; for example, unlike water, asylum seekers possess consciousness and individual will.

Here, too, one could consider the link between these fallacies and populism: characteristics of populist ideology are reinforced by the use of fallacies. Vlaams Belang constructs an 'enemy stereotype' by equating the population with 'the Fleming,' as if Flemings have a single, unified will. Asylum seekers are portrayed as largely fraudulent, likened to a natural disaster, and depicted as broadly unwelcome by the Flemish population.

[31] Text in Dutch: Tom Van Grieken: "We moeten eindelijk eens de keuze maken. Wie op illegale wijze ons grondgebied binnenkomt, verliest het recht op verblijf. Dat is maatregel nummer 1 die je moet nemen. 2. We weten van al die asielzoekers dat zes op de tien asielbedriegers zijn. Verkort die procedure en zet die mensen uit de asielcentra, dan heb je meer plek. En 3, last but not least, maak toch eens werk van een effectief terugkeerbeleid. Op de vraag waar moeten die uitgeprocedeerden dan naartoe: naar hun eigen land terug. Procedure is afgelopen. U krijgt het bevel om het grondgebied te verlaten, dan moet daar gevolg aan gegeven worden. Dat wil de bevolking. Geen spreidingsplannen (smalend). Dat is als uw straat overstroomt, een dijkbreuk, ze afkomen met: je moet evenveel water in je kelder hebben. Daar vraagt geen Vlaming om."

We continue our analysis of fallacies with an examination of a statement made by the chairman of OpenVLD, the liberal party.

> Moderator: "Why single men and not single women [who are denied access to asylum reception and thus must sleep on the streets] ...?"
> Tom Ongena: "I think, we should do everything we can to find a humane solution for each of these people ..."
> Moderator: "Why has this group been chosen?"[32]

Tom Ongena commits the fallacy of *ignoratio elenchi*, as his answer does not address the question of selection criteria, even if it is tangentially related. The moderator therefore presses on, repeating the question.

Tom Van Grieken's next intervention once again contains multiple fallacies.

> Tom Van Grieken: "For the party Groen, it will never be enough, that [*sic*] the whole of Flanders becomes a mini-Brussels. Groen has 5,000 to 6,000 members. If every Groen member took in one [asylum seeker], it would be solved, but you don't do that. It is in working-class neighbourhoods, where problems already exist, that more people should be added [according to Groen]. The debate here is always about more asylum places, because then it will get solved; it won't, because we don't need more asylum places, we need fewer asylum seekers. The country is full, and it's not me saying that. 75% of mayors, including those from CD&V and OpenVLD [= right-liberal party], believe they have enough reception places."[33]

By proposing that the asylum crisis could be resolved if each member of the party Groen housed an asylum seeker, Van Grieken commits *ignoratio elenchi*, as his suggestion, while loosely related, does not contribute to the debate's focus on structural, community-based solutions; rather, it individualises the responsibility. Furthermore, by implying that Groen members do not act on their stated beliefs, he engages in the *tu quoque* fallacy, a variant of the *argumentum ad hominem*, by suggesting hypocrisy. In attributing to Groen a desire to con-

---

[32] Text in Dutch: "Moderator: Waarom alleenstaande mannen wel en alleenstaande vrouwen niet ...?
Ongena: "Ik denk, we moeten er alles aan doen om voor elk van die mensen een menswaardige oplossing ..."
Moderator: "Waarom is die groep er uitgekozen?"

[33] Text in Dutch: Tom Van Grieken: "Voor de partij Groen zal het nooit voldoende zijn, dat heel Vlaanderen een mini-Brussel wordt. Groen heeft 5000 à 6000 leden, als ieder Groen-lid enen binnenpakt, is het opgelost, maar dat doet u niet. Het is in de volkswijken, waar al problemen zijn, dat er nog meer mensen moeten bijkomen. Het debat wordt hier altijd gevoerd over meer asielplekken, want dan zal het opgelost geraken, dat is niet, want we hebben niet meer asielplekken nodig, we hebben minder asielzoekers nodig. Het land zit vol, en dat zeg ik niet hé. 75 % van de burgemeesters, ook die van CD&V en OpenVLD, vinden dat ze voldoende opvang hebben."

centrate asylum seekers in working-class neighbourhoods, he commits a strawman fallacy, as this is not the party's standpoint. By further claiming that 75% of mayors agree that the country is full, he again evades the burden of proof while also invoking *argumentum ad populum* by appealing to a purported majority opinion.

### *2.5. Creating and Identifying Fallacies in a Political Debate Exercise*

The next step in the learning pathway on fallacies involves an in-class debate exercise on contemporary political topics. Recent examples of debate statements, relevant to Belgian or Flemish politics, include: "Mandatory military service for young people should be reintroduced," "Parents should be penalised if their teenagers repeatedly commit crimes," and "Politicians should be permitted to criticise judges' rulings."

For the debate exercise, the class is divided into four groups: a pro party, a contra party, a jury, and observers. The format consists of two rounds of debates over two lessons, allowing each student to participate twice as a debater. At home, students prepare for their assigned debate position by researching arguments in support of one side. Their preparation must also include crafting a fallacious argument in favour of their position. During in-class preparation, each party selects a specific fallacy to incorporate into their argumentation, which they then disclose to the jury. In the course of the debate, the observers are tasked with identifying the fallacy employed by each party and discussing them following the debate.

Before I developed this learning path, students only reviewed the course text on fallacies (see § 2.1) before participating in the debate exercise (§ 2.5). As a result, they often opted for a 'simple' *ad hominem* fallacy in their argumentation. Now that they are following the additional steps in the learning path (§ 2.2–2.4), they select more sophisticated fallacies for their argumentation.

### *2.6. Philosophical Reflection on Fallacies in Political Discourse*

*The final stage in the learning path focuses on a philosophical examination of* fallacies within political and populist discourse, as well as their interrelations. Possible topics for discussion include:

- Is it always clear whether an argument is fallacious? Why or why not?
- When and why are fallacies employed?
- How important is it to recognise fallacies within political discourse and in everyday life? What are the implications?

- Are fallacies within political discourse potentially harmful? If so, in what ways?
- What is the relationship between political discourse and truth? Should politicians always adhere to the truth? Why or why not?
- How do fallacies and political discourse interact? (cf. connection to persuasion and rhetoric within politics)
- What is the relationship between specific fallacies on the one hand and populism as a style and as an ideology on the other hand?

Below are some preliminary insights for addressing the question regarding the connection between fallacies and populism (for the characteristics of populism, see §1.1).

- Fallacies such as hasty generalisations, false dilemmas, and the strawman can be associated with the oversimplified analyses that often typify populist style. The strawman fallacy, in particular—wherein the arguments of political opponents are misrepresented—can serve as a populist strategy to delegitimise those opponents.
- In populist discourse, where the personalities of politicians are given prominence, attacking the personality of political opponents through *argumenta ad hominem* may serve as an effective strategy. When such personal attacks highlight the perceived elitist traits or ideas of opponents, they align with populism's anti-elitist stance.[34]
- The *argumentum ad populum*, or 'populist fallacy,' attempts to justify a standpoint by asserting that it is widely held. This fallacy complements the populist belief that politicians should reflect the will of the people[35] and aligns with the use of broad, inclusive terms such as 'the people' within a mediatised democratic context.

[34] The relation between the argumentum ad hominem and the populist dimension of anti-elitism is mentioned in Blassnig et al., "Populism and Informal Fallacies," 124.
[35] The relation between the argumentum ad populum and the evocation of the will of the people by populist politicians is mentioned in Blassnig et al., "Populism and Informal Fallacies," 124.

Daniela Zumpf (Paderborn, Deutschland)

# Das Spiel mit dem Volkswillen
# Kritische Gedanken zu einem Unterrichtskonzept am Beispiel des Brexit

„We send the EU £ 350 million a week. Let's fund our NHS instead. Vote Leave. Let's take back control",[1] lautete eine zentrale Botschaft der ‚Leave'-Kampagne, die im Vorfeld des Brexit-Referendums in der britischen Öffentlichkeit verbreitet wurde und u. a. auf einem Bus zu lesen war. Darin zeigen sich Facetten gegenwärtigen Populismus: Kennzeichnend dafür ist, dass das moralisch integre Volk der Briten gegen die kontrollierende, bevormundende und finanziell ausbeuterische EU-Elite rhetorisch in Stellung gebracht wird.[2] Kennzeichnend für Populismus als ‚demagogische Strategie' ist die Ignoranz der Faktenlage und das Geben falscher Versprechen.[3] Kennzeichnend für den Rechtspopulismus ist der Hintergrund der Botschaft „Let's take back control", denn er verbindet die Ablehnung der EU mit der Ablehnung von Immigration: Nicht nur von Brexit-Befürwortern, sondern auch in den britischen Medien wurde ab 2010, nachdem die konservative Regierung ihr angekündigtes Ziel verfehlt hatte, die Anzahl der Immigrant:innen auf 10.000 Personen pro Jahr zu begrenzen, von „unkontrollierter Masseneinwanderung", insbesondere aus ärmeren EU-Ländern, gesprochen, und es gelang den Brexit-Befürwortern, der Öffentlichkeit zu vermitteln, die Kontrolle über die Einwanderung sei nur durch den Austritt aus der EU zu erlangen.[4]

Um das Phänomen des gegenwärtigen Populismus mit Schülerinnen und Schülern der Mittelstufe zu erarbeiten und zu reflektieren, hat Dieter Marxmeier ein Unterrichtskonzept für das Fach Praktische Philosophie/Ethik/Werte und Normen/LER für die Jahrgangstufe 9/10 entwickelt, das den Titel ‚Ich sage das,

[1] Patrick Gensing, „Das 350-Millionen-Pfund-Versprechen", in https://www.tagesschau.de/faktenfinder/brexit-vote-leave-campaign-101.html [15.07.2024].

[2] Vgl. Jan-Werner Müller, *Was ist Populismus? Ein Essay*, Suhrkamp: Berlin, 2016, 42.

[3] Erstens können es rechnerisch höchstens 250 Millionen Pfund gewesen sein, zweitens sind die Zahlungen der EU an den Staat Großbritannien nicht gegengerechnet worden und drittens sind die Einsparungen, die mit dem EU-Austritt einhergehen, nicht zu den Auswirkungen auf den Handel und die britische Wirtschaft ins Verhältnis gesetzt worden (vgl. Gensing, „Das 350-Millionen-Pfund-Versprechen).

[4] Vidhya Ramalingam, „Die UKIP – Ein fruchtbarer Boden für die radikale Rechte in Großbritannien", in: https://www.bpb.de/themen/parteien/rechtspopulismus/242060/die-ukip-ein-fruchtbarer-boden-fuer-die-radikale-rechte-in-grossbritannien/ [27.06.2024].

was die Leute denken!' – Populismus als Herausforderung für die Demokratie trägt und 2018 im Raabe Verlag erschienen ist.

Das Unterrichtskonzept verfolgt die Ziele, dass die Schülerinnen und Schüler die Begriffe des Populismus, des Rechtspopulismus und des Rechtsextremismus klären und reflektieren, gesellschaftliche und politische Bedingungen von Populismus erfassen, in einem Gruppenprojekt eine populistische Partei oder Person eigenständig untersuchen, die Wirkung von Populismus durchdringen und gesellschaftliche und politische Strategien zum Umgang mit Populismus diskutieren können.[5] Der Schwerpunkt liegt auf der gesellschaftlichen didaktischen Perspektive, die Materialien und Methoden eignen sich ebenso für den Politikunterricht.[6]

## Zum Begriff des Populismus

Populismus ist ein vielgestaltiges Phänomen, das sich einer eindeutigen und gleichzeitig umfassenden Bestimmung entzieht.[7] In Marxmeiers Unterrichtskonzept erarbeiten die Schülerinnen und Schüler zum Einstieg zwei konträre Formen von Populismus, die ‚demagogische Strategie' und die ‚aufrichtige Interessenvertretung'. Populismus als ‚demagogische Strategie' verdeutlicht ein Cartoon, in dem ein Kind die Mutter fragt, was Populismus sei, und die Mutter dem Kind antwortet, Populismus sei, wenn sie ihm für den Fall, dass es brav sei, erlaube, jederzeit und so lange es wolle, mit dem Handy zu spielen, und das Kind ihr diese Aussage glaube.[8] Als Ergänzung und Hilfestellung zur Übertragung auf den politischen Kontext dient die Begriffserklärung aus dem Fremdwörterbuch des Duden, der Populismus als „eine von Opportunismus geprägte, volksnahe, oft demagogische [...] Politik, deren Vertreter durch Dramatisierung

---

[5] Vgl. Dieter Marxmeier, *„Ich sage, was die Leute denken!" Populismus als Herausforderung für die Demokratie*, Raabe: Stuttgart, 2018.

[6] Vgl. Marxmeier, *„Ich sage, was die Leute denken"*, 4-5.

[7] Es ist zum Beispiel nicht eindeutig bestimmbar, wie sich Populismus zur jeweiligen staatlichen Ordnung, zu Gewalt und Extremismus und zum Terrorismus verhält. Im letzten Drittel des 19. Jahrhunderts formierten sich Bewegungen, die sich selbst als *Populisten* verstanden und an denen dies deutlich wird, nämlich die *narodniki* in Russland und in den USA die *populist party*: Während sich die *narodniki* als Revolutionäre verstanden, die einen politischen Systemwechsel anstrebten, einen terroristischen Flügel beinhalteten, der ein tödliches Attentat auf Zar Alexander II. verübte, und der Utopie einer Bauernkooperative folgten, stand die *populist party* mit der Verfassung und der wirtschaftlichen Ordnung der USA im Einklang und forderte einige sehr konkrete Gesetzesänderungen, die die demokratische Partei später aufgriff, was zur Auflösung der *populist party* führte (vgl. Jutta Scherrer, „Populismus", in *Historisches Wörterbuch der Philosophie*, Bd. 7, hrsg. v. Joachim Ritter & Karlfried Gründer, völlig neubearbeitete Ausgabe des ‚Wörterbuchs der der philosophischen Begriffe' von Rudolf Eisler, Wissenschaftliche Buchgesellschaft: Darmstadt, 1989, Sp. 1100).

[8] Vgl. Marxmeier, *„Ich sage, was die Leute denken"*, 6.

der politischen Lage die Gunst der Massen zu gewinnen suchen", definiert.[9] Populismus als ‚aufrichtige Interessenvertretung' wird durch ein Aufsatzzitat („Wer als ‚Populist' bezeichnet wird, gilt im positiven Sinne als jemand, der die Probleme der ‚kleinen Leute' versteht, sie ausspricht und direkt mit dem Volk kommuniziert. Im negativen Sinn als jemand, der dem Volk nach dem Mund redet und dem Druck der Straße nachgibt",[10] verbunden mit einem Karikaturenzitat: „‚Sie sind Populisten und reden nur Unsinn!' – B: ‚Danke für's Kompliment ... man tut, was man kann!'") auf den Punkt gebracht.[11] Um diese Unterscheidung an Beispielen zu veranschaulichen, bieten sich die Beispiele der Leave-Kampagne zum Brexit-Referendum und der Occupy Wallstreet-Bewegung an. Durch eine anschließende Diskussion über den Unterschied zwischen den Begriffen des ‚Überzeugens' und des ‚Überredens' lässt sich die Gegenüberstellung vertiefen. Es bietet sich an, Sokrates' Position zur Rhetorik als eine ‚Schmeichelei', die auf Überredung zielt,[12] in die Diskussion einzubeziehen.

In Marxmeiers Konzept bezieht sich das darauffolgende Material nicht mehr auf den Populismus insgesamt, sondern auf den gegenwärtigen Rechtspopulismus. Um zu erarbeiten, was den Populismus näher kennzeichnet, bietet sich ein Auszug aus dem von Marxmeier zur weiteren Verwendung vorgeschlagenen Aufsatz von Karin Priester an:[13]

> „Populismus [geht davon aus], dass die Gesellschaft in zwei homogene, antagonistische Gruppen getrennt ist, das ‚reine Volk' und die ‚korrupte Elite', [...] und macht [geltend], dass Politik ein Ausdruck [...] des allgemeinen Volkswillens sein soll'. [...]
> Aus populistischer Sicht ist der ‚gesunde Menschenverstand' dem Reflexionswissen von Intellektuellen [...] überlegen, weil er auf konkreter, lebensweltlicher Erfahrung beruhe [...] und daher noch einen unverfälschten, ‚gesunden' Zugang zu Recht und Wahrheit habe. Populismus beruht [...] auf der Aversion gegen die ‚Bevormundung' des Volkes durch Funktionseliten. [...] Ein weiteres Merkmal ist die Antipolitik. Populisten mobilisieren vor allem [...] Teile der Bevölkerung, die Politik schlechthin für ein ‚schmutziges Geschäft' halten. Sie treten daher als antipolitische Sprachrohre und Seismografen des common sense auf, sei es als grobschlächtiger, im Dialekt sprechender ‚Mann von der Straße' wie Umberto

---

[9] Duden Fremdwörterbuch. Band. 5. 9., neu bearb. und erweiterte Aufl. Mannheim 2009, zitiert nach Marxmeier, *„Ich sage, was die Leute denken"*, 6.

[10] Florian Hartleb, „Totengräber oder Korrektiv der Demokratie?", in: *Aus Politik und Zeitgeschichte* 5/6 (2012), 22–29 (23), zitiert nach Marxmeier, *„Ich sage, was die Leute denken"*, 6.

[11] Marxmeier, *„Ich sage, was die Leute denken"*, 6.

[12] Vgl. Platon, *Gorgias*, in *Platon. Werke in acht Bänden, griechisch und deutsch*, hrsg. v. Gunther Eigler, Wissenschaftliche Buchgesellschaft: Darmstadt, 1973, 463 a – 466 a.

[13] Vgl. Marxmeier, *„Ich sage, was die Leute denken"*, 3.

> Bossi (italienische Lega Nord) [oder] als ‚einfache' Hausfrauen wie Pia Kjaersgaard (Dänische Volkspartei) und Sarah Palin (Tea Party-Bewegung in den USA). […]
> Populisten [fordern] eine ungefilterte politische Willensartikulation. […] In Europa treten sie für Plebiszite und Referenden ein, halten es aber in der Schwebe, ob diese die parlamentarisch-repräsentative Demokratie lediglich ergänzen oder nicht eher ersetzen sollen."[14]

Die erste Aufgabe besteht darin, die Merkmale von Populismus, wie von Marxmeier vorgesehen, in einem Schaubild zur Übersicht zu bringen. Daran sollte eine vertiefende Auseinandersetzung mit dem populistischen Demokratieverständnis und eine Problematisierung von ungefilterter politischer Willensartikulation anschließen. Dazu eignet sich eine nähere Fokussierung der Funkionen von Volkssouveränität und Rechtsstaatlichkeit. Dass reine Volkssouveränität zu einer ‚Tyrannei der Mehrheit' führen und Regierungsprinzipien ohne rechtsstaatliches Fundament überhaupt zur Degeneration neigen können, kann durch den auf Polybios zurückgehenden Zyklus der Verfassungen verdeutlicht werden, dem zufolge die Demokratie aufgrund des Verfalls der Staatsbürger*innentugenden zur Ochlokratie degeneriert.[15] Die Bedeutung der Rechtsstaatlichkeit kann mittels Montesquieus Darstellung der Gewaltenteilung erarbeitet,[16] aber auch mittels des Artikels 20 des Grundgesetzes verdeutlicht werden.[17]

Auf dieser Grundlage lässt sich eine übergeordnete Problemfrage für das Unterrichtskonzept formulieren: Stellt der Populismus eine Gefahr für Demokratie, Rechtsstaatlichkeit sowie den gesellschaftlichen Zusammenhalt dar?

## Zum parteiförmigen Rechtspopulismus in Europa

Die Einführung in den parteiförmigen Rechtspopulismus erfolgt in Marxmeiers Unterrichtskonzept durch vier Zitate europäischer rechtspopulistischer Politiker:innen:

---

[14] Karin Priester, „Wesensmerkmale des Populismus", in: *Aus Politik und Zeitgeschichte* 5/6 (2012), 3-8 (3); vgl. zudem Götz Distelrath, „Fundamentalismus und Populismus. Impulse zur begrifflichen Klärung vor und nach Unterrichtsbeginn", in: *Zeitschrift für Didaktik der Philosophie und Ethik* 3 (2016), 69-74 (73).

[15] Vgl. Karl-Wilhelm Welwei, „Demokratie und Masse bei Polybios: Helmut Berve in Verehrung zum siebzigsten Geburtstag", in: *Historia: Zeitschrift für Alte Geschichte* 15 (1966), 282-301.

[16] Vgl. Montesquieu: *Vom Geist der Gesetze*. Auswahl, Übers. u. Einl. v. Kurt Weigand, Reclam: Stuttgart, 2011, Buch 11, Kapitel 6.

[17] Vgl. Grundgesetz für die Bundesrepublik Deutschland, Art. 20, in: https://www.gesetze-im-internet.de/gg/art_20.html [18.10.2024].

1. „Eines der Dinge, die zu sagen uns nicht mehr erlaubt wird, ist, dass unsere Kultur bestimmten anderen Kulturen überlegen ist“[18] von Geert Wilders, Partij voor de Vrijheid, Niederlande,
2. „Sie entmündigen die Österreicher und verhöhnen sie gleichzeitig auch noch, sind abgehoben [...], indem sie hergehen und sagen: Wir hier im Parlament haben die Gescheitheit mit dem Löffel gefressen! [...] Sie haben Angst vor dem Volk, das Volk hat aber ein gutes Gespür für Recht und Unrecht. Und dort, wo Unrecht zu Recht wird, werde ich meine Stimme laut erheben, und da wird Widerstand zur Pflicht!“ von Heinz-Christian Strache, FPÖ, Österreich,[19]
3. „Ich bin kein Politiker, ich kümmere mich nicht um Kritik. Ich sage das, was die Leute denken“,[20] von Silvio Berlusconi, Forza Italia, Italien, und
4. „Wir haben es einfach satt, dass uns täglich von den Blockwarten der Political Correctness vorgeschrieben wird, was man sagen darf und was nicht. Zur Demokratie gehört das Recht auf Meinungsfreiheit auch für Freiheitliche, Patrioten und Islamkritiker“[21] von Judith Wolter, der ehemaligen Fraktionsvorsitzenden der Partei Pro Köln, Deutschland.[22]

Die Aufgabenstellung kann vor dem Hintergrund der bereits erarbeiteten Bestimmung des Populismusbegriffs gegenüber dem Unterrichtskonzept von Marxmeier dahingehend präzisiert werden, dass zunächst die Merkmale von Populismus in allen vier Äußerungen identifiziert, anschließend die Merkmale rechter Ideologie in den Äußerungen von Wilders und Wolter genauer in den Blick ge-

[18] Dokumentation der Rede von Geert Wilders, „Die Freiheit verteidigen“ vom 02.10.2010 in Berlin, in https://jungefreiheit.de/politik/deutschland/2010/geert-wilders-die-freiheit-verteidigen/ [18.10.2024].

[19] Aus der Rede Rede Heinz-Christian Straches auf der Nationalratssitzung am 9. April 2008, zitiert nach Priester, „Wesensmerkmale des Populismus“, https://www.bpb.de/shop/zeitschriften/apuz/75848/wesensmerkmale-des-populismus/ [18.10.2024].

[20] Matteo Tonelli, Casa, pensioni, Iraq e tante altre autosmentite di Berlusconi, in: *La Repubblica* vom 15.11.2005, zitiert nach Priester, „Wesensmerkmale des Populismus“, https://www.bpb.de/shop/zeitschriften/apuz/75848/wesensmerkmale-des-populismus/ [18.10.2024].

[21] Judith Wolters Rede im Rahmen von „Marsch für die Freiheit“ im Mai 2011, zitiert nach Priester, „Wesensmerkmale des Populismus“, https://www.bpb.de/shop/zeitschriften/apuz/75848/wesensmerkmale-des-populismus/ [18.10.2024].

[22] Priester, „Wesensmerkmale des Populismus“, 6, zitiert nach Marxmeier, *„Ich sage, was die Leute denken“*, 7.

nommen werden. In Wolters Aussage ist insbesondere die Wahl des Ausdrucks „Blockwarte der Political Correctness" hervorzuheben.[23]

In Marxmeiers Unterrichtskonzept werden die Merkmale des Rechtspopulismus zusammen mit denen des Populismus erarbeitet. Dieses Material ersetze ich durch folgende Charakterisierung des Rechtspopulismus:

> „Ein meist ethnisch, kulturell oder religiös definiertes ‚Wir' wird gegen ‚die Anderen' in Stellung gebracht. Zugleich wird der gesellschaftliche Diskurs moralisch aufgeladen, indem Untergangsszenarien beschworen und politische Gegner dämonisiert werden. [...] Im Gegensatz zum klassischen Rassismus, der bestimmte Menschen oder ‚Rassen' für höher- oder minderwertiger als andere hält, ist die Islamfeindlichkeit der Rechtspopulisten eher kulturell begründet. Nicht Rassen oder Menschengruppen werden als minderwertig klassifiziert, sondern eine bestimmte Kultur beziehungsweise Religion. So wird der Islam per se als rückständig, frauenfeindlich, als nicht ‚zu uns passend' bezeichnet. [...]
> Nicht umsonst ist ‚Lügenpresse' eines der Schlagwörter der Rechtspopulisten und wird auf deutsch inzwischen selbst in den USA gebraucht, um bestimmte Medien zu verunglimpfen. [...] Außerdem gehört es zur Strategie der Rechtspopulisten, einen Kampf um die Sprache zu führen. Insbesondere gegen angeblich vorherrschende ‚Denkverbote' und gegen eine ‚political correctness'. [...]
> Europaweit haben sich einige rechtspopulistische Parteien explizit als Anti-EU-Parteien gegründet. [...] Die Regierungen der europäischen Nationalstaaten werden beschuldigt, nationale Interessen an eine vermeintlich ‚volksfeindliche' Europäische Union verkauft zu haben. [...] Anstelle der EU soll wieder ein ‚Europa der Nationalstaaten' entstehen. Einheimischen eines Landes (‚autochthone' Bewohner) soll Vorrang eingeräumt werden gegenüber Migranten oder Flüchtlingen. Die heimische Wirtschaft soll bevorzugt und nach außen abgeschottet werden. Die Politik der Regierung soll sich noch mehr an ‚nationalen Interessen' orientieren".[24]

Als erste Aufgabenstellung bietet es sich an, das Schaubild zum Begriff des Populismus um die Merkmale des Rechtspopulismus zu ergänzen und die Merkmale des Rechtspopulismus farblich von denen des Populismus abzugrenzen.

Zur Vertiefung eignet sich eine Auseinandersetzung mit dem Film Brexit – Chronik eines Abschieds,[25] in dem das Making-Of der ‚Leave'-Kampagne sowie der Wahlkampf zum Brexit-Referendum als eine Satire mit Elementen der

---

[23] Zu einer Auseinandersetzung mit dem Vokabular des Rechtspopulismus eignet sich Robert Feustel/Nancy Grochel/Tobias Prüwer/Franziska Reif (Hrsg.), *Wörterbuch des besorgten Bürgers*, Ventil: Mainz, 2016.

[24] Thies Marsen, „Rechtspopulismus: Wie er funktioniert", in: https://www.planet-wissen.de/gesellschaft/politik/rechtspopulismus/rechtspopulismus-elemente-100.html [01.07.2024].

[25] Toby Haynes, *Brexit – Chronik eines Abschieds / Brexit – The Uncivil War*, GB, 2019.

Komödie und des Dramas inszeniert wird. Der Film veranschaulicht, wie – besonderes durch den Einsatz digitaler Medien – Menschen manipuliert und der politische Diskurs beeinflusst werden. Herausgearbeitet werden sollte erstens die Genese von ‚Let's take back control', d. h. wie der Zusammenhang zwischen der ablehnenden Haltung gegenüber der EU und gegenüber Immigration hergestellt wird. Zweitens bietet es sich an, das Verhältnis zwischen Rechtspopulisten und den Medien zu thematisieren: Massenmedien werden einerseits als zum Establishment gehörig abgelehnt, andererseits sorgen Rechtspopulisten für Schlagzeilen und wirken daher als Agendasetter der Massenmedien. Außerdem verfügen Rechtspopulisten über eine große Anzahl eigener, digitaler Kommunikationskanäle, über die sie die Öffentlichkeit ungefiltert erreichen; Rechtspopulisten zeichnen sich darüber hinaus durch eine hohe sowie professionalisierte Aktivität in den sozialen Medien aus.

## Zur Unterscheidung zwischen Rechtspopulismus und Rechtsextremismus

Der in Marxmeiers Unterrichtskonzept vorgesehene Text zur Unterscheidung zwischen Rechtspopulismus und Rechtsextremismus stellt einige wesentliche Merkmale des Rechtsextremismus, vorwiegend am Beispiel der NPD, heraus, aber es lässt sich das bedeutende Kennzeichen der Ablehnung der freiheitlich-demokratischen Grundordnung nur indirekt entnehmen.[26] Deutlicher auf den Punkt bringt es ein von Marxmeier zur Vertiefung vorgeschlagener Auszug aus einem Beitrag von Gabriele Nandlinger zum Begriff des Rechtsextremismus:

> „Als (rechts)extremistisch bezeichnet wird eine extreme, radikale politische Einstellung, die gezeigt, bezeugt, vertreten oder verfochten wird usw. Rechtsextremismus ist demnach Extremismus im Sinne der Ideologie der äußersten Rechten. Generell gilt: Rechtsextremisten lehnen die freiheitliche demokratische Grundordnung ab und wollen – auch unter Anwendung von Gewalt – ein autoritäres oder gar totalitäres staatliches System errichten, in dem nationalistisches und rassistisches Gedankengut die Grundlage der Gesellschaftsordnung bilden sollen.
>
> Das rechtsextreme Weltbild ist gekennzeichnet durch Nationalismus, Fremdenfeindlichkeit, völkische Ideologie, Antisemitismus, Geschichtsklitterung, einhergehend mit der Verherrlichung des NS-Regimes und Relativierung bis zur Leugnung des Holocaust, Diffamierung und Ablehnung des demokratischen

[26] Vgl. Karin Priester: „Fließende Grenzen zwischen Rechtsextremismus und Rechtspopulismus in Europa?", in: https://www.bpb.de/shop/zeitschriften/apuz/32423/fliessende-grenzen-zwischen-rechtsextremismus-und-rechtspopulismus-in-europa/ [16.07.2024], zitiert nach Marxmeier, *„Ich sage, was die Leute denken"*, 8.

> Rechtsstaats und seiner Institutionen. Nach einer Definition des Bundesverfassungsschutzes ist ‚Rechtsextremismus in Deutschland nicht ideologisch homogen. Eine Überbewertung ethnischer Zugehörigkeit und eine gegen den Gleichheitsgrundsatz gerichtete Fremdenfeindlichkeit sind allerdings bei allen Rechtsextremisten festzustellen.‘ [...]
> Rechtsextremistische bzw. rechtsextreme Ideologieansätze wurzeln im Nationalismus und im Rassismus. Sie sind von der Vorstellung geprägt, dass die ethnische Zugehörigkeit zu einer Nation oder Rasse die größte Bedeutung für das Individuum besitzt, und dem sind dann entsprechend die Rechte des Einzelnen untergeordnet.
> Ideologisches Bindeglied zwischen den verschiedenen Strömungen des Rechtsextremismus ist häufig der Antisemitismus. Letzterer wird entweder durch offene Hetze ausgedrückt oder kommt verbrämt, in Andeutungen zutage.
> Das Fundament des rechtsextremen Modells der autoritären ‚Volksgemeinschaft“ ist in der Regel ein aggressiver, expansionistischer Staat, gepaart mit völkischem Gedankengut. Ein solcher Staat ist mit der freiheitlichen demokratischen Grundordnung unvereinbar“[27].

Die erste Aufgabenstellung sollte, wie in Marxmeiers Unterrichtskonzept vorgesehen, in der Gegenüberstellung der Gemeinsamkeiten und Unterschiede von Rechtsextremismus und Rechtspopulismus bestehen.[28]

Eine Vertiefung des Verhältnisses zwischen Rechtsextremismus und Rechtspopulismus bietet eine vergleichende Betrachtung der Beispiele der NPD,[29] die extremistisch und nicht populistisch ist, der UKIP/Brexit Party/Reform Party,[30] die populistisch und nicht extremistisch ist, und der NSDAP an[31] die extremistisch und populistisch war. Daran schließt die Aufgabe an, zu diskutieren und zu beurteilen, inwiefern die AfD populistisch und extremistisch ist.

---

[27] Gabriele Nandlinger, „Wann spricht man von Rechtsextremismus, Rechtsradikalismus oder Neonazismus...?“, in: https://www.bpb.de/themen/rechtsextremismus/dossier-rechtsextremismus/41312/wann-spricht-man-von-rechtsextremismus-rechtsradikalismus-oder-neonazismus/?p=all, [01.07.2024].

[28] Vgl. Marxmeier, *„Ich sage, was die Leute denken“*, 8.

[29] https://www.bpb.de/themen/rechtsextremismus/dossierrechtsextremismus/500796/nationaldemokratische-partei-deutschlands-npd/ [05.07.2024].

[30] Vgl. Matthew Goodwin, „Explaining the Rise of the UK Independence Party“, in: https://eu.boell.org/sites/default/files/uploads/2014/06/ukip_eu.pdf [05.07.2024].

[31] Vgl. Arnulf Scriba, „Die Nationalsozialistische Deutsche Arbeiterpartei (NSDAP)“, in: https://www.dhm.de/lemo/kapitel/weimarer-republik/innenpolitik/nsdap [05.07.2024].

## Die Untersuchung einer populistischen Partei oder Person

In Marxmeiers Unterrichtskonzept findet die eigenständige Untersuchung einer populistischen Partei oder Person nach der Auseinandersetzung mit den gesellschaftlichen und politischen Bedingungen statt, die Populismus begünstigen.[32] Da die Untersuchung eine Anwendung des begrifflich Erarbeiteten ist und die vergleichende Betrachtung der drei Parteien Beispiele dafür geben, worauf es bei der Untersuchung ankommt, ist es sinnvoll, sie unmittelbar daran anzuknüpfen.

Zunächst werden Gruppen gebildet, die je einen Untersuchungsgegenstand wählen. Marxmeier schlägt die AfD (scheidet in diesem Fall aus), den „Rassemblement National", die FPÖ, Oskar Lafontaine, Donald Trump und Recep Tayyip Erdogan vor, betont aber, dass die Gruppen ihren Untersuchungsgegenstand selbst wählen sollten.[33]

Ziel der Untersuchung ist es, am Beispiel des ausgewählten Untersuchungsgegenstandes deutlich zu machen, wie Populismus konkret aussieht, und die Ergebnisse im Rahmen eines fünfminütigen Vortrags zu präsentieren. Die eigenständige Organisation und Durchführung der Untersuchung fördern eine Reihe wesentlicher Fähigkeiten im Rahmen selbstorganisierten Arbeitens in Gruppen, darunter die Fähigkeiten zur Recherche, zur Auswahl, Beurteilung und Aufbereitung von Informationen und zur Präsentation.

## Zu den gesellschaftlichen und politischen Ursachen von Populismus

Einen großen Anteil am Erfolg der Brexit-Befürworter hatte der Umstand, dass rassistische Vorurteile und Ablehnung von Immigration seit den 1960er Jahren in der britischen Gesellschaft stark verbreitet sind.[34] Zur Hinführung zur Erarbeitung der gesellschaftlichen und politischen Ursachen von Populismus kann, abweichend von Marxmeiers Konzept, eine Auseinandersetzung mit der tiefen gesellschaftlichen Verankerung einer ablehnenden Haltung gegenüber Minderheiten dienen,[35] weil diese einen großen Teil des gesellschaftlichen Nährbodens

[32] Vgl. Marxmeier, *„Ich sage, was die Leute denken"*, 11-14.

[33] Folgende Übersicht über die im EU-Parlament vertretenen Parteien bietet eine Auswahl möglicher Untersuchungsgegenstände: https://www.europawahl-bw.de/parteien-rechtspopulismus-eu [05.07.2024].

[34] Vgl. Vidhya Ramalingam (2017): „Die UKIP – Ein fruchtbarer Boden für die radikale Rechte in Großbritannien", in: https://www.bpb.de/themen/parteien/rechtspopulismus/242060/die-ukip-ein-fruchtbarer-boden-fuer-die-radikale-rechte-in-grossbritannien/ [27.06.2024].

[35] Andreas Zick und Beate Küpper: „Alltagsdiskriminierung als Form gruppenbezogener Menschenfeindlichkeit", in: *„Ich habe nichts gegen Ausländer, aber…". Alltagsrassismus in Deutschland*, hrsg. v. Britta Marschke u. Heinz Ulrich Brinkmann, Lit: Berlin, 2015, 93-115.

des gegenwärtigen Populismus ausmacht. Ein weiterer Aspekt, der an dieser Stelle vertieft werden kann, ist die Frage nach der grundsätzlichen Empfänglichkeit für populistische Demagogie. Dazu bietet sich eine Auseinandersetzung mit dem Populismusbarometer an,[36] einer empirischen Studie, die ermittelt, wie populistisch Wähler:innen und Nichtwähler:innen eingestellt sind. In der Erhebung sollen Proband:innen acht Aussagen entweder voll und ganz zustimmen, eher zustimmen, eher nicht zustimmen oder überhaupt nicht zustimmen. Wer allen acht Aussagen entweder eher oder voll und ganz zustimmt, gilt als populistisch eingestellt.[37] In einer Auseinandersetzung mit den Items der Erhebung können die Merkmale von Populismus in den Aussagen identifiziert werden.[38] Darüber hinaus bietet es sich an, die Zustimmungsfähigkeit der Aussagen bei näherem Hinsehen zu diskutieren.

Mit Blick auf das Unterrichtskonzept ist es sinnvoll, die Reihenfolge der Materialen zu ändern und zuerst den Auszug aus dem Aufsatz „Wesensmerkmale des Populismus“ von Karin Priester einzusetzen, da er einen eher hinführenden Charakter hat. Darin wird dargelegt, dass Populismus als gesellschaftliches und politisches Warnsignal gelesen werden soll, das auf demokratisch nicht legitimierte Experten hinweisen, auf die vermeintliche Alternativlosigkeit der Volksparteien reagieren, auf bürgerferne Eliten aufmerksam machen, tabuisierte oder vernachlässigte Themen ins öffentliche Bewusstsein rücken, auf ein Ungleichgewicht zwischen Rechtsstaatlichkeit und Volkssouveränität hinweisen und auf selbstreferenzielle ‚Parteienherrschaft‘ aufmerksam machen kann.[39]

Zur Erarbeitung ist die Rekonstruktion des Textes gemäß dem Think-Pair-Square-Share-Verfahren vorgesehen:[40] Nach der stillen Lektüre und der Formulierung von Überschriften zu den Absätzen in Einzelarbeit (think) erfolgt ein Austausch über die gefundenen Überschriften und ggf. deren Korrektur in Partnerarbeit (pair). Daraufhin einigen sich zwei Paare auf eine gemeinsame Version von Überschriften, anschließend wird in dieser Vierergruppe der Argumentationsgang rekonstruiert (square) und die Ergebnisse der Viererteams im Plenum diskutiert (share).

---

[36] Robert Vehrkamp & Wolfgang Merkel, *Populismusbarometer 2020: Populistische Einstellungen bei Wählern und Nichtwählern in Deutschland 2020*, Wissenschaftszentrum Berlin für Sozialforschung, Bertelsmannstiftung, 2020, file:///C:/Users/Admin/Downloads/ZD_Studie_Populismusbarometer_2020-1.pdf, [16.06.2024].
[37] Ebd.
[38] Zu den Items vgl. ebd., 16.
[39] Vgl. Priester, „Wesensmerkmale des Populismus“, 8.
[40] Vgl. Marxmeier, *„Ich sage, was die Leute denken“*, 14-15.

Daran schließt eine Auseinandersetzung mit einer gesellschaftlichen Diagnose des Soziologen Wilhelm Heitmeyer an, der zufolge eine zunehmende soziale Spaltung der Gesellschaft besteht, die unbeachtet bleibt und aus der für den armen Bevölkerungsteil die Zunahme sozialer und gesundheitlicher Probleme, Gewalt sowie die Unfähigkeit zur Artikulation der eigenen Interessen resultieren, während die politischen und wirtschaftlichen Eliten als Akteure der Spaltung identifiziert werden und im wohlhabenden, bürgerlichen Bevölkerungsteil soziale Abstiegsängste, der Eindruck, sozial benachteiligt zu sein, bestehen, ein ökonomistisches Denken vorherrscht sowie die Tendenz zur Abwertung des armen Bevölkerungsteils. Daraus resultiert die Forderung nach dem Abbau des sozialen Sicherungssystems, Werte wie Gleichheit und Gleichwertigkeit geraten ins Hintertreffen und die Gesellschaft ist von Zersetzung bedroht.[41]

Die Erarbeitung erfolgt gemäß einer abgewandelten Form des kooperativen Verfahrens der Strukturlegetechnik: Der Text wird in Einzelarbeit gelesen, dann innerhalb von Dreiergruppen in drei Abschnitte geteilt und die Abschnitte unter den Mitgliedern aufgeteilt. Jedes Mitglied notiert die Hauptaussagen seines/ihres Textabschnittes, und zwar immer genau eine Aussage auf eine DIN A7-Karte. Daraufhin referieren alle Mitglieder ihre erarbeiteten Hauptaussagen. Im nächsten Schritt werden die Karten umsortiert, sodass eine neue Textstruktur entsteht, in der aber alle Hauptaussagen erhalten bleiben. Im letzten Schritt formuliert die Dreiergruppe auf der Grundlage der neuen Textstruktur einen gemeinsamen Text über die gesellschaftlichen Bedingungen für das Entstehen oder Erstarken von Populismus.[42]

Nach der Auseinandersetzung mit den Perspektiven von Priester und Heitmeyer ist die Möglichkeit gegeben, die Problemfrage unter der Berücksichtigung aller erarbeiteten Ergebnisse zu diskutieren und differenziert zu beantworten.

## Zur Wirkung und zum Umgang mit Populismus

Zur Erarbeitung der Wirkung von Populismus sieht das Unterrichtskonzept die Auseinandersetzung mit der Beschreibung des ‚populistischen Teufelskreises' von Klaus Bachmann vor, eines sich selbst verstärkenden Mechanismus,[43] in dem Populisten Themen in den Fokus der öffentlichen Aufmerksamkeit rücken, von denen bekannt ist, dass sie für Angst und Verunsicherung in der Bevölkerung sorgen, unabhängig davon, ob dies begründet ist oder nicht, weil

[41] Vgl. Wilhelm Heitmeyer, „Rohe Bürgerlichkeit", in: *DIE ZEIT* (28.09.2011), zitiert nach Marxmeier, *„Ich sage, was die Leute denken"*, 24-25.
[42] Vgl. Marxmeier, *„Ich sage, was die Leute denken"*, 13.
[43] Marxmeier, *„Ich sage, was die Leute denken"*, 20.

nicht das tatsächliche Vorhandensein eines Problems für Beunruhigung in der Bevölkerung sorgt, sondern die Tatsache, dass es Gegenstand öffentlicher Debatten ist. Aus der Beunruhigung resultieren die Forderungen nach Maßnahmen und mehr Zuspruch für populistische Agendasetter seitens der Bevölkerung. Um den Populisten nicht das Feld zu überlassen, tendieren etablierte Parteien dazu, die populistische Rhetorik zu adaptieren, wodurch die Beunruhigung in der Bevölkerung weiter zunimmt.[44]

Nach der Rekonstruktion des ‚populistischen Teufelskreises' in einer Skizze sieht das Unterrichtskonzept die Diskussion von Möglichkeiten vor, diesen zu durchbrechen. Diese Diskussion bietet den Anlass zu einer Abschlussreflexion zum Phänomen des Populismus, seinen Spielarten, den Hintergründen und der Frage nach einem geeigneten Umgang damit. In diesem Zusammenhang sollte auch die Strategie der strikten Abgrenzung der deutschen Regierungsparteien zur AfD diskutiert und beurteilt werden,[45] indem sie der gegenteiligen Strategie gegenübergestellt wird, die in Österreich und den Niederlanden umgesetzt wurde, nämlich die populistische Partei zu integrieren mit dem Ziel, sie zu zwingen, sich inhaltlich zu positionieren und sie dadurch zu entzaubern.[46]

---

[44] Vgl. Klaus Bachmann, „Strategien zur Eindämmung populistischer Parteien", in: *Populismus in Europa - Krise der Demokratie?,* hrsg. v. Rudolf von Thadden & Anna Hofmann, [Genshagener Gespräche, Bd. 7. (c)], Wallstein: Göttingen, 2005, 65-100, zitiert nach Marxmeier, *„Ich sage, was die Leute denken"*, 20.

[45] Olaf Scholz bemerkte am 17.06.2024 in einem ARD-Interview zur Nominierung Ursula von der Leyens für die EU-Kommissionspräsidentschaft: „Ganz klar ist, im Parlament darf es keine Unterstützung der EU-Kommissionspräsidentschaft geben, die sich auf rechte und rechtspopulistische Parteien stützt."

[46] Vgl. Frank Decker, „Die populistische Herausforderung. Theoretische und ländervergleichende Perspektiven", in: *Populismus. Gefahr für die Demokratie oder nützliches Korrektiv?,* hrsg. v. Frank Decker, VS Verlag für Sozialwissenschaften: Wiesbaden, 2016, 9-32 (S. 22); vgl. auch Klaus Bachmann, „Strategien zur Eindämmung populistischer Parteien", 65-100, zitiert nach Marxmeier, „Ich sage, was die Leute denken", 22.

Riccardo Sirello (Savona, Italie)

# La classe expérimentale Réflexions sur le terme expérimentation et questions ouvertes

Avant de donner une définition de la « classe expérimentale », permettez-moi de réfléchir au terme « expérimental » et d'être en mesure de réfléchir à certaines prémisses fondamentales à l'égard de ceux qui mènent des expériences éducatives.

La racine grecque nous aidera à comprendre son fondement. πείρω [peira] rappelant les tentatives de vouloir essayer, d'apprendre par l'expérience.

λαμβάνω : plus proprement test. Dans le sillage de πείρω, le monde latin s'est ultérieurement orienté à donner une plus grande vitalité au terme de 'pĕrīcŭlum' entendu comme « expérience, essai, tentative » mais aussi comme « risque, danger, responsabilité ». Juridiquement, nous nous sommes orientés vers le procès, l'accusation et le protocole des magistrats. Mais il faut aussi tenir compte du suffixe « ex », c'est-à-dire « hors de, éloigner, élever » mais aussi « négation, privation et libération ».

Cela nous fait prendre conscience que le terrain de l'expérimentation est très complexe et que l'équilibre et la responsabilité de l'action doivent être de premier ordre et tout autant prudents. Il faut clairement se demander pourquoi, comment expérimenter et à quelles fins, afin d'éviter une nouveauté séduisante qui aurait pour but d'abandonner la tradition jugée démodée, inadéquate et monotone.

En principe, nous entendons par « classe expérimentale » un cadre éducatif dans lequel sont appliquées des méthodes et des approches innovatrices en matière d'enseignement et d'apprentissage. Si les approches sont innovantes, cela signifie que celles pratiquées jusqu'à présent ne sont plus considérées comme totalement adéquates. Les techniques elles-mêmes ne sont plus considérées comme appropriées pour obtenir de meilleurs résultats. Je voudrais insister sur le fait que la technique est un moyen pour atteindre une fin qui doit toujours être précise pour ne pas tomber dans l'inversion des rôles, c'est-à-dire lorsque la technique pratiquée est elle-même une fin en soi. C'est ce que j'appellerais un désir de changement. Le désir produit ce rythme incessant de changement une fois satisfait. Il va de soi que le désir doit être authentique et inconditionnel. La technique qu'on utilise pour atteindre des objectifs, la volonté de nous orienter constamment vers un devenir en constante évolution nous fait oublier tout ce qui est stabilité et équilibre. En ne suivant que les seules flatteries technologiques, l'expérimentation deviendrait une philosophie du changement à tout prix. La technique ne doit pas avoir de fin en soi, mais elle doit passer par les résultats et les poursuivre, même si nous savons que les résultats obtenus ne sont pas exempts des objectifs sur lesquels nous nous sommes concentrés. Ce qui est un résultat apparaît tôt ou tard inapproprié. La technique vise une auto-potentialité permanente et l'être humain n'aura pas à se soumettre à un seul modèle de calcul. Tout calculer à travers l'instrument technique conduit à une simple logique de pouvoir et de profit.

L'homme et la technologie devront tôt ou tard harmoniser un problème ouvert, celui de l'ontologie de l'être.

La classe peut faire appel à diverses techniques telles que l'apprentissage par projet, l'utilisation de la technologie, l'intégration de différentes disciplines et l'expérience pratique, mais les maîtres des fins doivent toujours rester les sujets humains dans le sens anthropologique qui se réfère au sujet en tant que personne, c'est-à-dire ceux qui réalisent et pratiquent l'expérimentation.

### Principales raisons et objectifs de l'expérimentation en classe

Sans aucun doute, l'objectif des personnes qui expérimentent est d'améliorer l'engagement des étudiants, de développer des compétences critiques surtout créatives en favorisant un environnement d'apprentissage actif.

Les classes expérimentales peuvent être utilisées à différents niveaux du système éducatif, de l'école primaire à l'université, et peuvent inclure des étudiants de différents âges et de milieux différents. Il est important que ces expériences soient évaluées et documentées afin de comprendre l'efficacité des approches adoptées et d'apporter d'éventuelles améliorations. Dans tous les processus expérimentaux, l'accent doit être mis sur les méthodes brevetées pour atteindre des objectifs jugés meilleurs que ceux atteints dans le passé. Il s'agit, dans ce sens, d'un point commun à l'Italie et à la France.

En France, rappelons-nous les classes Freinet où la libre expression est associée à la libre découverte avec un programme plus libre et souple, mais aussi Decroly avec son méthode de lecture globale et l'observation de la nature avec une méthode applicable aux jeunes et aux adultes, ou encore les écoles Steiner-Waldorf, avec leur apprentissage par les mains, la tête et le cœur, ou enfin les écoles Montessori qui se caractérisent par le refus d'imposer des programmes standardisés avec des étapes obligatoires fixées par les éducateurs, au bénéfice de l'exaltation de l'indépendance. Cette dernière est une pédagogie de l'action, de la pratique, divulguée par plus de 60.000 écoles dans le monde.

Toutes ces écoles sont orientées vers une « éducation nouvelle » qui s'appuie sur une philosophie et une pédagogie internationale actives.

La nouvelle éducation met l'accent sur les intérêts, les expériences et les besoins de l'étudiant en tant que sujet et non en tant qu'expression d'activités autoréférentielles. Par cette prémisse, l'activité d'apprentissage devient fondamentale, non pas comprise passivement et comme simple réception, mais comme une implication et une participation constante à chaque phase. La collaboration est importante et est stimulée par un dialogue ouvert. L'éducation intégrale est l'expression de tout changement dans l'individu au sens holistique du terme et dans l'intégralité des différents aspects psychophysiques, émotionnels, intellectuels et sociaux. Les contenus eux-mêmes ne peuvent être présentés comme des expressions inculquées de manière mnémotechnique, mécanique, mais ils doivent suivre une réforme minutieuse qui vise à mettre à jour les programmes d'études, des programmes d'orientation engageants et qui dirigent l'attention des étudiants vers des expériences significatives pour la vie elle-même. La planification de l'activité devient une priorité à tout moment de l'activité d'apprentissage ; le contact avec la nature et les voyages sont sans aucun doute importants à chaque étape du développement de l'élève

En Italie, il existe de nombreuses classes expérimentales qui concernent principalement l'étude des langues, mais pas seulement. Je dirais que toutes les disciplines y sont enseignées et les options internationales de chinois, d'espagnol, d'allemand et d'anglais ainsi que les expériences d'utilisation des nouvelles technologies d'enseignement y sont très actives.

Dans la classe expérimentale, c'est en premier lieu la motivation à être prise en compte, puis le parcours avance prudemment compte tenu de la charge de travail quotidien et l'importance des activités de formation continue constante pour les enseignants qui y sont impliqués.

L'accent est mis non seulement sur la motivation mais, comme je l'ai déjà dit, également sur les méthodes utilisées pour atteindre les objectifs visant à la participation active de chaque étudiant.

Une expérimentation à grande échelle mais sur des horizons plus limités qui, cependant, ont en commun le fait de s'intéresser à l'efficacité ou non des interventions proposées en classe.+

Plus que jamais je considère encore actuelles les observations insérées dans un des projets expérimentaux qui ont été mis en place en Italie. L'expérimentation en classe peut fournir des réponses aux questions posées ci-après en ouvrant la porte à une nouvelle didactique ainsi qu'à une éducation à la citoyenneté indispensable.

Il ne faut pas oublier[1] que « l'école n'est plus, comme par le passé, la seule agence éducative qui forme la mémoire et l'identité collectives, car il existe d'autres matières qui, bien qu'elles n'aient pas de fonctions éducatives spécifiques, exercent un rôle décisif dans la formation des consciences individuelles et collectives et dans la définition des identités. Il suffit de penser à l'usage public de l'histoire [mais aussi de la philosophie] dans les mass media, avec des opérations culturelles (et donc formatrices) qui ont une pénétration capillaire et envahissante dans la vie intellectuelle et matérielle des citoyens et une efficacité communicative bien supérieure à la transmission scolaire.

Mais les choses sont encore plus compliquées en ce qui concerne la question de l'identité, par la cohabitation souvent conflictuelle de différents groupes ethniques dans les mêmes sociétés européennes, par la pression exercée pour mettre en place des « défenses » ethniques et culturelles contre les immigrés alors qu'à l'inverse, des noyaux islamiques extrémistes s'enracinent.

La culture de la division et de la guerre se développe, même si les jeunes manifestent en masse pour la paix. Ainsi, la question de la démocratie et de la coexistence civilisée qui semblait avoir été réglée après les abominations totalitaires du XXe siècle, se pose largement même en Occident. Si, d'une part, on constate le relativisme des valeurs dans la société moderne, d'autre part, le racisme, l'intolérance et les aspirations autoritaires réapparaissent, ce qui implique également les questions de valeurs de la part des jeunes.

L'école, selon les enseignants eux-mêmes, ne transmet plus de valeurs communes, et donc sur quelle base fonder l'éducation aux droits et à la citoyenneté ? Quelle peut être la base de réflexion pour la fonction enseignante et pour le projet de l'école italienne [ N.d.A. mais pas seulement]

## Venons-en à l'expérimentation vécue

En ce qui concerne la philosophie, son expérimentation et son insertion obligatoire au sein des différentes sections d'études, je peux exposer mon expérience avec l'inspectrice Anna Sgherri du Ministère de l'Education, expérience que j'ai pratiquée pendant plusieurs années, tant au niveau théorique que didactique.

Avec l'équipe de l'inspectrice Anna Sgherri, nous avons inauguré la figure de l'*enseignant-chercheur* et de l'*étudiant-chercheur* par la recherche en labora-

---

[1] Traduction française par l'auteur. Cahier 2, publié par le Ministère de l'éducation, de l'université et de la recherche, Département du développement de l'éducation, Direction générale des règlements scolaires. Directeur général : Silvio Criscuoli. Directeur de projet : directrice de l'école Maria Francesca Amici. Responsable scientifique : Anna Sgherri, Rédaction : Riccardo Sirello. Personnel administratif : Aldo Pastore, Antonella Ruina, Texte de Laurana Lajolo, p. 115, Rome, éd. mai 2004.

toires, une véritable révolution dans les paradigmes de l'enseignement de la philosophie en Italie.

La recherche et le fait de savoir comment rechercher en s'orientant parmi les différentes sources fut le point de départ pour éclipser une étude limitée à l'utilisation du manuel scolaire menée en classe par de nombreux enseignants et souvent éloignée des intérêts et des expériences des étudiants. L'appel à la lecture directe des sources accompagnée par la problématisation philosophique de la lecture elle-même a porté des fruits très positifs.

*L'étudiant – en recherche* a la possibilité de trouver de nouveaux horizons pour une subjectivité ressentie et non modelée sur des normes déjà données.

Il s'agit de valoriser un élève protagoniste qui, par sa recherche, pose des questions, devient un témoin historique actif. Dans les textes originaux et choisis, les élèves ont extrapolé leurs expériences et ont ensuite pratiqué une véritable ascension sémantique en valorisant les aspects non seulement universels mais aussi de l'individu-autre. Le point de départ d'un choix fondamental a été celui de l'inter-subjectivité qui a évité de percevoir les problèmes comme lointains et peu communs. Notre équipe a appris grâce à cette expérimentation que si les problèmes ne se déclarent pas par curiosité en nous-mêmes, qu'ils ne sont pas filtrés dans notre être intérieur, et que notre ontologie de l'être n'est pas affectée, rien ne change réellement dans notre façon d'être.

Comme on peut le comprendre, le manuel scolaire n'a plus de fonction première, mais reste un simple outil d'aide à l'information parmi tant d'autres. A noter que l'utilisation du manuel scolaire est obligatoire dans les classes italiennes.

La création de la *Cité des philosophes*, basée au lycée " Ariosto" de Ferrare, est devenue un exemple de diffusion d'une nouvelle philosophie du projet en abordant de nombreuses questions philosophiques contemporaines. La ville de Ferrare elle-même s'est transformée en une ville aux objectifs philosophiques.

Le *Pôle de philosophie* créé au lycée de Savone "G. Chiabrera" et toujours actif aujourd'hui, est suivi par de nombreuses classes de philosophie de plusieurs lycées qui produisent chaque année des recherches sur un thème commun choisi au début de chaque année scolaire et qu'elles discutent lors d'une journée à la fin de l'année scolaire pour enfin partager et débattre des résultats communs obtenus.

Ce *Pôle de Philosophie* est devenu un forum de discussion entre différents acteurs de la société civile. Les élèves sont enthousiastes à l'idée de voir leurs idées argumentées et comparées à celles des autres. Le résultat est une pensée-autre chargée de la synthèse des différences mais qui atteint une unité non négligeable. Le Pôle Philosophie est devenu un centre de confrontation entre différentes écoles philosophiques et, comme dans le cas de la ville de Ferrare, la ville de Savone elle-même s'est ouverte à de multiples expériences culturelles.

## Réflexions finales possibles

Pour faire face à des risques, il faut une planification minutieuse, une formation appropriée et un suivi constant pendant la phase d'expérimentation afin d'adapter les stratégies et les approches en fonction des résultats obtenus et du retour d'information des élèves et des enseignants.

L'expérimentation est intimement liée à la didactique et aux méthodes pratiquées et jugées adaptées à une implication réelle des étudiants. En ce sens, l'ouverture aux produits des nouvelles technologies éducatives devient une nécessité mais aussi un terrain de réflexion. Il s'agit sans aucun doute d'une sélection attentive des ressources qui n'en privilégie pas seulement le spectaculaire même si on les juge indispensables, mais qui a pour objectif un apprentissage de plus en plus actif, multiforme et non pas guidé par l'habitude d'une utilisation exclusivement technique en soi et pour soi. L'aspect purement technique doit toujours être un moyen et jamais une fin.

Renouveler des programmes en oubliant complètement le passé et une tradition bien ancrée présente toujours des risques et peut devenir un défi. Les ressources elles-mêmes peuvent s'avérer insuffisantes au cours de l'expérimentation. Quand on expérimente, il est toujours nécessaire de se tenir au courant des événements non seulement internes au processus, mais aussi externe à celui-ci. Les enseignants devront également se tenir au courant étant donné que des outils pédagogiques spécifiques et jamais génériques sont toujours nécessaires. Nous savons comment la résistance au changement peut entraver un parcours qui utilise le renouvellement comme principe, qui doit viser des choix égalitaires parce que les nouveaux outils technologiques jugés appropriés doivent être en possession de tous les étudiants sans aucune discrimination pour les étudiants moins aisés.

En outre, il faut tenir compte des différences résultant de l'apprentissage luimême; chaque élève s'exprime avec son propre style et les mêmes méthodes ne sont pas toujours adaptables à tous ; là aussi, il faut veiller à ne pas pénaliser ou exclure ceux qui se révèlent critiques ou indifférents aux nouvelles approches pédagogiques. De nouvelles procédures d'évaluation devront être mises en place, sans lesquelles il n'est pas possible de vérifier si les objectifs fixés sont atteints. Enfin, il existe d'autres risques liés au comportement des étudiants qui, au sein du groupe, peuvent entraîner des conflits et des incompatibilités, l'intégration et l'inclusion étant considérées comme des conditions essentielles à la bonne entente. Les réflexions visant à réaliser une expérimentation adéquate requièrent une attention particulière quant aux effets qui pourraient s'avérer imprévisibles à long terme si toutes les variables susmentionnées n'étaient pas prises en compte.

Il ne fait aucun doute que la formation philosophique pratiquée à travers des voies expérimentales qui se sont affranchies de méthodes et de fins incertaines et séduites par les seules règles du marché incite à des stratégies populistes. Les inégalités sociales et économiques et l'incapacité à penser de manière critique agissent comme un levier pour la colère et la violence sociale ouvrant la porte au populisme comme ressource alternative au présent.

Une expérimentation qui n'est pas mise en place sérieusement entre les mains de professionnels peut facilement tomber dans cette déviance que l'on pourrait appeler le 'pĕrīcŭlum' contemporain où la seule logique qui domine est celle du marché et d'un devenir d'une technique comme une fin, porte ouverte au nihilisme.

*Markus Twittmann (Ennepetal, Deutschland)*

# Aristoteles vs. Trump: Ein virtueller Trainingsraum zur Abwehr fehlerhafter Argumente und populistischer Überzeugungsmittel

Um sich mit den in der heutigen politischen Debatte vor allem von populistischen Parteien verwendeten Argumentationsstrategien auseinandersetzen zu können, ist es notwendig, Fertigkeiten im Umgang mit verführerischen, aber in die Irre führenden Argumentationen und Redetechniken aufzubauen. In einem digitalen Trainingsraum, wie er hier vorgestellt wird, erhalten die Lernenden Gelegenheit dazu.

Seit Beginn ist es ein Ziel der Philosophie, nicht nur über faszinierende Fragestellungen nachzudenken, sondern dabei gleichzeitig das Vermögen zu schulen, auf eine systematische und reflektierte Weise nachdenken und über die Richtigkeit des Gedachten Rechenschaft ablegen zu können: Wer im Argumentieren sicher ist, entwickelt die Fähigkeit, sich eine eigene Meinung zu bilden und sie mit guten Gründen zu vertreten. Daraus entstehen in einer demokratischen Gesellschaft wie nebenbei Autonomie und Diskursfähigkeit.

Heute hat diese Notwendigkeit, sich der eigenen Argumentationsfähigkeit systematisch zu vergewissern, noch mehr zugenommen: Der politische Diskurs wird zunehmend hitzig geführt; die ins Parlament gewählten Parteien stehen sich zunehmend unversöhnlich gegenüber; die gesamte Demokratie steht unter Druck.

Ein erstaunliches Phänomen erhöht diesen Druck noch: Argumente und die Notwendigkeit, sie mit Vernunftgründen und Fakten belegen zu müssen, werden zunehmend entwertet; wir befinden uns seit einigen Jahren in einem ‚postfaktischen' Zeitalter, in dem unglaubwürdige Positionen auch dann noch vehement vertreten werden, wenn nach allen akademischen Maßstäben vollkommen klar ist, dass sie keine Gültigkeit beanspruchen können. Dennoch gelingt es manchen Politikern, Menschen von ihrer Sache zu überzeugen, auch wenn ihre Argumente schlecht oder schlicht gar nicht vorhanden sind. Man fragt sich: Wie kann es sein, dass etwas überzeugend wirkt – gänzlich ohne Argumente?

## Überzeugen, ohne zu argumentieren

Hier lohnt es, einige von Aristoteles stammende Unterscheidungen[1] aufzugreifen: Er nimmt an, dass es (im Bereich politischer Urteilsbildung) drei Überzeugungsdimensionen gibt – Logos, Ethos und Pathos -, von denen der Bereich sachlichen Argumentierens nur einer ist; er führt außerdem den Begriff der „Überzeugungsmittel"[2] ein, der zum Begriff der „Argumente" einen Oberbegriff bildet: Argumente sind zwar das wirksame und einzig gültige Überzeugungsmittel im Raum der Wissenschaft; im Raum des politischen Diskurses aber spielen die beiden weiteren Überzeugungsdimensionen und die mit ihnen verbundene Vielzahl weiterer Überzeugungsmittel eine außerordentlich wichtige Rolle. Wer also den politischen Diskurs in seiner charakteristischen Vielfalt verstehen will, muss demnach wissen, dass Argumente nicht die einzige Währung sind, und dass es auch weitere Überzeugungsmittel gibt. Die Überzeugungsmittel, deren sich Populisten bedienen, und die Trainingseinheiten, in denen sich die Lernenden mit ihnen auseinandersetzen, sollen im Folgenden schwerpunktmäßig vorgestellt werden. Zuvor einige Erläuterungen über Art und Aufbau des Trainingsraums.

## Ein virtueller Trainingsraum

Der Trainingsraum, der im Folgenden vorgestellt wird, hat das Ziel, den Sinn für ‚echte', gültige Argumente zu schärfen. Das geschieht häufig (ex negativo) auf dem Weg, dass Argumentationen vorgestellt werden, mit denen etwas nicht stimmt.

Die Trainierenden begegnen dabei einigen argumentationstechnischen Herausforderungen und können ihre Kräfte erproben. Die Inhalte der Trainingsräume orientieren sich an einigen notorischen Fehlschlüssen der klassischen Philosophie, die gerne und immer wieder auftauchen; die im engeren Sinne politischen Überzeugungsmittel verdanken sich Beobachtungen des aktuellen politischen Diskurses. Die Trainingseinheiten sind also nicht in Stein gemeißelt, sondern passen sich den Interessen von Unterrichtenden und Lernenden, dem Unterrichtsgang, dem aktuellen Geschehen und den fortschreitenden Erkenntnissen über populistisches Argumentieren an.

Der von mir verwendete virtuelle Trainingsraum hat zur Zeit zehn Trainingseinheiten und findet sich z. B. in der App „Taskcards" unter der Adresse:

---

[1] Sie finden sich z. B. in Aristoteles, *Rhetorik*, Reclam: Stuttgart 1999, 12 (1355b35-1356a4).

[2] gr. πίστις – Überzeugungsmittel, Beweismittel, Beglaubigung.

https://www.taskcards.de/#/board/5a45278f-0d52-40aa-8777-44c89fd87adc?token=8b2cefdd-dff0-4e5c-a523-6dc8e1e26281

**Ein Überblick über die einzelnen Trainingseinheiten:**

| Trainingseinheit | Behandelte Technik |
|---|---|
| 1. Sind Menschen von Natur aus untreu? | Sein-Sollen-Fehlschluss |
| 2. Was ist Liebe? | Definitionen; Begriffsanalyse (J. Wilson) |
| 3. Gott existiert! | Gültige u. ungültige Schlüsse (J. Rosenberg) |
| 4. Gott existiert nicht! | Genealogischer Fehlschluss |
| 5. Auch du bist ein Cyborg! | Graduelle u. kategorische Begriffe |
| 6. Leben wir in der Matrix? | Ockhams Rasiermesser |
| 7. Schaffst du es, deiner Schwester ungestraft einen Schokopudding wegzufuttern? | Eristische Argumente |
| 8. Ohne Argumente überzeugen: Pathos und Ethos | Ethos: Verbundenheit und Freund-Feind-Denken als Überzeugungsmittel |
| 9. Du gehörst zur Elite! | Radikale Narrative |
| 10. Kannst du populistische Überzeugungsmittel entlarven? Trumps Rede am 6.1.2021 | Eristische Argumente; Ethos; Narrative |

Wie sich vielleicht schon den Titeln der Übungen entnehmen lässt, sollen die Lernenden im Trainingsraum auf eine niedrigschwellige und möglichst motivierende Weise mit Kenntnissen zur Argumentationstheorie in Berührung kommen.

Vorbild dafür waren weniger die akademischen Logikübungen des philosophischen Grundstudiums als das anregende digitale Schach-Trainingsprogramm Fritz und Fertig und ein etwas trashiger, aber auch sehr unterhaltsamer Martial-Arts-Film mit dem Titel Die 36 Kammern der Shaolin.

Die einzelnen Trainingseinheiten sind als Challenges gestaltet: Der Trainer formuliert eine Aufgabe, mit der gezielt eine bestimmte Fähigkeit trainiert wird, gibt Hilfestellungen und verrät – und erläutert – die Lösungen. Im Sinne der Motivation, aber auch um eine lebensweltliche ‚Philosophieauffindefähigkeit' der Lernenden anzusprechen, sind die Challenges recht alltagsnah formuliert: Philosophisch gibt es immer etwas zu lernen – sei es beim Metzger, im Gespräch mit der Vermieterin oder beim Streit um einen Schokopudding...

Die Einheiten können nach Belieben innerhalb und außerhalb des Unterrichts eingesetzt werden: etwa zur vertieften Auseinandersetzung mit einer Argumentationsstrategie, der man im Unterricht begegnet ist; als Material zur Förderung besonders interessierter Kursteilnehmer; als Gegenstand einer Sequenz zum Thema „Argumentieren"; als Material für ‚Extra'- oder Vertretungsstunden, wobei der spielerische Wettbewerbscharakter noch unterstützt werden könnte durch Preise für diejenigen, die den Parcours oder eine Challenge erfolgreich gemeistert haben.

Das Format einer Materialsammlung auf einer Internet-Plattform bietet verschiedene Vorteile: Die Lerninhalte sind weder an bestimmte Kurse noch an bestimmte Jahrgangsstufen gebunden; es gibt kaum Begrenzungen im Hinblick auf den zeitlichen und räumlichen Umfang und die Art der Medien; die Inhalte lassen sich leicht überarbeiten und erweitern; sie stehen den Lernenden jederzeit zur Verfügung.

Die Trainingseinheiten 7-10 konzentrieren sich auf politische Überzeugungsmittel und eignen sich für eine Beschäftigung mit dem Phänomen des Populismus im Rahmen einer Unterrichtsreihe zur Staatsphilosophie.

Da das Augenmerk in diesem Artikel auf den populistischen Überzeugungsmitteln liegt, sollen diese im Folgenden allgemein erläutert und dann ihre Umsetzung in Einheiten des Trainingsraums vorgestellt werden.

## Populistische Überzeugungsmittel

Wenn man bei Aristoteles nachfragt, wie es dazu kommt, dass die Menschen einem politischen Anführer glauben und ihm folgen, gibt er eine differenzierte Antwort: Natürlich ist die Expertise eines Politikers, seine Analyse der Sachzusammenhänge und seine Kenntnis des politischen, wirtschaftlichen und sozialen Systems wichtig, aber es kommen außer der sachlichen noch zwei weitere Dimensionen hinzu: Um Akzeptanz seiner Vorschläge und politische Gefolgschaft zu erzeugen, muss der Politiker die Menschen emotional berühren und sie in eine geeignete Stimmung versetzen. Und um dies leisten zu können, muss er sie auf zwischenmenschlicher Ebene erreichen. Menschen müssen Vertrauen zu ihm aufbauen können, er muss ihnen authentisch, integer und sympathisch erscheinen.

Für politische Führerschaft sind alle drei Überzeugungsdimensionen notwendige Bedingungen: ohne Sachzusammenhänge (logos) gibt es keine Ansatzpunkte und Vorschläge für konkretes politisches Handeln; ohne Gefühle (pathos) gibt es keine Motivation zu handeln, und wenn der Politiker nicht als Person überzeugt (ethos), müssten die Menschen befürchten, manipuliert oder betrogen zu werden, und würden ihm nicht folgen.

Die politischen Überzeugungsmittel, die in den Trainingseinheiten 7-10 erarbeitet werden, werden im Folgenden kurz allgemein charakterisiert. Dazu dienen beispielhaft Vorgänge und Meinungsäußerungen der Beteiligten rund um die Ereignisse beim Sturm auf das Kapitol am 6. Januar 2021, wie sie in einem Dokumentarfilm aus dem Jahr 2021 dokumentiert sind.[3]

### Grundlegendes Überzeugungsmittel: Radikale Narrative

Was mag am 6.1.2021 in Washington eine bedeutende Menge von Menschen dazu bewegt haben, das Kapitol zu stürmen und in einem nicht für möglich gehaltenen Ausmaß Rechtsbrüche zu begehen? Warum hatten die Leute dabei offenbar kein schlechtes Gewissen, und warum waren sie offensichtlich vollständig davon überzeugt, im Recht zu sein?

Man gewinnt den Eindruck, die am Sturm auf das Kapitol beteiligten Menschen seien in einem erheblichen Maß ‚verblendet' gewesen und hätten sich gewissermaßen in einem ‚falschen Film' befunden. Sie handelten wohl auf Grund von Überzeugungen, die von den anderen Menschen in der Menge geteilt wurden und so motivierend und stark waren, dass sie moralische Skrupel überwinden konnten. Es hat sich eingebürgert, für ein wahrnehmungs- und handlungsleitendes System von Überzeugungen das Wort ‚Narrativ' zu gebrauchen. Narrative in diesem Sinne sind Geschichten, in denen einzelne Überzeugungen zu einem großen sinnvollen Zusammenhang verwoben werden. Es gibt sie in verschiedenen Kontexten: Psychologen erforschen die identitätsstiftende Funktion von Erzählungen, wie sie z. B. Menschen haben, wenn sie über sich und ihr Leben als Ganzes im Sinne einer ‚Lebensgeschichte' reflektieren. Geschichten werden auch in der Politik erzählt: Die verschiedenen Parteien bieten verschiedene Erzählungen von der wirtschaftlichen und sozialen Wirklichkeit an,

[3] Eine Unterrichtsidee für die Erarbeitung der populistischen Überzeugungsmittel mit Hilfe des Dokumentarfilms *Sturm auf das Kapitol. Der Angriff auf die US-Demokratie* von Jamie Roberts (USA 2021) findet sich bei Markus Twittmann, „Eristik, Sympathie und radikale Narrative: Wie überzeugen Populisten – ohne echte Argumente? Eine Unterrichtssequenz zu Überzeugungsstrategien von Populisten unter Verwendung der Fernseh-Dokumentation Sturm auf das Kapitol?", in: *Zeitschrift für Didaktik der Philosophie und Ethik* 2/2023, 48-56.

in der wir uns befinden, und entsprechend verschiedene Handlungsempfehlungen.

Die Menschen, die das Kapitol stürmten, waren offensichtlich von einer besonders fesselnden Geschichte motiviert, die so suggestiv und emotional gewesen sein muss, dass sie dazu führte, dass sogar Gesetze gebrochen wurden. Diese Art von ‚radikalen Narrativen' findet sich nicht nur bei den Menschen vom 6. Januar, sondern auch bei Anhängern fundamentalistischer religiöser und politischer Bewegungen. Die Elemente radikaler Narrative gleichen sich dabei auffällig: Immer verstehen sich ihre Anhänger als Teil einer Elitetruppe. Immer befindet man sich im Kampf. Immer ist der Feind übermächtig und gehört zum verachteten Establishment. Immer gilt aktuell ein Ausnahmezustand, in dem die Grenzen der Legalität überschritten werden dürfen und müssen.

Radikale Narrative sind in ihrer Freund-Feind-Struktur und der immer gleichen Erzählung von einem gerechten Kampf grundsätzlich eher schlicht und leicht zu erkennen, aber sie stellen dennoch ein besonders wirkungsvolles Überzeugungsmittel dar: Wer möchte nicht gern Teil einer Elite sein und exklusives Wissen besitzen? Wer wäre nicht gerne ein Held und diente einer großen und gerechten Sache? Anhänger radikaler Narrative (auch hartgesottene Neonazis) sind davon überzeugt, aus den edelsten Motiven und Gefühlen zu handeln.

Man sieht leicht, wie radikale Narrative in allen von Aristoteles benannten Überzeugungsdimensionen wirksam sind: Sie vermitteln starke und edle Gefühle (Pathos); sie erlauben es, zu einer ausgewählten und tugendhaften Gemeinschaft zu gehören (Ethos); und sie bieten eine Gesamtsicht auf die Wirklichkeit, mit der die einzelnen Dinge auf eine solche Weise erklärt und eingeordnet werden können, dass das eigene Leben einen Sinn und einen besonderen Stellenwert erhält (Logos).

### Ethos als Überzeugungsmittel

Die Anführer einer radikalen politischen Bewegung können das Ethos auch als dominierendes Überzeugungsmittel anwenden: Hierzu verstärken sie das innerhalb des radikalen Narrativs erzeugte Selbstbild ihrer Anhänger als Helden in einem gerechten Kampf: Während sie die Geschichte von einem heldenhaften Kampf gegen das Böse erzählen, führt die klare Unterscheidung von Freund und Feind dazu, dass die Eigengruppe sich eng zusammenschließt. Sie bilden zusammen mit ihrem Anführer eine kleine Gemeinschaft Eingeweihter, die – anders als viele andere – das böse Spiel durchschaut haben und auf deren positive Eigenschaften es in dem vorausliegenden Kampf nun entscheidend ankommt: Solche Eigenschaften sind z.B. Aufrichtigkeit, Mut, Entschlossenheit und Treue. Der politische Anführer wird nicht müde, seine Anhänger für diese Eigenschaften zu loben: Auf diese Weise gibt er den Menschen die gewünschte Anerkennung und wird von ihnen im Gegenzug ebenso anerkannt und gemocht, ja sogar geliebt.

### Eristische Argumente als Überzeugungsmittel

Argumente scheinen für die Trump-Anhänger, die das Kapitol erstürmten, dagegen keine große Rolle gespielt zu haben: In ihren im Dokumentarfilm aufgezeichneten Antworten zeigen sie sich von der Richtigkeit ihrer Erzählung überzeugt, auch wenn man ihnen mit stichhaltigen Einwänden begegnet. Das liegt neben der unbedingten Treue zu ihrem Anführer auch daran, dass ein grundsätzliches Misstrauen gegenüber der Wahrheitsfähigkeit anderer Positionen besteht: Danach ist die Optik des gegnerischen Lagers grundsätzlich eingetrübt; von dort sind nur Falschmeldungen zu erwarten, denn eine unabhängige Berichterstattung (und damit einen objektiven und neutralen Standpunkt) gebe es grundsätzlich nicht, wie sich schon daran ablesen lasse, dass in den Weiten des Internets für jede Auffassung eine Gegenposition gefunden werden könne. Eine Position, die der eigenen widerstreitet, ist somit grundsätzlich dem gegnerischen Lager zuzurechnen.

Eine solche Strategie, wonach es möglich wird, prinzipiell davon auszugehen, dass die Wahrheiten des anderen ‚Fake' sind, und ein grundsätzliches Misstrauen in die Möglichkeit einer freien und unabhängigen Feststellung von Wahrheit zu erzeugen, folgt dem argumentationstechnischen Prinzip ‚Muddy the water': Säe ein allgemeines Misstrauen gegenüber der Möglichkeit, die Wahrheit zu erkennen, und keine Position lässt sich mehr kritisch hinterfragen – und damit auch die nicht, die du vertrittst; die Möglichkeit der Falschmeldungen wird generalisiert – es ist grundsätzlich niemandem zu trauen; die weitere Konsequenz ist, dass man besser in seiner Bubble verbleibt, verlässliche Nachrichten sind ja nur von Freunden zu bekommen.

Wenn der Anhänger populistischer Theorien auf diese Weise davon dispensiert ist, sich mit dem konkreten Wahrheitswert einzelner Vorwürfe im Detail auseinandersetzen zu müssen (denn alles ist grundsätzlich bezweifelbar und es wird sich bestimmt eine befreundete Auffassung finden, die die Vorwürfe widerlegt), ist es nun möglich, seinerseits zum Gegenangriff überzugehen:

Man bringt nun den Gedanken ins Spiel, dass der Gegner den Vorwurf jetzt nur deshalb aufbringe, um bestimmte Ziele zu verfolgen. Es handle sich um eine Kampagne aus niederen und selbstsüchtigen Motiven.

Die Strategie besteht darin, eine Sachfrage auf eine persönliche Ebene zu verschieben: Plötzlich steht gar nicht mehr die Frage im Raum, ob an dem sachlichen Vorwurf etwas dran ist, sondern welche Absichten und Zwecke der Gegner verfolgt. Da der Gegner notorisch schlechte Absichten hat und an der Redlichkeit der eigenen Ziele nicht zu zweifeln ist, sind die Vorwürfe nichtig, gehen an dem, was wirklich wichtig ist, vorbei und sind, wenn auch vielleicht nicht falsch, so doch maximal Nebensache.

Diese Strategie, eine Sachdiskussion um Sachfragen von vornherein zu vermeiden und sie auf die Diskussion von Motiven und unterstellten bösen Absichten des Gegners zu verschieben, ist eine Spielart des argumentum ad hominem. Der Fokus befindet sich hier nicht bei der Sache (ad rem), sondern bei der Person (ad hominem) und ihren vermeintlichen Motiven.

Das argumentum ad hominem ist ein beliebtes Werkzeug populistischen Argumentierens und gehört nicht in den Bereich klassischer und sachlicher Argumente. Argumente, die nicht dazu dienen, sich der Wahrheit zu nähern, sondern nur dazu, in einer Diskussion unter allen Umständen die Oberhand zu behalten, gehören in das Gebiet der ‚Eristik'. Der in der Philosophie bekannteste Überblick über diese in der akademischen Philosophie anrüchigen Techniken gibt Arthur Schopenhauer in seiner Schrift Die Kunst Recht zu behalten.

Die von Schopenhauer aufgeführten Techniken sind freilich der akademischen Diskussionspraxis entnommen; es ist eine augenzwinkernde Auseinandersetzung mit den Schattenseiten akademischer Praxis, und die Techniken sind (bei aller moralischen Verworfenheit) geistreich und subtil.

Das muss für die in der heutigen politischen Debatte verwendeten Argumentationsformen leider ganz und gar nicht gelten.

Die von Anführern radikaler politischer Bewegungen häufig benutzten Überzeugungsmittel (Radikale Narrative, Erzeugung von Verbundenheit durch Ethos und eristische Argumente), sind im virtuellen Trainingsraum Inhalte der Trainingseinheiten 7-10, die im Folgenden kurz dargestellt werden.

## Trainingseinheiten zu populistischen Überzeugungsmitteln

*Challenge #7: Schaffst du es, deiner Schwester ungestraft einen Schokopudding wegzufuttern?*

Dies ist die einzige Station im Trainingsparcours, die nicht in Einzelarbeit gelöst werden kann: Die eristischen Überzeugungsmittel sollen nämlich in voller Aktion kennengelernt werden – in einem möglichst lebhaften (und möglichst unfairen) Streitgespräch, das diesen Namen auch einmal verdienen darf.

Ausgangspunkt ist ein im Alltagsleben einigen Schüler:innen vielleicht vertrautes Setting: Von einer Party zurückgekommen, hat der ältere Bruder Hunger und findet im Kühlschrank einen verlockenden, unangetasteten Schokopudding, der dummerweise seiner Schwester gehört. Da nach der schönen Feier die Willenskraft des jungen Mannes etwas geschwächt ist, macht er sich über den Pudding her und weiß, dass ihm am nächsten Tag Ärger droht. Auf die anstehende Auseinandersetzung mit seiner Schwester bereitet er sich schon einmal vor und zwar nach (so will es die Aufgabenstellung) allen Regeln der Kunst. Er bedient sich im Internet einer riesigen Sammlung unfairer Argumentationsstrategien und darüber hinaus verrät ihm das ihm zur Verfügung stehende Aufgabenblatt noch die beiden Königsargumente der Populisten, das argumentum ad hominem und das whataboutism-Argument, die hier aus naheliegenden Gründen ‚Trumpf-Argumente' genannt werden. Die Schwester darf sich ebenfalls mit der Sammlung fieser Argumente vorbereiten (kleine Schwestern sind ja auch nicht wehrlos…) und erhält von einem dritten Mitspieler, der als Punktrichter fungiert, Extrapunkte, wenn sie es geschafft hat, die beiden Trumpf-Argumente zu identifizieren und in ihrer Funktionsweise richtig zu beschreiben.

Ziel der im Idealfall recht lebhaften Übung ist die Kenntnis einer größeren Zahl eristischer Argumente und der Möglichkeit und der prinzipiellen Unredlichkeit des Argumentierens ad hominem.

*Challenge #8: Ohne Argumente überzeugen: Pathos und Ethos*

Die in dieser Challenge ausgewählte Rede soll zeigen, dass der Anteil von sachlichen Argumenten in Reden zugunsten der Überzeugungsdimensionen Pathos und Ethos beeindruckend gering sein kann – auch bei sehr berühmten Reden.

Die Schüler:innen durften sich die Rede für diese Challenge selbst aussuchen – sie entschieden sich für eine, von der sie schon viel gehört hatten: Es handelt sich um die Rede, mit der Joseph Goebbels am 18. Februar 1943 im Berliner Sportpalast das deutsche Volk zum Durchhalten und auf einen „totalen Krieg" einschwor. Reden zu analysieren ist nicht Gegenstand des Philosophieunterrichts, genauso wenig wie rhetorische Mittel. Die Aufgabenstellung ist daher so gefasst, dass der Fokus für die Schüler:innen erkennbar auf die Frage gerichtet bleibt: Wie schafft der Politiker es, die Menschen von seinen Zielen zu überzeugen? Ziel ist es, die Überzeugungsdimension des Ethos kennenzulernen und sie in ihrer Funktionsweise verstehen zu können. Dazu ist der Text bereits farbig markiert: Es lässt sich nachvollziehen, wo der Redner logisch argumentiert und wo er auf die Gefühle seiner Zuhörer abzielt. Die Stellen, an denen er in der Dimension des Ethos überzeugen möchte, sind in einer dritten Farbe markiert: Die Schüler:innen sollen selbst Hypothesen darüber aufstellen, wie diese Überzeugungsdimension funktioniert und können sie mit Hilfe eines Informationsblattes überprüfen.

*Challenge #9: Du gehörst zur Elite!*

Um Menschen dazu zu bewegen, einer radikalen (politischen oder religiösen) Bewegung beizutreten, reicht eine Sammlung mit Argumenten, eine rein intellektuelle Motivation, nach dem Gesagten nicht aus. Zur Motivation zu Handlungen, die vom gesellschaftlichen Konsens (noch) weit abweichen und den Handelnden sozial isolieren könnten, braucht es starke Handlungsmotivation im persönlichen und emotionalen Bereich.

Radikale Narrative bieten solche Motivationen, indem sie:

- einen Orientierungsrahmen schaffen, der es dem Einzelnen ermöglicht, die komplexe Wirklichkeit zu verstehen;
- dem eigenen Leben eine Aufgabe geben und Sinn verleihen;
- Identität stiften;
- Anerkennung verschaffen;
- starke Gefühle (Empörung über Unrecht; Liebe / Nostalgie gegenüber einer vergangenen Zeit; Verbundenheit in einer Gemeinschaft) ermöglichen, die dem eigenen Leben Spannung und Dramatik verleihen.

Die 9. Challenge geht davon aus, dass radikalen Bewegungen Narrative zu Grunde liegen, die solche Motivationen ermöglichen, und dass sie gemeinsame inhaltliche Merkmale haben. Es handelt sich um folgende inhaltliche Elemente:

- Grundlegend ist die Auffassung, dass es einen Kampf geben sollte.
- Der Kampf ist gerecht, weil empörendes Unrecht vorausgegangen ist.
- Das Unrecht wurde begangen von Menschen, die man als Feinde betrachten muss, und die derzeit noch Macht haben.
- Ziel des Kampfes ist die Herstellung eines gerechten Zustandes, wie es ihn (in der Darstellung vieler Narrative) früher einmal gegeben hat.
- Die Handelnden empfinden sich als Teil einer Elite, die jetzt schon über Wissen verfügt, das andere noch nicht besitzen, und die über gemeinsame Wertvorstellungen und Tugenden verfügen, die sie miteinander verbinden und durch die sie den Feinden überlegen sind.
- Der Sieg ist möglich, muss aber hart erkämpft werden, schließt also u.U. die Anwendung von Gewalt und die Übertretung von Gesetzen ein. Da die derzeitigen Gesetze von den Feinden gemacht worden sind, ist eine

kampfbedingte Übertretung der Gesetze / eine verfassungsmäßige Umgestaltung des Staates verzeihlich oder sogar geboten.

Diese Elemente lassen sich in der 9. Challenge an zwei exemplarischen Narrativen nachweisen. Inwiefern sie auch für populistische Auffassungen zutreffend sind, soll, zumindest für die Position von Donald Trump, in der 10. Trainingseinheit, geklärt werden.

*Challenge #10: Kannst du populistische Überzeugungsmittel entlarven? Trumps Rede vom 6.1.2021*

Trumps Rede vom 6. Januar 2021, die den Tumulten im Kapitol vorausging, dürfte jetzt schon ‚historisch' genannt werden dürfen. Sie ist berühmt, und weil sie gegenwärtig (und wohl auch zukünftig) Gegenstand der Diskussion bleibt, wissen auch viele Schüler:innen von ihr. Dieser Umstand und die Tatsache, dass sie in enger Verbindung zu radikalem politischen Verhalten steht, macht sie zu einem geeigneten Kandidaten für einen zusammenfassenden ‚Abschlusstest'.

Der Textausschnitt gibt einen zutreffenden Eindruck von Trumps Rhetorik, auch von seiner Weitschweifigkeit und dem charakteristischen Gestus, die immer wieder gleichen Gesichtspunkte zu wiederholen – deshalb musste die Rede zwar gekürzt werden, um im Unterrichtskontext handhabbar zu werden, aber nicht so rigoros, wie es außerhalb eines virtuellen Trainingsraums vielleicht nötig gewesen wäre.

Da sich auch in der gekürzten Rede eine sehr große Zahl an Belegen für eristische Argumente, für Versuche, Verbundenheit im Sinne des Ethos zu erzeugen, und für Elemente eines radikalen Narrativs finden lassen, gilt die Aufgabe als gelöst, wenn für jede Art von Überzeugungsmittel jeweils zwei Beispiele gefunden werden.

# 4. Book Reviews / Rezensionen / Critiques

**Peter Unruh, Kant und der Weltföderalismus. Zur Grundlegung und Aktualität von Kants global-politischer Philosophie, Wissenschaftliche Abhandlungen und Reden zur Philosophie, Politik und Geistesgeschichte, Band 104, Berlin: Duncker & Humblot 2021**

In der Anmerkung am Schluss des weit verbreiteten Aufsatzes „Was heißt: sich im Denken orientieren" von 1786 formuliert Kant die oberste Regel des Denkens: "Sich seiner eigenen Vernunft bedienen will nichts weitersagen, als bei allem dem, was man annehmen soll, sich selbst fragen: ob man es wohl tunlich finde, den Grund, warum man etwas annimmt, oder auch die Regel, die aus dem, was man annimmt, folgt, zum allgemeinen Grundsatze seines Vernunftgebrauchs zu machen."[1] Es verwundert, dass Kant dieses zentrale Gebot des Denkens in eine Anmerkung setzt. Die Lösung ist wohl die, dass er hier den Kategorischen Imperativ, den er 1785 in der „Grundlegung zur Metaphysik der Sitten" erstmals vorgestellt hatte, auf das Denken überträgt und dass diese Übertragung eigentlich ausführlicher hätte erläutert werden müssen. Uns gibt diese Umwidmung allerdings einen wesentlichen Hinweis. Der Kategorische Imperativ ist seiner Natur nach eine juristische Friedensregel. Wenn sie hier auf das Denken selbst angewandt wird, bedeutet das, dass das regelgerechte Denken alle gedanklichen Irrwege, so gerade auch populistische Spinnereien und Verschwörungstheorien besiegt und schließlich zwangsweise d.h. logisch zu universeller wahrhafter, aufrichtiger und ehrlicher Friedfertigkeit führt.

Dieses kategorische Friedenskonzept prägt damit Kants ganzes Denken, das schließlich in Form einer Weltfriedensordnung Lebenswirklichkeit werden soll. Ist das realistisch? Sind das nicht Träumereien, die Kant schon 1766 „In den Träumen eines Geistersehers" ironisch ad Absurdum führen wollte, um dann doch nur im Skeptizismus zu enden?

So ist und bleibt es ein ureigenstes Geschäft der Juristen, die realistische Sinnhaftigkeit von Kants Friedensvorstellungen zu überprüfen. Schließlich

[1] Auffällig erinnert die Ausführlichkeit dieser Regel des Denkens an Kants Vorlage des Kategorischen Imperativs, die er als Toleranzregel bei Pierre Bayle fand. Zur Entwicklung von Kants Denken: Werner Busch, „Innere und äußere Freiheit bei Kant: Zum Irrealis „... hätte anders handeln können" und zur Wirksamkeit der Freiheit", in *Forum Philosophie International 72, Freedom and/or Security – Freiheit und/oder Sicherheit – Liberté et/ou sécurité*, ed. G. Münnix, B. Rolf, M. Wirtz, H. Bringeland, LIT Verlag: Zürich 2023, 143 -149. Siehe auch: Werner Busch, „Immanuel Kants Schrift „Zum ewigen Frieden" – Anregungen für den Unterricht", *in Forum Philosophie International 70, Peace/Frieden/Paix*, LIT Verlag: Zürich 2021, 120 – 128.

schätzte der Königsberger Philosoph in hohem Maße das Römische Recht und erfahrene Richter. Friedrich Schlegel stellte sogar fest, dass „Kanten die Jurisprudenz auf die inneren Teile gefallen“ sei [2], was ja gerade die oben zitierte Regel des Denkens deutlich bestätigt.

So passt es, dass sich der Göttinger Juraprofessor und Präsident des Kirchenamtes der Nordkirche in Kiel Peter Unruh noch einmal und wieder einmal Kants kurze Friedensschrift von 1795 vornahm, und zwar in Hinsicht auf das Problem eines Weltföderalismus. Das Besondere der nicht sehr umfangreichen Abhandlung Unruhs ist, dass man den Eindruck hat, dass der Autor Kant auf gute juristische Art den Prozess macht. Alle Argumente Kants werden sorgfältig geprüft, die Vorgeschichte wird geklärt, die zahlreichen bisherigen Interpreten und Gutachter werden berücksichtigt und schließlich wird geurteilt, ob Kants Theorie einer internationalen Rechtsordnung als gültig anerkannt werden kann. Dieses sorgfältige Verfahren zeigt sich daran, dass von den 120 Seiten des Büchleins allein 20 der angeführten Literatur gehören und der Text mit 409 Verweisen versehen ist. D.h. wer sich über den fast unübersichtlichen Forschungsstand zu Kants Friedensschrift informieren will, ist gut beraten, zu Unruhs Erörterung zu greifen.

Der Prozess, den Unruh Kant macht, hat nun eine ganz eigenartige Aktualität, selbst wenn der Text natürlich ausdrücklich auf die allgemeine Lage unserer globalen Staatengemeinschaft, in der irgendwo immer grausame Kriege und menschenverachtende Bürger- oder Bandenkriege toben, rekurriert. Das Vorwort ist auf April 2021 datiert. Am 24. Februar 2022 überfiel eine Vetomacht des UNO-Sicherheitsrats, der per definitionem der Friedenssicherung verpflichtet ist, einen souveränen Nachbarstaat. Im rasch folgenden Prozess vor dem Internationalen Gerichtshof in Den Haag trat in reiner Verhöhnung noch nicht einmal ein Vertreter des angeklagten Aggressors auf. Wenn man schon meint, dass der Völkerbund und die UNO von der Argumentation Kants stark beeinflusst waren und sind, bedeutet der aktuelle politische Kulturbruch nicht ein totales Scheitern von Kants Friedensideen und sind Unruhs Überlegungen nicht schon von Anfang an überholt?

Verfolgen wir die Einzelargumentationen Unruhs. Zur Vorgeschichte wird gezeigt, wie besonders der Abbé de Saint-Pierre eine viel belächelte europäische Lösung des Friedensproblems in Form eines durchorganisierten Staatenkongresses vorschlug, auf die Jean-Jacques Rousseau ambivalent mit Überlegungen zwischen absoluter Souveränität der basisbestimmten Kleinstaaten und

[2] Friedrich Schlegel, *Seine prosaischen Jugendschriften 1794 - 1802*, J. Minor: Wien 1882, 2, 194, Frgt. 77 Lesarten.

zwischenstaatlichen Vertragsverhältnissen antwortete. Dabei wird deutlich, dass Kants Friedenstheorie im Gegensatz zu denen seiner Vorgänger global formuliert ist und daher bis heute wirken kann.

Im Mittelpunkt von Unruhs Erörterungen steht nun das kontroverse Spannungsverhältnis zwischen der notwendigen Überwindung des hobbesschen Naturzustandes durch die rechtlich gebundene Staatsgewalt und der Verrechtlichung der zwischenstaatlichen Verhältnisse mit oder ohne zwingende Gewalt. Unruh legt dar, wie Kant zwischen der Theorie eines Staatenbundes und der Form eines Bundesstaates oder sogar eines Völker- oder Weltstaates schwankt, und wägt sorgfältig und ertragreich zwischen denen, die meinen, Kants Theorie sei wegen des Fehlens zentraler Macht im internationalen Feld widersprüchlich inkonsistent, und denjenigen ab, die die Lehre der vereinigten Gewalt der das Recht verteidigenden, vertraglich verbundenen souveränen Staaten in Analogie zu einem Bundesstaat für vertretbar halten. Unruh greift ebenso die Kritik auf, dass Kant ständig zwischen apriorischen Rechtsformen und pragmatischen Argumenten – z. B. der Nichtregierbarkeit eines Weltstaates – unsicher laviere, und findet die Lösung darin, dass sich die Staatengemeinschaft, getragen von positiven Geschichtszeichen, dynamisch zu einem Weltföderalismus hin entwickeln müsse und wohl irgendwann auch werde. Damit endet sein Prozess gegen Kant mit einem eindeutigen Freispruch.

Dieser Freispruch erster Klasse ermöglicht es Unruh, abschließend neun eigene Thesen aufzustellen, die eine ökonomische und ökologische föderale Weltfriedensordnung formulieren.

Nun drängt es sich auf, wie oben schon angedeutet, nach dem 24. Februar 2022 den Prozess gegen Immanuel Kant neu aufzurollen. Die anhaltenden Kriegsverbrechen in der Ukraine, eine auf totale Vernichtung ausgerichtete Militärdoktrin, die seit der Zerstörung Grosnys bekannt ist, die Missachtung aller internationalen Institutionen, und die verständnisvolle Schwäche der das Recht vertretenden Staaten scheinen Kants durch und durch profanen erfahrungsgesättigten anthropologischen Pessimismus, der von Thomas Hobbes zu Arthur Schopenhauer überleitete, wie schon Friedrich Paulsen meinte, voll und ganz zu bestätigen.[3] Obendrein ist Kants optimistisches Konzept ‚Wandel durch Handel' in Hinsicht auf viele Teile der Erde zur bitteren Lachnummer geworden. Nimmt man die ständige Bedrohung durch ABC-Waffen hinzu, liegt eine Weltfriedensordnung ferner denn je.

[3] Friedrich Paulsen, *System der Ethik, Vol. 1: Mit Einem Umriss der Staats-und Gesellschaftslehre*, 11. Und 12. Aufl. Stuttgart/Berlin 1921, 300. Zu Kants antinomischer Grundkonzeption: Siehe Anm. 1.

Führen wir einen neuen Prozess, sollte man neue Beweismittel einbringen, und diese könnten darin bestehen, Kants Weltfriedensordnung zum wiederholten Male in einen ausgeweiteten Horizont zu stellen. Diesen öffnet Kant selbst in § 83 der ‚Kritik der Urteilskraft', in dem Kant das friedliche Zusammenleben der Menschen in einem System aller Staaten dynamisch als letzten Zweck entwickelt. Dabei ist zu beachten, dass Kants gesamte Philosophie nur mit Hilfe seines Rückgriffs auf die aristotelische Naturzwecklehre zu begreifen ist. Gerade das rätselhafte Zusammenwirken apriorischer Formen mit der Sinnlichkeit im menschlichen Körper und der Erfahrungswelt ist ohne den Hintergrund dieser antiken Zwecklehre in Form der Selbstwirksamkeit der Organismen nicht zu verstehen. Dass alles zusammenpasst, erweist das Erfolgskonzept Vernunft in Wissenschaft, Technik, Kultur und nach Hannah Arendt [4] in Inseln des Rechts. [5] Reflektieren wir nun im Bereich der Zwecke, merken wir, welchen verschlungenen Weg der Organismus Mensch einschlagen muss, um sich als Gruppe am Leben zu erhalten, welche neuen Rechtsformen entwickelt werden müssen, um im Sinne des Lebens erfolgreich zu sein. Da tut sich tatsächlich ein weiter Spielraum auf zwischen Staatenbund, Bundesstaat, Weltstaat, komplexen vertraglichen Regelungen und Weltföderalismus und im aktuellen Fall des Überfalls auf die Ukraine ein neuer rechtlicher Raum für publikumswirksame internationale Gerichtsverfahren, Ausschlussverfahren, kollektive Hilfsmaßnahmen, Waffenlieferungen an die Angegriffenen, Embargos etc. Es kommt nur darauf an, dass der Weg auf eine zweckmäßige Herrschaft der rechtschöpfenden Vernunft gerichtet ist, und diesen gerade zeigt die vortreffliche Schrift Peter Unruhs zu Kant und dem Weltföderalismus.

*Werner Busch*

**Karl Hepfer: Verschwörungstheorien. Eine philosophische Kritik der Unvernunft, Bielefeld: transcript Verlag 2017, 3., aktualisierte und ergänzte Auflage 2021**

Verschwörungstheorien haben Konjunktur in Zeiten des Umbruchs. Die Strategie, verwirrende und damit Angst einflößende Ereignisse durch eine Verschwörung zu erklären, kann auf eine lange Geschichte zurückblicken und hat in den

[4] Hannah Arendt, *Vita Activa oder Vom tätigen Leben*, 6.Aufl., Piper Verlag: München 1989, 239f.
[5] Matthias Schramm, *Natur ohne Sinn? Das Ende des teleologischen Weltbildes*, Styria: Graz – Wien – Köln 1985. bes. 172ff.

letzten Jahren hat durch COVID-19 und das Aufkommen rechtspopulistischer Strömungen einen enormen Schub erfahren.

Für gewöhnlich sind Verschwörungstheorien ein Thema der Sozialwissenschaften, der historischen Forschung und der Psychologie. Karl Hepfer, Privatdozent für Philosophie an der Universität Erfurt, präsentiert einen neuen Zugang: Er setzt sich philosophisch mit ihnen auseinander, betrachtet sie aus erkenntnis- und wissenschaftstheoretischer Perspektive.

Seine Analyse besteht aus drei Teilen: Im ersten legt den Schwerpunkt auf erkenntnis- und wissenschaftstheoretische Auffälligkeiten, im zweiten befasst er sich mit typischen inhaltlichen und praktischen Kennzeichen von Verschwörungstheorien. Damit das Unternehmen nicht zu einer trockenen Übung wird, werden nach jedem theoretischen Abschnitt eine konkrete Verschwörungstheorien dargestellt und analysiert, insgesamt 14 – von den Iden des März in der römischen Antike über die Geheimgesellschaft der Illuminaten im 18. Jahrhundert und die Director's-Cut-Theorie in Bezug auf die erste Mondlandung 1961 bis hin zu Nine Eleven im Jahr 2001. In der dritten Auflage des Buches neu hinzugekommen ist ein Teil, der sich mit der sogenannten Corona-Lüge befasst.

Im theoretischen Teil betrachtet Hepfer Verschwörungstheorien u. a. aus der Sicht des philosophischen Skeptizismus, dessen Programm es ist, bisher für wahr gehaltene Meinungen systematisch in Zweifel zu ziehen und dies mit Gründen zu untermauern. Er legt dar, dass Verschwörungstheoretiker dieses Programm zwar einerseits übernehmen, aber im Unterschied zu Skeptikern wie René Descartes die Forderung nach Zweifelsfreiheit unterschlagen, wenn es um die eigenen Behauptungen geht – etwa die von Absprachen geheimer Mächte, welche die Absicht haben, der Allgemeinheit zu schaden. Insofern ist ihnen hier eine erkenntnistheoetische Asymmetrie vorzuwerfen.

An anderer Stelle zeigt Hepfer Defizite in der Beweisführung von Verschwörungstheorien auf. Diese können zwar in der Regel eine Fülle von empirischen Belegen für ihre Behauptungen anführen und profitieren dabei zunehmend auch von den neuen Möglichkeiten des weltumspannenden Datenaustauschs. Für den Erkenntnistheoretiker ist jedoch klar, dass sich aus einer Menge einzelner Aussagen niemals allgemeine Aussagen ableiten lassen. Induktiv begründete Aussagen gelten immer nur mit Wahrscheinlichkeit; Notwendigkeit können allein auf deduktivem Weg gewonnene Aussagen für sich in Anspruch nehmen – sofern die ihnen zugrundeliegenden allgemeinen Aussagen wahr sind. Für deren Gültigkeit können Verschwörungstheorien – so Hepfer – jedoch keine hinreichenden Beweise vorlegen. Während wissenschaftliche Theorien aus der Tatsache, dass keine Belege für ihre Behauptungen zu finden sind, ableiten, dass weitere Forschung nötig ist oder die Theorie aufgegeben werden muss, bewerten Verschwörungstheoretiker die Abwesenheit von Dokumenten, die ihre Behauptungen belegen können, als Beweis für ihre Behauptungen - sie zeige, wie lang der Arm der Verschwörer ist.

Im Umfeld der Pandemie beinhalten Verschwörungstheorien alternative Erklärungen zur Entstehung des Virus', etwa die Behauptung, es sei gezielt von finsteren Mächten in einem Geheimlabor hergestellt worden, um einen Anlass für ‚Zwangsimpfung' zu schaffen, bei der Menschen völlig unbemerkt mit einem Mikrochip versehen werden, um sie digital zu versklaven. Für Hepfer eskaliert das Verschwörungsdenken hier insbesondere dadurch, dass es sich in einem noch höheren Maße als zuvor von der eigenen Erfahrung entkoppelt. Da die direkten Begegnungen von Menschen im öffentlichen Raum eingeschränkt sind, verlagert sich die Meinungsbildung verstärkt in die virtuellen Räume mit ihren hermetischen Meinungsbiotopen und Echokammern, in denen eine erfolgreiche gesellschaftliche Auseinandersetzung über Sachfragen schwer oder gar unmöglich wird.

Weitere Aspekte, unter denen der Autor Verschwörungstheorien betrachtet sind: Wahrheit, Realität, Analogieschlüsse, Dogmen, Projektion, Nutzen und Motive, Wahn und politische Legitimation.

Mit diesem Buch legt Karl Hepfer eine – ganz im aufklärerischen Sinn – erhellende Kritik der Unvernunft vor. Er stellt interessierten Leserinnen und Lesern das theoretische Werkzeug zur Verfügung, um dem Verschwörungsdenken erfolgreich zu begegnen.

*Bernd Rolf*

### Bernd Stegemann, Das Gespenst des Populismus. Ein Essay zur politischen Dramaturgie, Berlin: Theater der Zeit 2017

Bernd Stegemanns Essay "Das Gespenst des Populismus" ist zwar schon vor einiger Zeit (2017) erschienen, hat seitdem aber an Aktualität nichts verloren. Der Essay liefert eine tiefgründige Analyse eines der drängendsten Phänomene der Zeit: des Populismus. Der Autor ist Professor für Dramaturgie an der Hochschule für Schauspielkunst „Ernst Busch" in Berlin und hat über die Systemtheorie Luhmanns promoviert. Diese berufliche Tätigkeit qualifiziert Stegemann besonders, da er im Essay sowohl die systemtheoretischen als auch die dramaturgischen Perspektiven integriert, um das Phänomen des Populismus zu beleuchten.

Der Essay lässt sich in drei Teile gliedern: Stegemann beginnt mit der Entwicklung einer systemtheoretischen Perspektive auf den Populismus. Diese Herangehensweise ermöglicht es, Populismus als ein System von Narrativen zu verstehen, die bestimmte gesellschaftliche Zustände reflektieren und beeinflussen. Er nutzt Luhmanns Systemtheorie, um die Wechselwirkungen zwischen politischen Systemen und der Gesellschaft zu analysieren. Im Anschluss betrachtet Stegemann im zweiten Teil des Essays drei Formen des Populismus: 1) Der Rechtspopulismus wird als Reaktion auf Migration und kulturelle Veränderungen beschrieben, wobei nationale Identität und traditionelle Werte betont werden. Er sei oft durch seine ablehnende Haltung gegenüber dem Establishment und den etablierten politischen Institutionen gekennzeichnet. 2) Der Liberale Populismus manifestiere sich in einem Übermaß an wirtschaftlicher Freiheit und Individualismus und sei oft verbunden mit einer starken Kritik an der staatlichen Regulierung und einem Streben nach mehr persönlicher Autonomie. 3) Der Linke Populismus ziele auf soziale Ungleichheit ab und richte sich gegen eine neoliberale Politik, die die Arbeiterklasse und sozial Schwächere vernachlässige. Linker Populismus versuche, soziale Gerechtigkeit und wirtschaftliche Gleichheit durch staatliche Interventionen zu fördern. Im letzten Teil („Das politische Sprechen") analysiert Stegemann die Art und Weise, wie populistische Akteure kommunizieren. Er zeigt auf, dass Populismus nicht nur inhaltlich, sondern auch formal die Art und Weise verändere, wie politische Botschaften vermittelt werden.

Insgesamt ist Stegemanns Essay ein durchdachter Beitrag zur Diskussion über Populismus, der nicht nur die aktuellen politischen Entwicklungen beschreibt, sondern auch tiefer liegende Ursachen untersucht.

*Stefan Düfel*

# The Authors / Zu den Autoren / Les auteurs

Johannes **Balle** ist Gymnasiallehrer am Rhein-Gymnasium Köln, Fachmoderator für Philosophie und Lehrbeauftragter an der Universität zu Köln, an der Fresenius Hochschule sowie der Kölner Hochschule für Polizei und Verwaltung. Forschungsgebiete: Phänomenologie, Anthropologie und Philosophie des Geistes, Metaethik, Philosophiedidaktik. E-Mail: joballe@web.de

Dr. Werner **Busch,** Studium der Germanistik, Geschichte und Philosophie in Bonn, Poitiers und Marburg. Bei Klaus Reich in Marburg promoviert mit einer Arbeit zur Entstehung der kritischen Rechtsphilosophie Kants. 1982-2006 Leiter des Gymnasiums Wellingdorf in Kiel. 2006-2012 Präsident der AIPPh. Co-chair der Sektion Philosophieunterricht bei den Weltkongressen der Philosophie 2013 in Athen und 2018 in Peking. Seit 2019 Ehrenpräsident der AIPPh.

Prof. Dr. Edwige **Chirouter** est professeure des universités pour la philosophie de l'éducation à Université de Nantes. Elle est également titulaire de la Chaire UNESCO: "Pratiques de la philosophie avec les enfants, une base éducative pour le dialogue interculturel et la transformation sociale". https://chaireunesco philoen fants.univ-nantes.fr/

M.A. Stefan **Düfel** ist Philosophiedidaktiker und unterrichtet als OStR am Ricarda-Huch-Gymnasium in Hagen/Westfalen die Fächer Philosophie und Deutsch.

Prof. Dr. Griet **Galle** is an Associate Professor at the Institute of Philosophy, KU Leuven. She wrote a doctoral dissertation in medieval natural philosophy. She teaches philosophical skills, philosophy didactics, and philosophical conversation with children and adolescents and is co-chair of VEFO, the Flemish Network for Contemporary Philosophy Education. She conducts research in philosophy didactics and is the supervisor of the project 'Bringing Up Thinking: Philosophy and Philosophy Education in Textbooks for Secondary Education'.

Prof. Dr. Georgi **Kapriev s**tudierte und promovierte im Fach Philosophie an der Universität Sofia, war DAAD-, Humboldt-, KAAS- und Melon-Stipendiat in Köln und Paris. Er lehrt als Professor für Philosophie an der Universität Sofia. Seine Forschungsschwerpunkte sind mittelalterliche (byzantinische und lateinische) Philosophie, orthodoxe Theologie, Philosophie und Soziologie der Kultur und Philosophie der Kunst des 20. Jahrhunderts.

Dr. Gabriele **Münnix** studierte Philosophie, Mathematik und Physik an der Universität Köln und promovierte in Philosophie an der Humboldt-Universität Berlin. Dozentin für Philosophie zunächst in der Lehrkräftefortbildung, dann in der PhilosophieleherInnenausbildung an der Universität Münster; daneben Vorlesungen und Seminare zur interkulturellen Philosophie an der Universität Innsbruck. Schul- und Sachbuchautorin, im Ruhestand freiberufliche Autoren- und Vortragstätigkeit (s. www.muennix.de). Früher Präsidentin, heute Ehrenpräsidentin der Association Internationale des Professeurs de Philosophie und senior editor des „Forum Philosophie International".

Prof. Dr. Ewa **Nowak** ist ordentliche Professorin an der Adam-Mickiewicz-Universität in Poznań (Polen) und Leiterin des Lehrstuhls für Ethik. Sie promovierte und habilitierte über die klassische deutsche Philosophie. Stipendiatin u. a. der Alexander von Humboldt-Stiftung, des DAAD, der ESKAS und TFK (Deutschland, Schweiz, USA). Schwerpunkte der Forschung: Moralische Urteilskompetenz, Angewandte Ethik, Rechtsphilosophie, Fichte und Hegel. Kontakt: ewanowak@ amu.edu.pl

Prof. Dr. Dorothy **Oluwagbemi-Jacob** is a lecturer in the Department of Philosophy, University of Calabar, Calabar, Nigeria. Her areas of research include political philosophy, gender studies, logic/critical thinking and intercultural philosophy. E-Mail: dorothyolujacob@unical.edu.ng

Prof. Dr. Riccardo **Pozzo** holds the chair of the History of Philosophy of Tor Vergata University of Rome, Department of History, Humanities and Society. Graduated from the State University of Milan in 1983, he completed his education in Germany - Dr. phil. at the University of Saarland in 1988 and Habilitation at the University of Trier in 1995. In 1996 he was appointed at the Catholic University of America in Washington, D.C. In 2003 the University of Verona called him back to the chair of the History of Philosophy. From 2009 to 2012 he directed the Institute for the European Intellectual Lexicon and History of Ideas of the National Research Council of Italy. From 2012 to 2017, when he was head of the Department of Human and Social Sciences, Cultural Heritage of the National Research Council, he implemented Italy's participation in the European research infrastructures for social and cultural innovation.

Dr. Bernd **Rolf** war Gymnasiallehrer und Fachleiter für Philosophie am Zentrum für schulpraktische Lehrerausbildung in Kleve und Krefeld; 2003 bis 2012 Vorsitzender des Fachverbandes Philosophie; Schulbuchautor und Verfasser von Aufsätzen zur Didaktik der Philosophie.

Prof. Dr. Stefan **Rummens** is a Professor of Political Philosophy at the Institute of Philosophy, KU Leuven. He wrote a doctoral dissertation on Jürgen Habermas' deliberative model of democracy. His academic work is mainly concerned with a philosophical analysis of the nature of our democratic regime and the problems it is currently facing. He has published in leading academic journals on a diversity of topics such as representation, deliberation, populism, freedom of speech and the constitutional structure of the European Union.

Dr. Petra **Šebešová** studied philosophy and aesthetics at Charles University in Prague. Her Ph.D.-thesis focused on the didactics of philosophy in secondary education. She taught civics and basics of social sciences at a grammar school. Since 2013, she teaches didactics of philosophy at Charles University in Prague. Recently, she has focused on teaching critical thinking and its relationship to philosophy, lecturing both also at the Faculty of Education at University of Southern Bohemia in České Budějovice. She has selected and translated into Czech important texts from German didactics of philosophy in an anthology Why and How to Teach Philosophy at Secondary Schools?

Prof. Dr. Riccardo **Sirello**, Professeur de philosophie de nationalité italienne et française, ancien secrétaire général de l'AIPPh. Actuellement, membre d'honneur. Il a participé aux congrès mondiaux de philosophie de Pékin (2018) et de Rome (2024), où il est intervenu dans la section « Philosophie de l'éducation ». Il enseigne la philosophie à l'Uni Savona. Il a à son actif plusieurs projets et publications nationaux et internationaux.

Prof. Dr. Mohamed **Turki**, geb. in Gabès (Tunesien), studierte Philosophie, Romanistik und Soziologie in Münster, lehrte von 1980 – 2008 Philosophie an verschiedenen Universitäten in Deutschland (Bremen, Frankfurt, Gießen und Kassel) Mauretanien (Nouakchott) und Tunesien (Sfax und Tunis). Zahlreiche Veröffentlichungen in arabischer, deutscher und französischer Sprache.

Markus **Twittmann** ist Lehrer für Philosophie, Deutsch, Latein und Theater am Reichenbach-Gymnasium Ennepetal, stellvertretender Vorsitzender des Fachverbands Philosophie NRW. E-Mail: markustwittmann@ aol.com

Dr. Daniela **Zumpf** ist wissenschaftliche Mitarbeiterin in der Didaktik der Philosophie an der Universität Paderborn, zuständig für das Praxissemester; Forschungsgebiet: Antike Philosophie, Moral- und Sozialphilosophie, Philosophiedidaktik. E-Mail: daniela.zumpf@upb.de